Judging a Book by Its Cover

The Connection Between Physical Traits and Psychology

Marissa A. Harrison, Ph.D.

Susan M. Hughes, Ph.D.

ISBN: 9798607677725

DEDICATION

In loving memory of

Joseph P. Hughes, George T. Geueke, Jr., and Julia C. Pennington

CONTENTS

Acknowledgments   i

1   Introduction   1

2   Face   10

3   Bilateral Symmetry   32

4   Voice   54

5   Fingers   88

6   Toes   117

7   Body Ratios   129

8   Body Scent   166

9   Minor Physical Anomalies   194

10   Conclusion   210

ACKNOWLEDGMENTS

We would like to extend our sincerest gratitude to the people, places, and organizations that made this book possible. Thank you to our families and our friends; our Alma Mater, the University at Albany, State University of New York (SUNY); our professors and mentors, especially Dr. Gordon G. Gallup, Jr., and Dr. Donn Byrne; the NorthEastern Evolutionary Psychology Society (NEEPS), a champion for evolutionary psychological research, its scholars, and its students; and Penn State University and Albright College. Thank you to all our students, coauthors, and colleagues, particularly Dr. Brett Pelham and Dr. Steve Platek for their support of this text.

Thank you so much to the people who permitted us to use their photos in this book. Unsurprisingly, we had 100% participation when we asked, "Can we use your photo in a book about beauty? You won't get paid, but you will be presented as beautiful in perpetuity!" To wit, all images presented herein are printed and disseminated with the express permission of those we behold herein.

Also, Harrison thanks Hughes and Hughes thanks Harrison for over two decades of friendship and collaboration.

Chapter 1

INTRODUCTION

Biological explanations of human behavior can be scary.

-Pratt, Turanovic, and Cullen (2016)

The idiom, "Don't judge a book by its cover," tells us that you cannot determine something's true character from its external appearance. You need to explore something further, beyond the surface, to understand its true nature. But *can you actually* judge a book by its cover? Evidence from biopsychology, particularly evolutionary psychology, suggests that perhaps you can. For many years, the field has produced studies yielding compelling evidence that there is a connection between morphology (i.e., physical form and structure) and psychology. That is, from someone's physical traits, it may be possible to predict attitudes, actions, and other attributes. Researchers from all over the world from multiple laboratories and institutions have provided evidence that traits like body symmetry, facial appearance, and body ratios are predictably related to various behaviors and mental processes.

Perhaps biological psychology is intimidating in the sense that it challenges us to consider our animal roots (Kalat, 2016). Ancient Greeks understood that the brain was the seat of reason. The science of biopsychology (i.e., behavioral neuroscience) arguably continued to grow from there, but not without taking steps backwards on occasion. That is, the study of the biology of behavior, unfortunately, is tainted by pseudoscientific history. Franz Joseph Gall (1758–1828), a German physician, developed *phrenology* in the late 1700s. He posited that skull configuration (i.e., the "bumps" on your head) can be assessed to determine mental abilities and personality. Since the brain is the organ of the mind and specific neural functions are localized, it was thought that the size of these sites speaks to the brain's strengths and weaknesses in terms of behaviors and mental processes (Flourens, 1846).

At least Gall attempted to employ some empiricism by actually examining the heads of friends and colleagues to derive data. However, as Parker Jones and colleagues (2018) astutely noted, the "digital technology" he used was his fingers. Gall studied prison inmates and individuals in mental health asylums, and he delineated the head into regions that, when felt, supposedly informed the observer about the cranial possessor's "organs" of murder and theft. Later in phrenology, somewhat less severe labels were used for these assessments, such as secretiveness, inquisitiveness, destructiveness, sublimity, and wit (Encyclopedia Britannica, 2018).

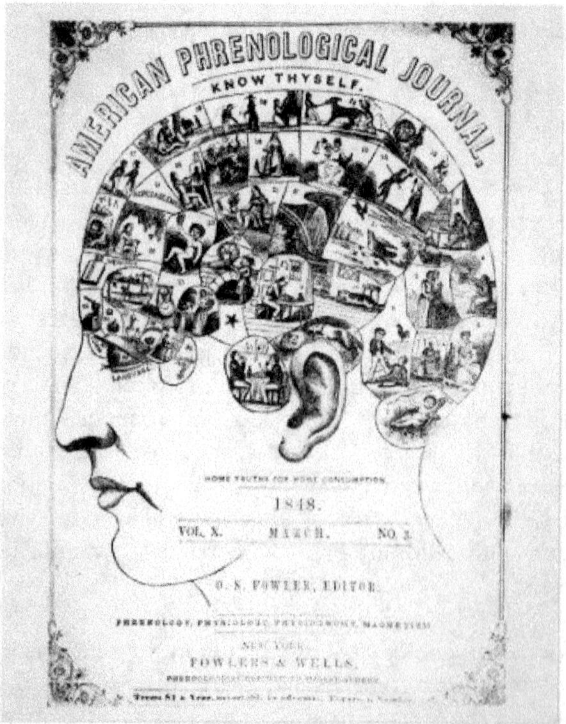

Image in public domain

Given the history of phrenology, modern day scientists, now equipped with sophisticated brain imaging techniques, have been able to confirm that head bumps, in fact, do not relate to behavior (Parker Jones, Alfaro-Almagro, & Jbabdi, 2018). As Dempsey-Jones (2018) emphasized, "there is no way lumpy bits of brain are pushing the skull out to create surface bumps—the skull does not mirror the brain surface." We have come a long way since phrenology. The connection between physical traits and psychology is still examined by contemporary scientists, but the process is scientific and rigorous. True biopsychology (i.e., behavioral neuroscience) continues to grow with each passing day, and increasingly advanced research techniques help open the door to understanding the complexity of the human organism.

Evolutionary Psychology

Much of the research regarding physical traits and their associated behaviors presented in this book was crafted by evolutionary psychological scholars. Whereas evolutionary psychology (EP) falls under the umbrella of biopsychology, it is not a subdivision of psychology per se. EP is a framework through which one can view <u>all</u> behavior and mental processes. We (Harrison and Hughes) each have been researchers and teachers in the field for well over 20 years as of this writing, earning our degrees in biopsychology with a specialization in evolutionary psychology.

Largely based on Darwinian principles, EP contends that just as our bodies have experienced millions of years of anatomical adaptations, our minds have experienced psychological adaptations. All these adaptations— arguably most of what we are and do—have an ultimate, reproductive significance. That is, our behaviors and mental processes are rooted in the need to maximize our chance at reproducing (i.e., what evolutionary psychologists call *fitness*). How we think and behave often can have reproductive consequences—even decisions like which job you take, if you go to college, or even if you stay out late on a Saturday with your friends. Hence, EP can be thought of as a field that examines how the physiology, behavior, and cognitions of modern human beings have been shaped by our ancestral past, and it considers different human traits as evolved adaptations.

We can use a basic tenet in the study of learning and conditioning to think about how selection of certain traits occurs. Consider Thorndike's Law of Effect on a large scale (Thorndike, 1927). Behaviors that are rewarded are more likely to be repeated. This chocolate chip cookie tastes good; I want to eat another cookie. A behavior, trait, or emotion that is conducive to reproductive success is likely to be repeated. If organism A possesses this trait or exhibits this behavior, and organism B does not possess this trait or exhibit this behavior, it is organism A that will leave more descendants. The genes of organism A will be passed down to subsequent generations, who will have the biological proclivity to behave in that way. We call this an *adaptation*. Why do we get jealous? The simple answer is that people who got jealous were more likely to guard their mate to assure fidelity, thereby ensuring that they left more of their own descendants. Why do we bond with our children? People who bonded with children helped assure the survival of those children to grow and reproduce themselves, thereby leaving more descendants. These adaptations worked over millions of years in the ancestral past, so they are repeated in modern humans today, independently of whether or not they may be advantageous today (Buss & Schmitt, 1993; Buss, 1999; Tooby & Cosmides, 1990).

Adaptations are indeed difficult to ponder, as they are products of accidents. It may be challenging to tell your friends, neighbors, students, and children that their existence is the sum of accidents. Evolution does not occur by design. Adaptations are the product of genetic mutations—a substitution, deletion, duplication, or mutagen that caused a change in the DNA sequence—that gave rise to a change in behavior or mental process. Couple the incidence of mutations with selective pressure and you see the emergence of a trait within a gene pool. Thinking of yourself and your family as the sum result of millions of years of genetic accidents might not be comforting, but at least some of those accidents have led to your capacity to love, care, have compassion, and be happy. Again, random, genetic mutations leading to the ability to love and care, etc., gave organisms that possessed those mutations a reproductive advantage over those who did not love and care. That's why people today possess those genes and think and act in those ways. So, evolution does not strive to make you happy. You are happy because humans have evolved to feel that emotion.

Another difficult concept to master in EP is that of deep time. We are not talking about a consideration of events since last year, or since the days of Janis Joplin, or since Queen Victoria's reign, or since Romans built the aqueducts. Often teens and young adults have a difficult time even comprehending the vast lifespan of their parents and professors compared to their own. We are talking about millions of years of biological and psychological human evolution, since the days that hominins Ardi (*Ardipithecus ramidus*) and later Lucy (*Australopithecus afarensis*) roamed the ancient Earth at the dawn of civilization. The pressures they faced in their social landscape help shape our contemporary human psychology.

That is not to say we are beholden to our evolutionary heritage. As an example, consider reproductive drive. Men produce millions of sperm daily from puberty onward, and women are born with all the ova (eggs) they will ever have, releasing only a few hundred from puberty to menopause. This fundamental reproductive sex difference has given rise to behavioral adaptations conducive to maximizing fitness in cardinally different ways for men and women. Men have the desire to have sex with more partners than do women, as their gametic abundance allows for wide-spread fertilization of partners (Trivers, 1972; Buss, 1993). Women, on the other hand, more often have the desire to bond with one partner and are more discriminating when selecting a partner than are men. With ova being very rare, women must be careful who fathers their children. It is a one-shot deal, with a pregnancy taking a woman out of reproductive commission for perhaps one to two years (between pregnancy and lactation). Furthermore, women only have a limited reproductive lifespan until menopause approaches.

That being said, we modern humans are endowed with frontal lobes that help us choose what we want to do. Men may have the drive to have sex with multiple people, but some choose to marry and be committed to a single person for life (which also has its reproductive advantages). Women may have the drive to pair-bond, but if a woman wants to have sex with everyone she knows, that is her prerogative (which, again, also has its reproductive advantages). We may even elect not to have children at all. Again, EP does not convey or condone genetic determinism. Having a genetic foundation for a trait or behavior does not mean you are certain—or doomed—to express it.

A bit more background is warranted in terms of the tenets of EP. EP contends that we are physically attracted to someone because of *proximate* cues. A hormonally mediated masculine or feminine face looks good to us. The *ultimate* reason, however, for our attraction is that it allows us to choose a mate who is in our reproductive best interest. We are attracted to cues of good genes, and if we reproduce with that person, our offspring will have high-quality genes. After all, the name of the game in evolution is passing on your genes, having your offspring reproduce and pass on their genes, and so on. Whether consciously or not, we have evolved to care about our genetic legacy. Even if we are cognizant of it and opt not to reproduce, and this drive is manifested in our interest in sex and mating choices.

In this book, we review research on the connection between physical traits and behavior, with much of the research that we cover addressing evolved preferences for physical traits that can tell us about the psychology of the target and the perceiver. We discuss these phenomena and the strengths and weaknesses of the argument for their viabilities as predictors of human behavior.

In our research for over 20 years, the authors of this book have focused on the EP of human mating. The way that we feel and behave when we are attracted to someone, the type of person to whom we are attracted, the kind of person we would marry, the kind of person we would have sex with, our reactions to others' advances or rejections…all these examples are evolved adaptations that have helped humans navigate the social terrain of how to select a mate that is most favorable to passing on our genes. This line of research has been interesting, intriguing, challenging, and often controversial. The media will often pick up published research in the field for news stories, and as researchers we find ourselves delighted to present our findings to the world through popular media. However, we are at times challenged by media and must clarify misconceptions about evolutionary theory as it pertains to behavior.

For more reading about EP, we highly suggest an article by Confer and colleagues (2010) that summarizes some of the tenets and controversies of the field. We also recommend David Buss's (2016) *The Evolution of Human Desire: Strategies of Human Mating* which has been a staple of the field since 1994 and is now available in an updated edition. In addition, Donald Symon's (1979) *The Evolution of Human Sexuality* is considered one of the principle readings in the field. We further recommend Brett Pelham's (2018) witty and detailed *Evolutionary Psychology: Genes, Environments, and Time.*

Behavioral Neuroendocrinology and Developmental Biology

Although much research discussed in this book can be found in journals like *Evolutionary Behavioral Sciences*, *Evolutionary Psychology*, and *Evolution and Human Behavior*, this book provides a summary of some research where it will not always be clear whether traits that connect to behavior have adaptive significance. Some of the physical traits we discuss are consequences of ontogenetic (developmental) and hormonal processes and are likely not evolved to solve adaptive problems. For example, there is a connection between having digit syndactyly (having webbed fingers and toes) and having schizophrenia, a severe mental illness (Maynard, Sikich, Lieberman, & LaMantia, 2001). Syndactyly does not make you have schizophrenia. Schizophrenia does not give you syndactyly. Everyone who has syndactyly does not have schizophrenia, nor does everyone who has schizophrenia have syndactyly. We can think of no known reproductive benefits for syndactyly. The argument is that *something* is altering morphogenesis early on in utero, disrupting both central nervous system

(CNS) development and altering typical digit development. Of course, there are multiple genetic, developmental, and environmental factors creating a vulnerability for schizophrenia, but the connection between physical manifestations and schizophrenia provides very strong evidence for its biological underpinnings (Compton & Walker, 2008).

As another example, evidence suggests that pedophiles have shorter legs than nonpedophiles. Fazio, Dyshniku, Lykins, and Cantor (2017) studied "pedophilogenesis." They found that pedophiles tend to have shorter leg length and shorter overall height compared to nonpedophile sex offenders. Short legs do not make you a pedophile. All people with short legs are not pedophiles. Something has happened prenatally, or even during early childhood, that altered not only leg growth but also sexual cognitive processes or sexual orientation processes. Some theorist indeed argue that pedophilia is a sexual orientation and cannot be changed. Being that events occurring early in utero during sexual differentiation contribute to later sexual orientation (Bao & Swaab, 2011), pedophilogenesis might begin then as well. Again, here we can associate a physical trait with a behavior and mental process, but we certainly are not suggesting causality. Short legs are not a concrete red flag for pedophilia, nor are all the physical traits mentioned in our book iron-clad predictors of the behaviors and mental processes to which research has related them. Thus, as in all psychological science, we stress caution in attributing causal factors for correlational evidence. Alternatively, we caution that we should not be dismissive of correlational evidence, because it can often reveal important associations.

Caveat and Conclusion

We caution that people have used judgment of physical characteristics for nefarious purposes. Over the centuries, biological differences, whether perceived or real, have informed sexism, racism, and even Nazism (Pratt, Turanovic, & Cullen, 2016). Ernst Haeckel's (1868) book *Natural History of Creation* presented people in a hierarchy, with Island people being at the lowest and Caucasian people being at the highest rank. He is "credited" with having at least some responsibility for Nazi ideology (Richards, 2007), eventuating into some of the greatest crimes against humanity ever to take place. Systematic physical or psychological differences in people do not confer superiority. We therefore implore the reader to understand that we present evidence here as an interesting phenomenon and as another avenue to understand human psychology. We do not promote judgments of superiority or inferiority based on physical traits. Knowing is always preferable to not knowing, and therefore, we hope you will find the research presented in this text as intriguing as our students and we have for the many years that we have been conducting and studying it.

Why This Book?

People are currently reading scientific journals and attending conferences to hear research connecting physical traits to behavior and mental processes. The topics in this book (e.g., bilateral symmetry, facial attractiveness, 2D:4D finger ratios, shoulder-to-hip ratio, waist-to-hip ratio) are of interest to evolutionary and biological psychologists, and to the best of our knowledge, there is no single, contemporary source that presents a summary and synthesis of how physical traits relate to behavior and mental processes. We therefore hope this book will serve as a valuable source of information, a stimulus for discussion, and perhaps as a springboard for future research.

References

Bao, A., & Swaab, D. F. (2011). Sexual differentiation of the human brain: Relation to gender identity, sexual orientation and neuropsychiatric disorders. *Frontiers in Neuroendocrinology, 32*(2), 214-226. https://doi.org/10.1016/j.yfrne.2011.02.007

Buss, D. M. (1999). Sexual strategies theory: Historical origins and current status. *The Journal of Sex Research, 35*(1), 19-31. http://www.jstor.org/stable/3813162

Buss, D. M. (2016). *The evolution of human desire: Strategies of human mating.* New York, NY: Basic Books.

Buss, D. M., & Schmitt, D. P. (1993). Sexual strategies theory: An evolutionary perspective on human mating. *Psychological Review, 100*(2), 204–232.

Compton, M. T., & Walker, E. F. (2008). Physical manifestations of neurodevelopmental disruption: Are minor physical anomalies part of the syndrome of schizophrenia? *Schizophrenia Bulletin, 35*(2), 425-436. https://doi.org/10.1093/schbul/sbn151

Confer, J., Easton, J., Fleischman, D., Goetz, C., Lewis, D., Perilloux, C. & Buss, D. (2010). Evolutionary Psychology: Controversies, questions, prospects, and limitations. *American Psychologist, 65*(2), 110-126. DOI: 10.1037/a0018413

Dempsey Jones, H. (2018). Neuroscientists put the dubious theory of 'phrenology' through rigorous testing for the first time. *The Conversation.* Retrieved from https://theconversation.com/neuroscientists-put-the-dubious-theory-of-phrenology-through-rigorous-testing-for-the-first-time-88291

Encyclopedia Britannica. (2018). *Phrenology: Pseudoscientific practice.* Retrieved from https://www.britannica.com/topic/phrenology

Fazio, R. L., Dyshniku, F., Lykins, A. D., & Cantor, J. M. (2017). Leg length versus torso length in pedophilia: Further evidence of atypical physical development early in life. *Sex Abuse, 29*(5), 500-514. doi: 10.1177/1079063215609936

Flourens, P. (1846). *Phrenology examined*. Philadelphia, PA: Hogan and Thompson.

Maynard, T. M., Sikich, L., Lieberman, J., & LaMantia, A. (2001). Neural development, cell-cell signaling, and the "two-hit" hypothesis of schizophrenia. *Schizophrenia Bulletin, 27*(3), 457-476. https://doi.org/10.1093/oxfordjournals.schbul.a006

Parker Jones, O., Alfaro-Almagro, F., & Jbabdi, S. (2018). An empirical, 21st century evaluation of phrenology. *Cortex, 106*, 26-35. https://doi.org/10.1016/j.cortex.2018.04.011

Kalat, K. W. (2016). *Biological psychology, 12ed*. Boston, MA: Cengage.

Pratt, T. C., Turanovic, J. J., & Cullen, F. T. (2016). Revisiting the criminological consequences of exposure to fetal testosterone: A meta-analysis of the 2D:4D digit ratio. Criminology, 54(4), 587-620. https://doi.org/10.1111/1745-9125.12115.

Richards, R. S. (2007). Ernst Haeckel's alleged anti-Semitism and contributions to Nazi biology, *Biological Theory, 2*, 97-103. doi: 10.1162/biot.2007.2.1.97

Symons, D. (1979). *The evolution of human sexuality*. New York: Oxford University Press.

Thorndike, E. L. (1927). The law of effect. *The American Journal of Psychology, 39*, 212-222.

Tooby, J., & Cosmides, L. (1990). The past explains the present: Emotional adaptations and the structure of ancestral environments. *Ethology and Sociobiology, 11*, 375-424. https://doi.org/10.1016/0162-3095(90)90017-Z

Trivers, R. (1972). Paternal investment and sexual selection. In B. Campbell (Ed.), *Sexual selection and the descent of man* (pp. 136–179). Chicago, IL: Aldine-Atherton.

Chapter 2

FACE

What factors shape facial attractiveness and perceptions thereof? According to researchers, facial beauty, and preferences for specific facial features, can be tied to an ultimate, evolutionary significance of mate choice and reproduction. In this chapter, we present a discussion of what someone's face can tell us about their behaviors and mental processes, and of what preferences for these traits tell us about the perceiver (i.e., receiver psychology). We stress that we do not endeavor to present a systematic literature review. Rather, we focus on presenting some intriguing theory and research on the ultimate meaning of facial beauty.

As pointed out by Langlois and Roggman (1990), the question of "What makes a face beautiful?" has baffled philosophers and scientists throughout time (p. 115). Facial attraction is not a straightforward measure as is height or weight (Damon et al., 2019). As emphasized by Armstrong (2005), there is no single, mathematically derivable explanation for beauty. Evolutionary psychologists contend that what is beautiful to our conscious selves, and/or in our unconscious perception, are traits that facilitate the maximization of reproductive success.

Since the dawn of the field of evolutionary psychology, Symons (1979), Thornhill and Gangestad (1999), and others have dispelled the notion that physical beauty is arbitrary, and they promoted an argument for the selection of beauty through millions of years of human evolution. What we deem now to be attractive is shaped by sexual selection (Grammer & Thornhill, 1994); it is the solution to an adaptive problem in our ancestral environment (Grammer, Fink, Møller, & Thornhill, 2007; Thornhill & Gangestad, 1999). As evidence for its evolutionary underpinnings, facial attraction and the premium placed on facial beauty appear to be universal. People across cultures tend to agree on what faces are attractive, and facial attraction is critical to mate choice cross-culturally (Gangestad & Scheyd, 2005; Little, 2014). In fact, research has repeatedly shown that adults, infants, and even newborns prefer attractive faces over unattractive faces (e.g., Slater et al., 1998).

Why do we find certain faces beautiful?

Seeing an attractive face is proximately rewarding at the biological level. Viewing facial beauty activates our brain's reward circuitry, including the medial orbitofrontal cortex and the nucleus accumbens (Aharon et al., 2001; Bray & O'Doherty, 2007; Cloutier, Heatherton, Whalen, & Kelley, 2008; O'Doherty et al., 2003), areas also involved in drug pleasure and addiction. So, a beautiful face literally affects you like a drug does. This response is boosted when the attractive face is smiling (O'Doherty et al, 2003), perhaps attributable to opening the door for mutual interest.

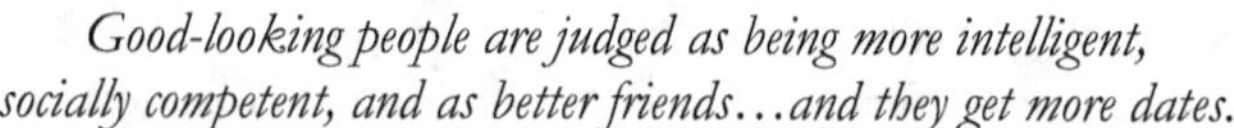

Good-looking people are judged as being more intelligent,
socially competent, and as better friends…and they get more dates.

Being attractive certainly has its benefits (Esel & Polat Esel, 2017). Social psychologists have long documented people's proclivity to believe that "what is beautiful is good" (Dion, Berscheid, & Walster, 1972). People who are facially beautiful are perceived to be more socially competent, intelligent, trustworthy, sexy, exciting, poised, distinct, as having a more desirable personality, and they get more dates (Dion & Dion, 1987; Eagly, Ashmore, Makhijani, & Longo, 1991; Little, Burt, & Perrett, 2006; Lorenzo, Biesanz, & Human, 2010; Shinners, 2009). Health care professionals consider good-looking people to be better patients (Nordholm, 1980). Hollywood films have attractive characters that tend to be more intelligent and friendly than unattractive characters (Smith, McIntosh, & Bazzini,

1999). Evidence shows that even teachers judge more attractive students as being more intelligent, having greater academic potential, and having better social skills than their unattractive counterparts (Ritts, Patterson, & Tubbs, 1992).

Speaking of beauty benefits, it has been known in the criminal justice system for many years that if you are good-looking, you have a better chance of being found not guilty, or at least of getting a less severe sentence (see Mazella & Feingold, 1994; Reynolds & Sanders, 1975). We recall the case of suspected serial killer Sharon Kinne, who was on trial and then acquitted of one of the murders she was alleged to have committed. Despite her background of being sexually involved and then jilted by the victim's husband (he tried to terminate their affair), evidence linking her gun to the crime, and evidence linking her car tires to the scene of the crime, the all-male jury, that some claimed were "smitten" with her, found her not guilty.

Sharon Kinne ("La Pistolera") was said to be
"the prettiest defendant ever tried for murder" in Kansas City

Image from KCMOPolice public files

The *Great Bend Tribune* (1961) on its front page said that Kinne was "probably the prettiest defendant ever tried for murder" in Kansas City, Missouri, U. S. After acquittal, she was photographed giving autographs to

13

the jury (The Salina Journal, 1961). She was later convicted of shooting and killing a man in Mexico, earning her the nickname "La Pistolera." The Investigation Discovery (ID) television series *A Crime to Remember* dedicated a 2016 episode to her, entitled, *"Luck Be a Lady"* (Season 4, Episode 2). In an interesting twist, La Pistolera disappeared from a Mexican prison and was never heard from again. Did her beauty help her escape?

Beautiful and Healthy

Thornhill and Gangestad (1999) cleverly described facial attractiveness as a "health certificate" (p. 452) and reminded us that there have been "beauty contests" throughout evolutionary history, whereby mechanisms of evolution have shaped the features we find attractive, and they have also shaped the receiver psychology of processing and judging these physical attributes. As Symons (1979) pointed out, smooth, clear skin, clear whites of eyes, and shiny hair provide evidence that someone is pathogen free. The argument is that the ability to detect these honest signals of health has evolved because it confers benefits to the perceiver (Gangestad & Scheyd, 2005). What we see now, in essence, won beauty contests across the millennia, and those selecting the winning contestants as reproductive partners left more descendants. Grammer and colleagues (2007) further reminded us that, whereas cultural standards of beauty can change across time and location, they all have been shaped by these common selection pressures.

Some researchers, however, have argued for an alternate mechanism of facial attraction. They theorize that attraction is a generalization of our biological object recognition system. Research has shown we tend to prefer a prototype after we learn a category. This perceptual bias would explain our proclivity to be attracted to average faces (see Fabrice et al., 2019, for a great summarization). In fact, Halberstadt and Rhodes (2003) showed that fish, cars, and birds are more attractive when manipulated for averageness, bolstering the prototype. (Now you are thinking of attractive fish.) Nonetheless, as noted by Fabrice et al. (2019), these two explanations need not be mutually exclusive, and one could be derived from the other, as perceptual biases could still signal mate quality (Rhodes, 2006).

Still, there is some evidence to suggest that evolutionary models of facial attractiveness as a signal of health are incorrect. Kalick, Zebrowitz, Langlois, and Johnson (1998) conducted a study using longitudinal data to trace attractiveness and health in over 300 men and women. Examining participants' health records in adolescence, middle adulthood, and later adulthood, they found that adolescent facial attractiveness ratings were not associated with actual health at any point during a person's lifetime. Moreover, raters mistakenly rated attractive targets as being healthier than their peers (Kalick et al. 1998). These data should be considered carefully in evaluating the health-certificate view of facial attractiveness.

Face Matters

There are many physical and environmental attributes that contribute to perceptions of what faces are beautiful. Evidence suggests that symmetry, averageness, and sex-specific hormonal profiles affect perceptions of facial attractiveness (Rhodes, 2006).

We (Hughes and Harrison) have conducted research on body symmetry and associated behaviors and mental processes (Hughes & Aung, 2018; Hughes, Harrison, & Gallup, 2002), so we devoted another chapter (Chapter 3) in this book entirely to this topic. For the sake of a cogent discussion, we touch on facial symmetry briefly here.

Facial bilateral symmetry means that both sides of your face are the mirror image of one another. That is, your two eyes, nostrils, cheekbones, mouth edges, and all other bilateral features of the face are the same size, position, and shape (Grammer & Thornhill, 1994). Symmetry is thought to be a sign of genotypic and phenotypic quality and predicts desirability as a mate (Hughes & Aung, 2018; Jones, Little, Penton-Voak, Tiddeman, Burt, & Perrett, 2001; Perrett et al., 1999). If someone is asymmetrical, this shows evidence of developmental instability vis-à-vis the inability to resist disease and parasites. Facial asymmetry is argued to be a sign of poorer genes. So, less fluctuating asymmetry (FA) means better genes. FA negatively correlates with ratings of attractiveness; in other words, less *asymmetry* means more attractiveness and higher mate quality (Møller & Thornhill, 1998; Scheib, Gangestad, & Thornhill, 1999).

We are indeed more attracted to people with symmetrical faces. We have evolved to detect symmetry as a feature of good genes (unconsciously) and therefore are attracted to targets that possess symmetry. This evolved psychological mechanism translates into our conscious perception of what we deem is beautiful. Remember, in evolutionary terms, physical attraction ("She is hot!") is the proximate cause of attraction to symmetry, and increased opportunity for reproduction with a quality partner is the ultimate cause. We are fairly certain you do not frequently approach a potential romantic or sexual partner with a digital caliper to measure traits and ascertain their mate value; it is an innate ability. However, that would be a novel approach to getting a date.

Average and Hot

Averageness is also implicated in facial attraction. Symons (1979) argued that averageness is associated with good genes, because selection is stabilized. Gangestad and Buss (1993) and Thornhill and Gangestad (1993) theorized that facial averageness signals protein heterozygosity, which is conducive to disease resistance and defense against parasite. The latter asserts that attractiveness is the adaptive solution to the problem of selecting a healthy mate.

Langlois and Roggman (1990) and Langlois, Roggman, and Musselman (1994) were amongst the first researchers known to us to document that composite (average) faces tend to be more attractive than the individual faces used to generate the image. Whereas numerous studies have shown preferences for averageness (e.g., Halberstadt & Rhodes, 2000; Rhodes & Tremewan, 1996), DeBruine and colleagues (2007) stressed that attractive faces are not always average, and extremes are also rated as attractive.

Some argued that the reason why experimentally averaged faces were found to be more attractive is because the composite cancels out asymmetry of the individual components. However, evidence suggests this is not exactly the case. Rhodes, Sumich, and Byatt (1999) provided data that showed averageness predicts unique variance in attractiveness ratings, beyond that which is predicted by symmetry. Valentine, Darling, and Donnelly (2004) also showed that averageness contributed uniquely to ratings of attraction by morphing facial profiles of women using a side view where bilateral symmetry could not be a factor. Indeed, even in this situation, faces morphed away from the average shape were still rated as less attractive (Valentine et al., 2004).

Of note, preferences for average faces may be uniquely human. Tomeo, Underleider, and Liu (2017) showed that rhesus monkeys prefer to view faces that vary from average. To gauge preference, these researchers considered length of glance to be a marker of monkey interest. Adult male monkeys looked longer at nonaverage male monkey faces. Tomeo et al. asserted these results show that preferences for average faces do not generalize to nonhuman primates. However, whereas this study provided valuable data and a rich source of consideration for future research, Tomeo et al. considered the preferences of only three monkeys in their study. There are several caveats to consider with respect to implications for attractiveness preferences. These three monkeys may have had unique taste. Male monkeys may view outliers as a threat to safety, thus staring longer in assessment. Male monkeys may have preferences different from those of female monkeys. More data are needed to assess this phenomenon, particularly to determine if it is conserved across species.

Sexual Dimorphism

Sexual dimorphism in faces refers to the phenomenon that men's faces are more masculine, and women's faces are more feminine. That is, men and women each have distinctive, sex-specific, expected appearances mediated by hormones.

Men undergo facial masculinization via mechanisms of the hormone testosterone. Testosterone influences the development of craniofacial features, including the jaw, chin, eyebrow ridges, and facial width. In men, these features are linked to salivary testosterone levels (Lefevre, Lewis, Perrett, & Penke, 2013; Penton-Voak & Chen, 2004) and signal formidability in intrasexual competition and immunocompetence (Penton-Voak & Perrett, 2000; Thornhill & Gangestad, 1999).

In women, a feminine face is marked by soft features, such as full lips, large eyes, and an unremarkable jaw. These are characteristics mediated by estrogens and that signal health and fitness (Singh, 1993; Perrett et al., 1998). Women with higher estrogen levels are indeed judged to have more feminine faces (Law Smith et al., 2005). Research conducted with static and dynamic stimuli showed that men tend to prefer women with feminine faces (Fraccaro, Feinberg, DeBruine, Little, Watkins, & Jones, 2010; O'Connor, Fraccaro, Pisanski, Tigue, & Feinberg, 2013). A feminine face is considered attractive, and what is attractive is a purported marker of fertility and health.

Researchers have provided evidence to suggest that the human preference for sexually dimorphic faces is evolutionary novel. Scott and colleagues (2014) conducted a large-scaled study of 12 populations with diverse economies. They found that preferences for sex-specific, exaggerated facial traits are found only in economically developed countries. This challenges the notion that facial dimorphism was an important signal in the environment of evolutionary adaptedness (EEA).

Interestingly, Scott and colleagues (2010) used geometric, morphometric methodology to detect sexual dimorphism in faces and created a discrimination index that correctly classified almost every face in their study as being that of a man or woman. However, they found no relationship between morphological masculinity and ratings of facial attractiveness. They suggested that current environmental conditions, such a slow life history (preference for fewer sexual partners), is more relevant to attractiveness assessments, and that preferences for masculine faces may more accurately reflect adaptive choices in the harsh conditions of the ancestral environment (Scott, Pound, Stephen, Clark, & Penton-Voak, 2010). As evolution does not equal genetic determinism, it is possible for the modern human to operate outside the parameters of ancestral tendencies.

Sexually dimorphic facial properties relate to certain assessments about a man. In our own work, we found that heterosexual men had greater overall masculine measured facial features than gay men, and the more masculine a man's facial features were, the more likely he was perceived by raters to have a heterosexual rather than homosexual orientation (Hughes & Bremme, 2011). It should also be noted that women judge men with less masculine faces to be more honest and better parents (Perrett et al., 1998) and faces that appear overly masculinize faces are associated with psychopathy and narcissism (Lyons, Marcinkowska, Helleb, & McGrath, 2015). Likewise, women perceive men with more masculinized facial features to be dishonest and cold with respect to parental investment (Perrett et al., 1998). It seems more manly faces are physically desirable but not always seen consciously as better. It does seem appropriate here to point out that the masculine men in the exemplar photo are known to the authors and do not exhibit psychopathy, narcissism, or dishonesty.

What makes a male face attractive? What makes a face masculine?

Is there accuracy in this perception of masculine faces? The drawback of high-testosterone men as partners is that they are likely less committed to their partners and their offspring, and they are more likely to have an unrestricted sociosexual orientation (greater preference for uncommitted sex; Boothroyd, Jones, Burt, DeBruine, & Perrett, 2008). In a study whose name we applaud for creativity, *"Bad to the Bone: Facial Structure Predicts Unethical Behaviour,"* Haselhuhn and Wong (2011) showed that men with wider faces (a larger facial width-to-height ratio, or facial WHR) were more likely to cheat and deceive counterparts for financial gain. Researchers suggested these men's sense of power influenced their moral decisions. Again, a wider face is a marker of testosterone exposure (Penton-Voak & Perrett, 2000). Nonetheless, we must keep in mind the wide individual variation in these traits, and there are many masculine men who are notable partners and fathers. It should be added that we are certain the subject in our example father photo, our friend, is an outstanding parent.

Can we predict from physical appearance who will be a great dad?

Preferences for feminine women's faces can be moderated by other factors. Marcinkowska and colleagues (2014) assessed preferences for women's faces in 1,972 heterosexual men from 28 countries. Whereas men globally preferred feminine women's faces, this preference correlated positively with the health of the nation of origin. The researchers theorized that in harsher environments (i.e., poor economic conditions and more cases of poor health), men gravitate to signs of resource access potential instead of signs of high fertility. In addition, Welling et al. (2008) found that men with higher testosterone prefer feminine women's faces. This makes sense, as when testosterone is higher, men pay closer attention to stimuli that is socially important (Van Honk et al., 1999; Welling et al., 2008).

Interestingly, your own attractiveness can influence your ratings of others' attractiveness. Little and colleagues (2001) asked women to rate their self-attractiveness and to judge male faces for a long-term relationship or for a short-term relationship (i.e., "one-night stand" or sexual "hookup"). Whereas masculinity preferences did not differ between relationship type, women who considered themselves attractive showed an increased preference for masculine faces for long-term relationships. The researchers suggested that women of high attractiveness, and therefore high mate value, make choices to maximize the likelihood they secure a mate with high phenotypic quality and therefore increased immunocompetence. The caveat exists that perceptions of your own attractiveness may not accurately match others' perceptions of your attractiveness.

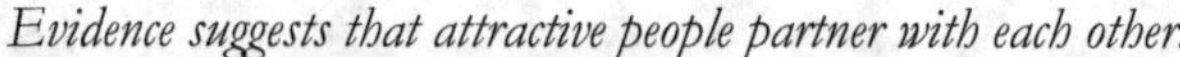

Evidence suggests that attractive people partner with each other.

Further, evolutionary psychologists, social psychologists, and sociologists have asserted for many years that people engage in *homophily*, or significant ties to people who match them in meaningful ways, like job, education level, and even facial attractiveness level. Some call this *the matching hypothesis*. The matching hypothesis predicts that, for example, if you are a "10 out of 10" on an attractiveness scale, chances are you are going to seek, and be partnered with, someone else who is a "10." There is some empirical support for the notion that people in romantic pairs have similar levels of facial attractiveness (Feingold, 1988; Taylor et al., 2011).

Changing Preferences (About Face)

It seems that what is beautiful…may not always be. Evidence shows that perceptions of a beautiful face can vacillate. For example, moral valence can affect attractiveness ratings. Participants found the same faces more attractive when they were altruistic nurses and less attractive when they were drug dealers. This effect is more pronounced for women perceivers compared to men perceivers (González-Álvarez & Cervera-Crespo, 2019).

Facial expressions also affect receiver psychology. People rate the same faces as more attractive when they are smiling as opposed to when having non-smiling neutral expression (Reis et al., 1990). In addition, attraction preferences increase when someone is looking at us and smiling (Jones et al., 2006). Raters attribute a variety of other positive attributes to a smiling individual such as sincerity, sociability, and competence. However, raters also attribute lower levels of independence and masculinity to smiling faces (Reis et al., 1990).

Batres and Perrett have conducted research demonstrating that harshness of environment affects facial preferences. Men in an Army (military) training camp, a markedly stressful situation, showed an increased preference for female facial adipose (Batres & Perrett, 2016). People in the developing country, El Salvador, had disparate facial preferences depending on whether they had Internet access. Those without Internet access prefer more feminine men and more masculine, higher adipose women. Those without Internet access also had less access to running water (Batres & Perrett, 2014). This supports the environmental harshness hypothesis, as these are robust traits signaling the ability to survive famine (Batres & Perrett, 2014; Brown & Konner, 1987).

Women seem to change their opinion of the same man's physical attractiveness depending upon his advertisement of his resources. For instance, the same men were rated by women on different occasions as appearing more attractive when the man wore high-end attire (i.e., suit and tie) as opposed to more casual clothing, when shown in pictures depicting high luxury home ownership, and when sitting in high status cars (see Hughes & Aung, 2017, for review).

Some evidence suggests that women's preferences for masculine faces changes across the menstrual cycle, in what has been called *the dual mating hypothesis*. According to this hypothesis, women's preferences shift during ovulation towards more masculine male faces (cues of fitness), whereas preference for more feminine male faces predominates during the non-fertile phases of the menstrual cycle. Roney and Simmons (2008) showed that women's estradiol and testosterone preferences fluctuate together across the phases of the menstrual cycle (women have high estradiol at ovulation and low estradiol during menstruation).

According to Jones, Hahn, and DeBruine (2019), this strategy presupposes cuckoldry, or tricking a man into investing in a child who does not carry his genes, as a primary feature. Jones et al. (2019) detailed several issues and highlighted several studies that challenge this hypothesis. Namely, studies testing women's preferences for masculine faces have many limitations in that: 1. they are typically underpowered (i.e., not a large enough participant sample size to facilitate best practices in statistical testing), with many very underpowered; 2. they tend to use women's self-reports to judge menstrual cycle status, which is an imperfect method; and 3. they largely use between-subject designs (i.e., comparing women in different phases of the menstrual cycle), which do not detect sensitive effects as do within-subject designs (i.e., comparing the same group across a cycle). Jones et al. also reported that many studies have produced null results when testing the dual mating hypothesis.

Bobst, Sauter, Foppa, and Lobmaier (2014) tested women in the low-fertility early follicular phase. Interestingly, naturally cycling women's preferences for masculine faces peaked with testosterone. This was not true for women using hormonal birth control. What is beautiful, then, is not a constant. Receiver psychology, it seems, is a dynamic phenomenon.

In our field, we argue that preferences for facial beauty are the product of our evolved genetic heritage. Then again, maybe they are not. Germine and colleagues (2015) asserted that individual preferences for facial aesthetics can be explained more by environmental factors than by genetic factors. Using an impressively large set of twin data from 547 monozygotic twin pairs (i.e., identical twins who share 100% genetic material) and 214 same-sex dizygotic twin pairs (i.e., fraternal twins who share an average of 50% genetic material), they found that unshared environment explained most of the variance in attraction ratings. That is, each person's unique environment was more important in determining what they deemed as attractive. There is a need for more research about environmental effects on attractiveness perceptions.

Other Issues to Face

Of note, the science of facial attractiveness is very nuanced, with increasingly sophisticated studies emerging to provide detailed evidence of the components of facial attractiveness. For example, limbal rings are dark rings around the iris (the colored part) of the eye and are related to higher genetic quality. In short-term mating choice tasks, women's choices evinced aversion to men without limbal rings (Brown, Sacco, & Medlin, 2019).

Facial skin color and health also can be used as a determinant of attractiveness (Jones, Little, Burt, & Perrett, 2004). Jones et al. (2004) conducted two studies to test the relation between skin health and male facial attractiveness, regardless of face shape. They found a small correlation between skin health ratings and facial attractiveness ratings. They also found that faces rated as healthier had skin that was rated as healthier. Evidence for this as a universal phenomenon has been mixed (Stephan, Scott, Coetzee, Pound, Perrett, & Penton-Voak, 2012; Han et al., 2018).

Of course, the face is not the only physical feature we use to assess potential mates. Our research team (see Hughes et al., 2002) for decades has stressed the importance of nonvisual modalities of mate assessment. Groyecka and colleagues (2019) underscored that in addition to visual cues, we rely heavily on auditory and olfactory (odor) cues to mate quality (as discussed in Chapters 4 and 8 in this book). In fact, as Groyecka et al. pointed out, information from multiple modalities (e.g., face, voice) of person assessment are integrated in a common neural region. The superior temporal sulcus (STS) is thought to be a "convergence zone" for the processing of affective cues (Watson et al., 2014). The STS is highly involved in emotion processing and represents a social cognition area underlying perspective-taking, empathy, and the processing judgments of trustworthiness and intention (Campanella & Belin, 2007; Watson et al., 2014; Winston, Strange, O'Doherty, & Dolan, 2002). Also, as we have been stating for decades (Hughes et al., 2002), mating in the EEA likely took place in the safety of night, and you cannot see very well what someone looks like in the dark. Communication mechanisms like voice, then, are critical tools of mate assessment. You can be heard in the dark.

In terms of reproductive success, the caveat exists that face information gives less fertility information than does body information (Confer, Perilloux, & Buss, 2010). To determine whether face or body would be more important in a short-term versus long-term mating situation, Confer and colleagues (2010) asked women and men to consider a hypothetical, short-term mating situation (i.e., hook-up). More men chose to evaluate a body cue over a face cue of a potential short-term mate versus a potential long-term mate. Women's choices were unaffected by hypothetical relationship condition.

Still, as noted by Bruce and Young (1986) decades ago, "a face is the most distinctive and widely used key to a person's identity" (p. 305), and the face plays a central role in social interactions. A face can tell us about a person's intention, mood, interest, and much more (Bruce & Young, 1986). Whereas face is not the only feature we use to assess potential mates, it appears to be one of the most critical targets for mate assessment (Candolin, 2003). Currie and Little (2009) empirically tested whether people used the face as the most prominent cue to evaluate others' mate value. Using general linear model analysis, they indeed found that facial attractiveness ratings were a better predictor of overall attractiveness perception (face and body combined) than were body attractiveness ratings. Currie and Little (2009) made a good speculation as to why the face is an extremely salient cue of mate value. In the face, a number of areas that are vulnerable to developmental perturbations exist closely to each other (e.g., nose, eyes, mouth). Thus, we can make a quick judgment by looking in a single area.

Again, we do not have a precise way to determine objectively what makes a face beautiful. However, some researchers have made attempts to derive a precise mathematical formula as to what makes up the perfect face. One such mathematical formula used is the Golden Ratio (also known as the "Golden Mean", "Divine Ratio", "Golden Section", and the "Fibonacci Ratio"). This mathematical equation signifies a 1.618 ratio ("Phi") and occurs when a line is divided into two parts such that the longer portion divided by the smaller portion is equal to the entire length divided by the longer portion. The Golden Ratio has been famed throughout history for its aesthetic properties, often used in architecture and paintings, and is claimed to be a universal natural phenomenon (see review in Green, 1995). For centuries, artists have used this formula to create beauty, perhaps because of its focus on symmetry.

Certain ratios of different features of the human face are thought to reflect the Golden Ratio (e.g., width of nose to width of mouth; width of mouth to distance between outer part of eyes; distance from pupil to bottom of nose to the distance from bottom of nose to the tip of chin). Adults rate faces with proportions that are farthest from the Golden Mean as less attractive than faces with proportions closer to it (Geldart, Maurer, & Henderson,

1999). Measurements of fashion models' faces also tend to come closer to the Golden Mean proportions than do faces from the rest of the population (Lowey, 1994). Modern actresses Amber Heard, Halle Berry, and Helen Mirren are said to have faces that closely approximate the Golden Ratio.

In a non-peer-reviewed paper, Schwind (2011) described Marquardt's Phi Mask, which is a creation of different facial proportions lines mapped together that can be overlaid onto an image of a face to assess deviations from the Golden Mean. This mask is thought to represent the ideal for a beautiful face. Some scholars have promoted its utility as a guide for judging beauty and even for planning plastic surgery of structures related to face, orthodontics, and dentistry (Jefferson, 1996; Prokopakis et al., 2012). However, some researchers have identified problems with applying Marquardt's Phi Mask or Golden Ratio facial proportions to judge or attain standards of beauty that vary on a feminine-masculine continuum (Holland, 2008). Our understanding of facial beauty may not be as exact as we would like.

Conclusion

We prefer beautiful faces. Evidence suggests that facial beauty signals to the perceiver that the target is a high-quality mate. Although there is no single way to determine beauty, our evolutionary heritage has provided physical and cognitive mechanisms whereby we know it when we see it.

References

Aharon, I., Etcoff, N., Ariely, D., Chabris, C. F., O'Connor, E., & Breiter, H. C. (2001). Beautiful faces have variable reward value: fMRI and behavioral evidence. *Neuron, 3*(8), 537-551. https://doi.org/10.1016/S0896-6273(01)00491-3

Armstrong, J. (2005). *The secret power of beauty: Why happiness is in the eye of the beholder.* London, UK: Penguin Global.

Batres, C., & Perrett, D. I. (2014). The influence of the digital divide on face preferences in El Salvador: People without internet access prefer more feminine men, more masculine women, and women with higher adiposity. *PLOS One, 9*(7), e100966. https://doi.org/10.1371/journal.pone.0100966

Batres, C., & Perrett, D. I. (2016). How the harsh environment of an army training camp changes human (Homo sapiens) facial preferences. *Ethology, 123*(1), 61-68. https://doi.org/10.1111/eth.12571

Bobst, C., Sauter, S., Foppa, A., & Lobmaier, J. S. (2014). Early follicular testosterone level predicts preference for masculinity in male faces – But not for women taking hormonal contraception. *Psychoneuroendocrinology, 41,* 142-150. https://doi.org/10.1016/j.psyneuen.2013.12.012

Boothroyd, L. G., Jones, B. C., Burt, D. M., DeBruine, L. M., & Perrett, D. I.

(2008). Facial correlates of sociosexuality. *Evolution and Human Behavior, 29*(3), 211-218. https://doi.org/10.1016/j.evolhumbehav.2007.12.009

Bray, S., & O'Doherty, J. (2007). Neural coding of reward-prediction error signals during classical conditioning with attractive faces. *Journal of Neurophysiology, 97*(4), 3036-3045. https://doi.org/10.1152/jn.01211.2006

Brown, P. J., & Konner, M. (1987) An anthropological perspective on obesity. *Annals of the New York Academy of Sciences, 499*, 29-46. doi:10.1111/j.1749-6632.1987.tb36195.x.

Brown, M., Sacco, D., & Medlin, M. M. (2019). Women's short-term mating goals elicit avoidance of faces whose eyes lack limbal rings. *Evolutionary Behavioral Sciences, 13*(3), 278-285. doi: 10.1037/ebs0000135

Bruce, V., & Young, A. (1986). Understanding face recognition. *British Journal of Psychology, 77*(3), 305-327. https://doi.org/10.1111/j.2044-8295.1986.tb02199.x

Campanella, S., & Belin, P. (2007). Integrating face and voice in person perception. *Trends in Cognitive Science, 11*(12), 535-543. doi: 10.1016/j.tics.2007.10.001

Candolin, U. (2003). The use of multiple cues in mate choice. *Biological Reviews, 78*(4), 575-595.

Cloutier, J., Heatherton, T. F., Whalen, P. J., & Kelley, W. M. (2008). Are attractive people rewarding? Sex differences in the neural substrates of facial attractiveness. *Journal of Cognitive Neuroscience, 20*(6), 941-951. https://doi.org/10.1162/jocn.2008.20062

Currie, T. E., & Little, A. C. (2009). The relative importance of the face and body in judgments of human physical attractiveness. Evolution and Human Behavior, 30(6), 409-416. doi: 10.1016/j.evolhumbehav.2009.06.005

Damon, F. et al. (2019). Preference for attractive faces is species-specific. *Journal of Comparative Psychology, 133*(2), 262-271. doi:10.1037/com0000148

DeBruine, L. M., Jones, B. C., Unger, L., Little, A. C., & Feinberg, D. R. (2007). Dissociating averageness and attractiveness: Attractive faces are not always average. *Journal of Experimental Psychology: Human Perception and Performance, 33*(6), 1420-1430. doi: 10.1037/0096-1523.33.6.1420

Dion, K., Berscheid, E., & Walster, E. (1972). What is beautiful is good. *Journal of Personality and Social Psychology, 24(*3), 285-290. http://dx.doi.org/10.1037/h0033731

Dion. K. L., & Dion, K. K. (1987). Belief in a just world and physical attractiveness stereotyping. *Journal of Personality and Social Psychology, 52*(4), 775-780.

Eagly, A. H., Ashmore, R. D., Makhijani, M. G., & Longo, L. C. (1991). What is beautiful is good, but…: A meta-analytic review of research on the physical attractiveness stereotype. *Psychological Bulletin, 110*(1), 109-128.

Esel, E., & Polat Esel, G. (2017). The neurobiology and evolutionary foundations of the perception of beauty. *Düşünen Adam: Journal of Psychiatry and Neurological Sciences, 30*(4), 368-388. http://dx.doi.org/10.5350/DAJPN2017300412

Feingold, A. (1988). Matching for attractiveness in romantic partners and same-sex friends: A meta-analysis and theoretical critique. *Psychological Bulletin, 104*(2), 226-235. http://dx.doi.org/10.1037/0033-2909.104.2.226

Fraccaro, P. J., Feinberg, D. R., DeBruine, L. M., Little, A. C., Watkins, C. D., &

Jones, B. C. (2010). Correlated male preferences for femininity in female faces and voices. *Evolutionary Psychology, 8*(3), 447-461. https://doi.org/10.1177/147470491000800311

Gangestad, S. W., & Buss, D. M. (1993). Pathogen prevalence and human mate preferences. *Ethology and Sociobiology, 14*(2), 89-96. https://doi.org/10.1016/0162-3095(93)90009-7

Gangestad, S. W., & Scheyd, G. J. (2005). The evolution of human physical attractiveness. *Annual Review of Anthropology, 34*, 523-548. doi: 10.1146/annurev.anthro.33.070203.143733

Geldart, S. Maurer, D. & Henderson, H. (1999). Effects of the height of the internal features of faces on adults' aesthetic ratings and 5-month-olds' looking times. *Perception, 28*, 839-850.

Germine, L., et al. (2015). Individual aesthetic preferences for faces are shaped mostly by environments, not genes. *Current Biology, 25*(20), 2684-2689. https://doi.org/10.1016/j.cub.2015.08.048

González-Álvarez, J., & Cervera-Crespo, T. (2019). Gender differences in sexual attraction and moral judgment: Research with artificial face models. *Psychological Reports, 122*(2), 525-535. doi: 10.1177/0033294118756891

Grammer, K., Fink, B., Møller, A. P., & Thornhill, R. (2003). Darwinian aesthetics: Sexual selection and the biology of beauty. *Biological Reviews of the Cambridge Philosophical Society, 78*(3), 385-407. https://doi.org/10.1017/S1464793102006085

Grammer, K., & Thornhill, R. (1994). Human (Homo sapiens) facial attractiveness and sexual selection: The role of symmetry and averageness. *Journal of Comparative Psychology, 108*(3), 233-242.

Great Bend Tribune. (1961 June 18). *KC murderess on trial.* Retrieved from www.newspapers.com

Green, C. (1995). All that glitters: A review of psychological research on the aesthetics of the golden section. *Perception, 24*, 937-968.

Halberstadt, J., & Rhodes, G. (2000). The attractiveness of nonface averages: Implications for an evolutionary explanation of the attractiveness of average faces. *Psychological Science, 11*(4), 285-289. https://doi.org/10.1111/1467-9280.00257

Halberstadt, J., & Rhodes, G. (2003). It's not just average faces that are attractive: Computer-manipulated averageness makes birds, fish, and automobiles attractive. *Psychonomic Bulletin & Review, 10*(1), 149-156.

Han, C., et al. (2018). Cultural differences in preferences for facial coloration. *Evolution and Human Behavior, 39*(2), 154-159. https://doi.org/10.1016/j.evolhumbehav.2017.11.005

Haselhuhn, M. P., & Wong, E. M. (2011). Bad to the bone: Facial structure predicts unethical behaviour. *Proceedings of the Royal Society B. 279*(1728), 571-576. https://doi.org/10.1098/rspb.2011.1193

Holland, E. (2008). Marquardt's phi mask: Pitfalls of relying on fashion models and the golden ratio to describe a beautiful face. *Aesthetic Plastic Surgery, 32*(2), 200-208. https://doi.org/10.1007/s00266-007-9080-z

Hughes, S. M., & Aung, T. (2017). Modern day female preferences for resources and provisioning by long-term mates. *Evolutionary Behavioral Sciences. 11*(3),

242-261. http://dx.doi.org/10.1037/ebs0000084

Hughes, S. M., & Aung, T. (2018). Symmetry in motion: Perception of attractiveness changes with facial movement. *Journal of Nonverbal Behavior, 42*(3), 267-283. https://doi.org/10.1007/s10919-018-0277-4

Hughes, S. M., & Bremme, R. (2011). The effects of facial symmetry and sexually-dimorphic facial proportions on the assessment of sexual orientation. *Journal of Social, Evolutionary, and Cultural Psychology, 5*(4), 214-230. http://dx.doi.org/10.1037/h0099261

Hughes, S. M., Harrison, M. A., & Gallup, G. G., Jr. (2002). The sound of symmetry: Voice as a marker of developmental instability. *Evolution and Human Behavior, 23*(3), 173-180. doi:10.1016/S1090-5138(01)00099-X

Jefferson, Y. (1996). Unraveling the mystery of facial beauty and its biological significance. *Journal of General Orthodontics, 7,* 7-25.

Jones, B. C., DeBruine, L. M., Little, A. C., Conway, C. A., & Feinberg, D. R. (2006). Integrating gaze direction and expression in preferences for attractive faces. *Psychological Science, 17*(7), 588-591. https://doi.org/10.1111/j.1467-9280.2006.01749.x

Jones, B. C., Little, A. C., Burt, D. M., & Perrett, D. I. (2004). When facial attractiveness is only skin deep. *Perception, 33*(5), 569-576. doi: 10.1068/p3463

Jones, B. C., Little, A. C., Penton-Voak, I. S., Tiddeman, B. P., Burt, D. M., & Perrett, D. I. (2001). Facial symmetry and judgements of apparent health: Support for a "good genes" explanation of the attractiveness–symmetry relationship. *Evolution and Human Behavior, 22*(6), 417-429. https://doi.org/10.1016/S1090-5138(01)00083-6

Kalick, S. M., Zebrowitz, L. A., Langlois, J. H., & Johnson, R. M. (1998). Does human facial attractiveness honestly advertise health? Longitudinal data on an evolutionary question. *Psychological Science, 9*(1), 8-13. https://doi.org/10.1111/1467-9280.00002

Langlois, J. H., & Roggman, L. A. (1990). Attractive faces are only average. *Psychological Science, 1*(2), 115-121. https://doi.org/10.1111/j.1467-9280.1990.tb00079.x

Langlois, J. H., Roggman, L. A., & Musselman, L. (1994). What is average and what is not average about attractive faces? *Psychological Science, 5*(4), 214-220. https://doi.org/10.1111/j.1467-9280.1994.tb00503.x

Law Smith, M. J., et al. (2005). Facial appearance is a cue to oestrogen levels in women. *Proceedings of the Royal Society B, 273*(1583), 135-140. http://doi.org/10.1098/rspb.2005.3296.

Lefevre, C. E., Lewis, G. L., Perrett, D. I., & Penke, L. (2013). *Evolution and Human Behavior,* 34(4), 273-279. https://doi.org/10.1016/j.evolhumbehav.2013.03.005

Little, A. C. (2014). Facial attractiveness. *WIREs Cognitive Science, 5,* 621-634. doi: 10.1002/wcs.1316

Little, A. C., Burt, D. M., Penton-Voak, I. S., & Perrett, D. I. (2001). Self-perceived attractiveness influences human female preferences for sexual dimorphism and symmetry in male faces. *Proceedings of the Royal Society B, 268,* 39-44. doi: 10.1098/rspb.2000.1327

Little, A. C., Burt, D. M., & Perrett, D. I. (2006). What is good is beautiful: Face preference reflects desired personality. *Personality and Individual Differences, 41*(6), 1107-1118. https://doi.org/10.1016/j.paid.2006.04.015

Lorenzo, G. L., Biesanz, J. C., & Human, L. J. (2010). What is beautiful is good and more accurately understood: Physical attractiveness and accuracy in first impressions of personality. *Psychological Science, 21*(12), 1777-1782. https://doi.org/10.1177/0956797610388048

Lowey, M. (1994). Beauty: Making sense of sex appeal, is there an ideal face? *Focus,* p. 20.

Lyons, M. T., Marcinkowska, U. M., Helle, S., & McGrath, L. (2015). Mirror, mirror, on the wall, who is the most masculine of them all? The Dark Triad, masculinity, and women's mate choice. *Personality and Individual Differences, 74*, 153-158. https://doi.org/10.1016/j.paid.2014.10.020

Marcinkowska, U. M., et al. (2014). Cross-cultural variation in men's preference for sexual dimorphism in women's faces. *Biology Letters, 10*(4), 20130850. https://doi.org/10.1098/rsbl.2013.0850

Mazella, R., & Feingold, A. (1994). The effects of physical attractiveness, race, socioeconomic status, and gender of defendants and victims on judgments of mock jurors: A meta-analysis. *Journal of Applied Social Psychology, 24*(15), 1315-1338.

Møller, A. P., & Thornhill, R. (1998). Bilateral symmetry and sexual selection: A meta-analysis. *The American Naturalist, 151*(2), 174-192. doi:10.1086/286110

Nordholm, L. A. (1980). Beautiful patients are good patients: evidence for the physical attractiveness stereotype in first impressions of patients. *Social Science & Medicine. Part A: Medical Psychology & Medical Sociology, 14*(1), 81-83.

O'Connor, J. J., Fraccaro, P. J., Pisanski, K., Tigue, C. C., & Feinberg, D. R. (2013). Men's preferences for women's femininity in dynamic cross-modal stimuli. *PLOS One, 8*(7), e69531. doi: 10.1371/journal.pone.0069531.

O'Doherty, J., Winston, J., Critchely, H., Perrett, D., Butt, D. M., & Dolan, R. J. (2003). Beauty in a smile: The role of medial orbitofrontal cortex in facial attractiveness. *Neuropsychologia, 41*(2), 147-155. https://doi.org/10.1016/S0028-3932(02)00145-8

Penton-Voak, I., & Chen, J. Y. (2004). High salivary testosterone is linked to masculine male facial appearance in humans. *Evolution and Human Behavior, 25*(4), 229-241. https://doi.org/10.1016/j.evolhumbehav.2004.04.003

Penton-Voak, I., & Perrett, D. I. (2000). Female preference for male faces changes cyclically: Further evidence. *Evolution and Human Behavior, 21*(1), 39-48. https://doi.org/10.1016/S1090-5138(99)00033-1

Perrett, D. I., Burt, D. M., Penton-Voak, I. S., Lee, K. J., Rowland, D. A., & Edwards, R. (1999). Symmetry and human facial attractiveness. *Evolution and Human Behavior, 20*(5), 295-307. https://doi.org/10.1016/S1090-5138(99)00014-8

Perrett, D. I., Lee, K. J., Penton-Voak, I., Rowland, D., Yoshikawa, S., Burt, D. M....Akamatsu, S. (1998). Effects of sexual dimorphism on facial attractiveness. *Nature, 394*(6696), 884-887. doi:10.1038/29772

Prokopakis, E. P. (2012). The golden ratio in facial symmetry. *Rhinology, 51*(18), 18-21. doi:10.4193/Rhino12.111

Reynolds, D. E., & Sanders, M. S. (1975). Effect of defendant attractiveness, age, and injury on severity of sentence given by simulated jurors. *The Journal of Social Psychology, 96*(1), 149-150. https://doi.org/10.1080/00224545.1975.9923277

Rhodes, G. (2006). The evolutionary psychology of facial beauty. *Annual Review of Psychology, 57*, 199-226.

Rhodes, G., & Tremewan, T. (1996). Averageness, exaggeration, and facial attractiveness. *Psychological Science, 7*(2), 105-110. https://doi.org/10.1111/j.1467-9280.1996.tb00338.x

Rhodes, G., Sumich, A., & Byatt, G. (1999). Are average facial configurations attractive only because of their symmetry? *Psychological Science, 10*(1), 52-58. https://doi.org/10.1111/1467-9280.00106

Ritts, V., Miles, L., & Tubbs, M. E. (1992). Expectations, impressions, and judgments of physically attractive students: A review. *Review of Educational Research, 62*(4), 413-426. https://doi.org/10.3102/00346543062004413

Roney, J. R., & Simmons, Z. L. (2008). Women's estradiol predicts preference for facial cues of men's testosterone. *Hormones and Behavior, 53*(1), 14-19. https://doi.org/10.1016/j.yhbeh.2007.09.008

Scheib, J. E., Gangestad, S. W., & Thornhill, R. (1999). Facial attractiveness, symmetry and cues of good genes. *Proceedings of the Royal Society B, 266*(1431), 1913-1917. https://doi.org/10.1098/rspb.1999.0866

Schwind, V. (2011). *The golden ratio in 3D human face modeling.* Stewart Media University. Retrieved from https://vali.de/wp-content/uploads/The-Golden-Ratio-in-3D-Face-Modelling.pdf

Scott, I. M., et al. (2014). Human preferences for sexually dimorphic faces may be evolutionarily novel. *Proceedings of the National Academy of Science (PNAS) of the United States of America, 7*(111), 14388-14393. doi:10.1073/pnas.1409643111

Scott, I. M. L., Pound, N., Stephen, I. D., Clark, A. P., Penton-Voak, I. S. (2010). Does masculinity matter? The contribution of masculine face shape to male attractiveness in humans. *PLOS One, 5*(10), e13585.

Shinners, E. (2009). Effects of the "what is beautiful is good" stereotype on perceived trustworthiness. *UW-L Journal of Undergraduate Research.* Retrieved from https://www.uwlax.edu/urc/jur-online/PDF/2009/shinners-erinPSY.pdf

Singh, D. (1993). Body shape and women's attractiveness: The critical role of waist-to-hip ratio. *Human Nature, 4*(3), 297-321. doi: 10.1007/BF02692203

Slater, A., Von der Schulenburg, C., Brown, E., Badenoch, M., Butterworth, G., Parsons, S., Samuels, C. (1998). Newborn infants prefer attractive faces. *Infant Behavior and Development, 21*(2), 345-354. https://doi.org/10.1016/S0163-6383(98)90011-X

Smith, S. M., McIntosh, W. D., & Bazzini, D. G. (1999). Are the beautiful good in Hollywood? An investigation of the beauty-and-goodness stereotype on film. *Basic and Applied Social Psychology, 21*(1), 69-80. https://doi.org/10.1207/s15324834basp2101_7

Stephan, I. D., Scott, I. M. L., Coetzee, V., Pound, N., Perrett, D. I., & Penton-Voak, I. S. (2012). Cross-cultural effects of color, but not morphological masculinity, on perceived attractiveness of men's faces. *Evolution and Human Behavior, 33*(4), 260-267. https://doi.org/10.1016/j.evolhumbehav.2011.10.003

Symons, D. (1979). *The evolution of human sexuality*. New York, NY: Oxford University Press.

Taylor, L. S., Fiore, A. T., Mendelsohn, G. A., & Cheshire, C. (2011). "Out of my league": A real-world test of the matching hypothesis. *Personality and Social Psychology Bulletin, 37*(7), 942-954. https://doi.org/10.1177/0146167211409947

The Salina Journal. (1961 June 23). *"Too many loopholes," so Sharon Kinne acquitted*. Retrieved from www.newspapers.com.

Thornhill, R., & Gangestad, S. W. (1999). Facial attractiveness. *Trends in Cognitive Science, 3*(12), 452-460. https://doi.org/10.1016/S1364-6613(99)01403-5

Thornhill, R., & Gangestad, S. W. (1993). Human facial beauty: Averageness, symmetry and parasite resistance. *Human Nature, 4*(3), 237-269. doi:10.1007/BF02692201

Tomeo, O. B., Underleider, L. G., & Liu, N. (2017). Preference for average faces does not generalize to non-human primates. *Frontiers in Behavioral Neuroscience, 11*(129), https://doi.org/10.3389/fnbeh.2017.00129

Valentine, T., Darling, S., Donnelly, M. (2004). Why are average faces attractive? The effect of view and averageness on the attractiveness of female faces. *Psychonomic Bulletin & Review, 11*(3), 482-487.

Van Honk, J., et al. (1999). Correlations among salivary testosterone, mood, and selective attention to threat in humans. *Hormones and Behavior, 36*(1), 17-24. doi: 10.1006/hbeh.1999.1521

Watson, R., Latinus, M., Noguchi, T., Garrod, O., Crabbe, F., & Belin, P. (2014). Crossmodal adaptation in right posterior superior temporal sulcus during face-voice emotional integration. *The Journal of Neuroscience, 34*(20), 6813-6821. doi: 10.1523/JNEUROSCI.4478-13.2014

Welling, L. L. M., Jones, B. C., DeBruine, L. M., Smith, F. G., Feinberg, D. R., Little, A. C., & Al-Dujaili, E. A. S. (2008). Men report stronger attraction to femininity in women's faces when their testosterone levels are high. *Hormones and Behavior, 54*(5), 703-708. https://doi.org/10.1016/j.yhbeh.2008.07.012

Winston, J. S., Strange, B. A., O'Doherty, J., & Dolan, R. J. (2002). Automatic and intentional brain responses during evaluation of trustworthiness of faces. *Nature Neuroscience, 5*(3), 277-283. doi:10.1038/nn81

Chapter 3

BILATERAL SYMMETRY

Measure and symmetry are beauty and virtue the world over.

-Socrates

There are some standards of beauty that exist universally across cultures, suggesting that beauty is not entirely arbitrary (Fink & Penton-Voak, 2002; Thornhill & Gangestad, 1999a). Evolutionary psychologists have long suggested that human preferences for beauty reflect psychological adaptations that attract us to traits that signal mate quality (Fink & Penton-Voak, 2002). In other words, we have evolved to be attracted to beautiful people, because beauty is a sign of good genes. One such reliable trait that relates to perceptions of beauty is bilateral symmetry.

Bilateral symmetry (i.e., when two sides of a face or body trait are identical) has been used to define beauty because it is thought to be a phenotypic marker indicating underlying genetic quality. It speaks to a person's ability to resist developmental and environmental stress, making symmetrical individuals desirable mates (Penton-Voak et al., 2001). We are very physically attracted to people who are symmetrical, and, as such, those who are symmetrical have more mating success (Penton-Voak et al., 2001; Grammer & Thornhill, 1994). Symmetry is not only important in human mate selection, but across multiple species those with lower levels of asymmetry are selected as ideal mates and have reproductive advantages (Grammer & Thornhill, 1994). The premium placed on bilateral symmetry is prima facie evidence that we, consciously or unconsciously, do "judge a book by its cover." This chapter provides an overview of research on bilateral symmetry.

Leonardo da Vinci created The Vitruvian Man (15th Century), an "idealized" male body, with geometrically perfect (symmetrical) proportions (Richman-Abdou, 2018).
Public domain.

Types of Bilateral Symmetry

All multicellular organisms show some degree of bilateral symmetry in various organs; however, organisms often fail to develop and display perfect symmetry in their bilateral organs (Kowner, 2001). Three different types of asymmetry have been classified: directional asymmetry, antisymmetry, and fluctuating asymmetry (Kowner, 2001; Van Valen, 1962). First, *directional asymmetry* typically refers to a greater development of a trait on one side than the other (e.g., heart and brain). Second, *antisymmetry* is similar to directional asymmetry, but one finds it difficult to predict which side of an organism shows greater development (e.g., human hands). Third, *fluctuating asymmetry (FA)* refers to randomly produced deviations from perfect symmetry of organisms whose bilateral asymmetry in morphological traits is zero. A higher FA measure indicates lower bilateral symmetry for a particular trait. It is called "fluctuating" because the direction of variability is not controlled by genes (Kowner, 2001; Van Valen, 1962). Nonetheless, FA has been shown to have a small but statistically significant heritable component as analyzed in a meta-analysis of 34 studies examining 17 different species (Møller & Thornhill, 1997). Relatives tend to resemble one another in *magnitude* in their asymmetry rather than in the *direction* of their asymmetry (Van Valen, 1962). FA is the type of symmetry measure that is commonly of focus when studying human traits related to mate selection and is primarily referenced in this chapter.

Symmetry and Genetic Quality

From the viewpoint of sexual selection (mate choice driving the evolution of traits), underlying bilateral symmetry in men and women can signal higher genetic and developmental quality (Little, Jones, DeBruine, & Feinberg, 2008; Livshits & Kobyliansky, 1991; Thornhill & Møller, 1997). Higher bilateral symmetry reflects higher developmental stability for an organism as it is affected by numerous stressors throughout development in which one must cope (Leary & Allendorf, 1989; Watson & Thornhill, 1994). Such stressors could include genetic perturbations (i.e., mutations, chromosomal abnormality, homozygosity of deleterious recessives; Parsons, 1990); heterozygosity (Lerner, 1954; Thornhill & Gangestad, 1993); environmental factors such as extreme temperatures (Parsons, 1990), maternal effects (e.g., maternal infection, high maternal age, dietary deficiency; Thornhill & Møller, 1997), and pollutants, poor habitats, and parasites (Gangestad, Thornhill, & Yeo, 1994; Thornhill & Gangestad, 1993). Thus, bilateral symmetry is thought to reflect immunocompetence and the genetic ability to deal with perturbations during development (Thornhill & Møller, 1997). As such, FA is associated with a host of physical, health, psychological, and behavior outcomes that further connotes the desirability of an individual as a mate. Below we discuss some of the physical and psychological correlates of symmetry.

Symmetry and Physical/Health Outcomes

Health. Lower FA (i.e., greater symmetry) is linked to greater health and to various "favorable" physiological outcomes. For instance, low FA predicts lower rates of morbidity and men with higher FA tend to get sick more frequently (Waynforth, 1998). In both men and women, the higher one's FA, the more likely the person had reported having two or more medical conditions (Milne et al., 2003). Both facial and body FA are related to the number of respiratory infections participants had over the last three years. Facial asymmetry, in particular, is positively associated with the number of days infected and antibiotic use (Thornhill & Gangestad, 2006). Symmetry also appears to be related to disease resistance. Women with higher levels of asymmetry not only showed higher blood pressure, more diabetes, and more additional illnesses, they also bore children with higher FA, supporting the heritable component of FA (Livshits et al., 1988). Physical attraction to someone with low FA, then, means that the perceiver is unconsciously tuning into signals of good genes.

In utero, alcohol exposure also alters directional asymmetry of several craniofacial features. Those diagnosed with fetal alcohol syndrome (FAS) have greater asymmetry than controls (Klingenberg et al., 2010) and FA could be another potential facial dysmorphology that could be useful for diagnosing FAS.

It is important to note that not all studies have confirmed the link between symmetry and physiological fitness. Measures of several health-related physiological performance tests that included measurements of resting blood pressure (e.g., MAP; mean arterial pressure), lung functioning, vertical jump, blood lipid (e.g., cholesterol), mean grip strength, sit-and reach exercises and gas-analyzed maximal oxygen uptake using cycle ergometry all failed to show a difference between symmetric and asymmetric individuals (Tomkinson & Olds, 2000).

Fertility.   In addition to overall health, bilateral symmetry can be a predictor of fertility in both sexes. Lower FA in men is linked to more offspring and higher sperm per ejaculate, as well as sperm speed and migration (Manning, Scutt, & Lewis-Jones, 1998).   Symmetrical men examined in rural villages of Belize who live a transition mode of subsistence had fathered more offspring than their asymmetrical counterparts and also had a lower age of first reproduction and more lifetime partners (Waynforth, 1998). Symmetrical women have higher levels of estradiol across their menstrual cycles which increase the probability of conception (Jasienska, Lipson, Ellison, Thune, & Ziomkiewicz, 2006). Women with higher breast symmetry have more offspring (Møller, Soler, & Thornhill, 1995) and have earlier age at first birth (Manning, Scutt, Whitehouse, & Leinster, 1997).

Furthermore, FA for some soft tissue traits varies across the menstrual cycle and these fluctuations have been referred to as *cyclical asymmetry*, or CA (Manning, Scutt, Whitehouse, Leinster, & Walton, 1996). Women tend to experience a 24-hour mid-cycle increase in soft-body symmetry of their breasts when they are fertile. This decreased FA associated with ovulation is possibly attributed by increased estrogen, follicle-stimulating hormone (FSH), and luteinizing hormone (LH). Alternatively, increases in FA appear to occur in the infertile period of a woman's cycle, possibly related to increased progesterone (Scutt & Manning, 1996). Thus, some bilateral features related to soft tissue FA are influenced by hormones and are important in predicting human performance in fecundity and reproduction.

Masculine Vigor. Symmetry has been linked to increased masculinity and vigor in men (Gangestad & Thornhill, 1997a). Symmetrical men tend to get into more fights with other men and have the propensity to escalate a negative encounter with violence (Furlow, Gangestad, & Armijo-Prewitt,

1998). Further, as male body weight increases, asymmetry decreases. It is thought that men with the best genes are able to develop and maintain a large body size (Manning, 1995). Men with lower FA also show a lower resting metabolic rate (Manning, Koukourakis, & Brodie, 1997) which was advantageous in our ancestral past where feeding was often occurred on a feast or famine basis (Knight, 2011).

FA also relates to locomotor ability. For instance, the symmetry of certain lower body parts relates to sprinting performance. Jamaican track and field athletes have been measured to have more symmetrical knees and ankles than controls (Trivers et al., 2014). In fact, the measured knee symmetry of Jamaican children of both sexes predicted their sprinting speeds 14 years later (Trivers, Palestis, & Manning, 2013).

Feminine Vigor. In women, greater body symmetry is often linked to lower body weight as measured by body mass index, BMI (Manning, 1995; Milne et al., 2003). FA tends to increase as women increase in height, body mass, breast volume, and age (Møller, Soler & Thornhill, 1995). Breast asymmetry, in particular, appears to play an important role in mate selection, and women with symmetrical breasts are considered more attractive and healthier (Singh, 1995). Møller and colleagues (1995) found that breast FA is lower in married females, and higher among women without children and women who were of an older age when giving birth for the first time. The authors suggested that men prefer women with symmetrical breasts because it signals higher fecundity, and the trait may be passed on to their daughters as well.

Symmetry and Behavioral/Psychological Traits

Mental Health. Symmetry can also be used as an index of one's quality of mental health (Kowner, 2001) and may be indicative of certain abnormal personality traits. For example, an analysis of asymmetry for finger ridge counts in twins revealed that patients with schizophrenia had greater FA than controls, and their symptom severity positively correlated with FA (Markow & Wandler, 1986). Depression scores, as measured by the Beck Depression Inventory (BDI), have also been shown to be positively related to FA in men (Martin, Manning, & Dowrick, 1999).

Personality. Having greater bilateral symmetry can create a favorable impression of a person. Women with symmetrical faces were rated higher on positive personality characteristics (i.e., sociable, intelligent, lively, self-confident, balanced), whereas women low in symmetry were rated as being more anxious and neurotic (Fink, Neave, Manning, & Grammer, 2006;

Noor & Evans, 2003). Another study showed that these perceptions are indeed accurate. Researchers found positive correlations between facial symmetry some of Big Five Personalities scores, such as agreeableness and openness (Fink, Neave, Manning, and Grammer (2005), extraversion (Pound, Penton-Voak, and Brown, 2007).

However, we should point out that other researchers have questioned FA's relationship to major personality domains (e.g., The Big Five), and found no consistent associations found with FA; low FA was only weakly associated with conscientiousness and openness to experience (Hope, Bates, Penke, Gow, Starr, Deary, 2011).

FA seems to a more reliable predictor of personality traits associated with assertiveness, aggression, and anger in men. Men who have greater facial symmetry tend to be more assertive, but not necessarily more dominant. This is thought to be an advertisement of desirable traits of high status in men that women find attractive (Borraz-Leon & Cerda-Molina, 2015). Even at younger ages, symmetrical boys show higher aggression, particularly physical aggression (Manning &Wood 1998). Holtzman and colleagues (2011) conducted a study examining the relation between more than 200 personality traits and symmetry and those with more facial and bodily symmetry had increased aggression. While Muñoz-Reyes, Gil-Burmann, Fink-Turiegano (2012) could not confirm the association between FA and physical aggression in adolescent boys, low FA boys had showed greater anger. Likewise, a negative association between FA and hostility was found only in older adolescent women ages 17-19 years.

Jealousy. When it comes to the trait of jealousy, asymmetrical individuals tend to be significantly more jealous in mating contexts, but not during nonromantic contexts (Brown & Moore, 2003). Because asymmetrical individuals are considered to have a lower mate value, they may feel more threatened by other potential mates thereby demonstrating higher levels of jealousy. Further, in competitive mating contexts, symmetrical individuals seem to use different behavioral tactics to attract a mate than the less symmetric counterparts. Men who are put into a competing situation with another same-sex individual to get a date with an attractive opposite-sex interviewer had used more direct competition tactics (Simpson, Gangestad, Christensen, & Leck, 1999). These tactics included being more likely to assert their superiority over the competitor by directly comparing themselves with him, being less likely to use humor, or claiming to be particularly likable or communal, and they engaged in some pretense by not trying to just be themselves. These behavioral displays may be advantageous in the game of intersexual competition.

Risk-Taking. Higher risk-taking behavior is also associated with lower FA. For instance, people who had tattoos or non-conventional piercings, compared to controls, also had lower FA (Koziel, Kretsfchmer, & Pawlowski, 2010). Tattooing can be considered a risk-taking behavior as it increases the possibility of contact with blood and bodily fluids and the exposure to viral and microbial infections. Koziel and colleagues argued that people with higher genetic quality can afford to get more tattoos than those with lower genetic quality.

Intelligence. Body symmetry is also predictive of a person's psychometric intelligence (Furlow, Armijo-Prewitt, Gangestad, & Thornhill, 1997) and general (g) intelligence (Prokosch et al. 2005; for a meta-analysis see Banks, Batchelor, & McDaniel, 2010). In fact, about 20% of the variance in g can be explained by FA, suggesting that general intelligence may be an honest signal of fitness (Luxen & Buunk, 2006). Even the relationship between head size and IQ has been shown to be mediated by FA, such that individuals with low mutation rates may be able to sustain the development of a larger brain as well as life longevity (Luxen & Buunk, 2006). The association between intelligence and FA is not sex-specific, which implies sexual selection pressures for both highly intelligent men and women (Bates, 2007).

The theory of developmental instability offered by Yeo and colleagues (2016) suggests that variation in general cognitive ability reflects an organism's ability to buffer brain development from certain environmental and genetic perturbations. As such, they found a negative relationship between measured FA of regions of the cortical surface area of the brain with general cognitive ability. In light of these findings, selecting mates with higher general cognitive abilities may be wise in the sense that they are more resilient to environmental and genetic threats to the environment and genetic threats to development, which is also linked to better health.

Sexual Behaviors. Sexual behaviors have been linked to bilateral symmetry. For both men and women, those with lower FA tend to have more sex partners throughout a lifetime when controlling for age (Thornhill & Gangestad, 1994). Men with lower FA tended to have first sex at an earlier age (Thornhill & Gangestad, 1994), a higher numbers of extra pair copulations, and a greater number of times being chosen as an extra-pair partner by women (Gangestad & Thornhill, 1997b). Women report having higher rates of experiencing orgasms when having sex with symmetrical men than with less symmetrical men, which has been argued as an adaptive outcome toward sperm competition in order to sire offspring from higher genetic quality men (Thornhill, Gangestad, & Comer, 1995). Female orgasm is believed to be a cryptic semen retention mechanism enacted under sexual situations with men of high genetic quality (Baker & Bellis, 1995; Thornhill, Gangestad, Miller, Scheyd, McCollough, & Franklin, 2003). Apparently, symmetry means better sex, also.

A more recent study which used a large representative sample and more comprehensive measures of body asymmetry was unable to find the same relationships between sexual behaviors and fluctuating asymmetry (Kordsmeyer & Penke, 2017). In fact, more asymmetric women indicated higher numbers of lifetime sexual partners and one-night stands, but not extra-pair partners or times having been and extra-pair partner. Further replication studies utilizing larger samples and aggregated measures of fluctuating body asymmetry are needed to get a clearer picture of the association between developmental stability and mating behaviors.

Symmetry and Sexual Orientation

Both symmetry and sexual orientation are thought to be influenced by factors that operate during prenatal development; therefore, it may be possible that the two are related. However, there is some dispute in the literature for the existence of a relationship between FA and sexual orientation. Some researchers have documented such a relationship such as Miller, Hoffman, and Mustanski (2008) who found that as ear breadth FA and two composite FA scores increases, so did men's scores on a modified Kinsey scale (where higher numbers indicate increased preference for homosexuality). This relationship was only evident for men but not for women. Hall and Schaeff (2008) were able to identify a link between FA and sexual orientation for both sexes whereby FA was significantly higher in both males and females with a homosexual orientation than those with a heterosexual orientation.

Yet another study found differences but in the exact opposite direction; homosexual individuals actually exhibited a lower FA in for certain bilateral hand measures (when correcting for directional asymmetries of the traits measured) than heterosexual individuals, contradicting the theory that increased developmental instability is the cause of atypical sexual orientation (Martin, Puts, & Breedlove, 2007).

Still other studies have found that sexual orientation does not relate to any measures of FA and homosexuality is not a result of a disruptive prenatal development (Rahman, 2005; Rahman & Wilson, 2003a). For instance, there was no relationship between sexual orientation and fluctuating asymmetry when based upon finger digit measures (Rahman & Wilson,

2003a) or upon a composite of nine different bilateral body traits (Rahman, 2005). Thus, it is not certain that elevated levels of developmental stress as reflected by FA are linked to shifts in sexual orientation.

Dermatoglyphic (Fingerprint) Asymmetry. Another measure of symmetry that has been used to compare individuals with different sexual orientations is dermatoglyphic asymmetry. *Dermatoglyphics* refers to the study of the ridge counts and patterns of the finger, palms, and soles (e.g. fingerprints) which are determined between the 8th and 16th week of fetal life (Holt, 1968). These ridge patterns emerge during prenatal period and are not affected by development or the environment and can only be altered by severe mechanical damage (Cummins & Midlo, 1961). Therefore, these measures are a good source of information about the timing of prenatal events, and influences of later sexual orientation are thought to occur prenatally, as well (see Rahman & Wilson, 2003b). A higher frequency of atypical lateralization for at fingerprint ridges was found in those with a reported homosexual orientation compared to those with a reported heterosexual orientation (Hall & Kimura, 1994). But, again, there is conflicting evidence as to whether dermatoglyphic asymmetry is a correlate of sexual orientation because Mustanski, Bailey, and Kaspar (2002) were unable to replicate the relationship between the two.

The 1912 fingerprint card of Juan Vucetich, a police officer from Argentina who invented a viable system of fingerprint identification.

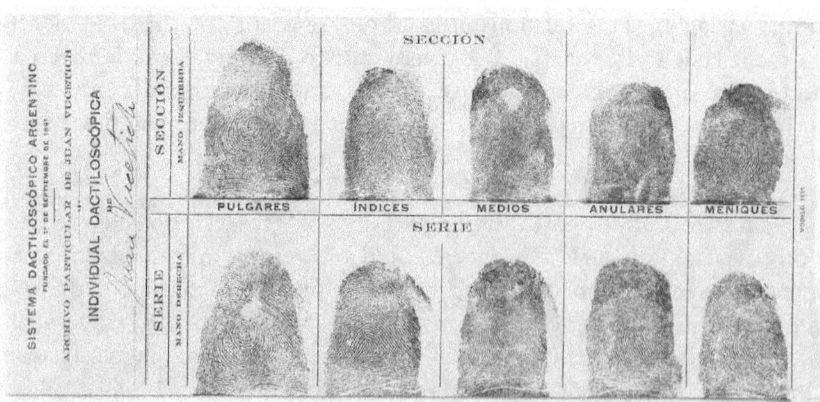

Imagine in public domain from U.S. National Library of Medicine, National Institutes of Health (2014)

Cerebral Asymmetry. Asymmetry of the brain hemispheres (i.e., cerebral asymmetry) has also been examined in relation to sexual orientation. But it appears that differences in brain hemispheric asymmetries are based more upon the biological sex to which one is more attracted. Both heterosexual men and homosexual women (i.e., those attracted to females) showed greater variance in the volume between the two hemispheres with a larger right hemisphere, whereas homosexual men and heterosexual women (i.e., those attracted to males) tended to show less lateralization and have more equal or symmetric volumes between their two hemispheres (Savic & Lindstrom, 2008).

In addition to the lateralization in the brain, some studies have also demonstrated patterns of atypical lateralization for handedness for people with a homosexual orientation (Lalumiere, Blanchard, & Zucker, 2000). They had greater propensity to be non-right-handed compared to the population, which gives evidence of prenatal influences. However, these findings could later only be replicated for homosexual women who had highly significant increases in non–right-handedness compared with same-sex heterosexual controls (Mustanski et al., 2002). Of note, cortical asymmetry is mediated by sex steroid hormones (Gerendai & Halász, 1997; Wisniewski, 1998), as is sexual orientation (Bao & Swaab, 2011), explaining a potential common pathway for the connection.

"Gaydar" Abilities. Whether or not FA and sexual orientation are indeed linked, symmetry appears to be used as a gaydar (i.e., "gay radar") cue to assess another's sexual orientation. In our research, we showed that the more likely raters perceived someone to hold a heterosexual orientation, the more symmetrical that person's facial features were (Hughes & Bremme, 2011). Hence, individuals seem to be using cues of symmetry to make assessments about one's sexual orientation and it may be one feature that comprises one's gaydar abilities.

But are people accurate in using cues of symmetry to assess sexual orientation? Because, as our data showed, actual measures of facial symmetry differed between those who are heterosexual and those who are homosexual (Hughes & Bremme, 2011), we may be able to conclude that using symmetry as a cue for assessing a target's sexual orientation enhances accuracy, although future studies testing this conjecture are warranted. It is also likely that most are not aware that they are gathering information about how symmetrical a person's face is in order to assess sexual orientation given that bilateral facial symmetry can be somewhat perceptually inconspicuous trait.

Symmetry and Attractiveness

We are very physically attracted to people who are more symmetrical, both facially and bodily. In evolutionary terms, an attraction to this trait leads us to select mates with high quality genes. We discuss some of the literature on this topic below.

Facial Symmetry. Numerous studies over decades have shown that symmetrical faces are rated as being more attractive than asymmetrical faces (Fink et al., 2006; Grammer & Thornhill, 1994; Hume & Montogomerie, 2001; Mealey, Bridgestock, & Townsend, 1999; Penton-Voak et al., 2001; Perrett et al., 1999; Rhodes, Proffitt, Grady, & Sumich, 1998), and this is the case in even non-Western cultures which supports the argument that preferences for symmetry are biologically based (Rhodes, Yoshikawa, Clark, Lee, McKay, & Akamatsu, 2001). However, there are a few studies that have not yielded significant associations between facial symmetry and attractiveness (Hönekopp, Bartholomé, & Jansen, 2003; Samuels, Butterworth, Roberts, Graupner, & Hole, 1994; Swaddle & Cuthill, 1995).

Our friend volunteered to have her picture taken for a symmetry measurement demonstration.

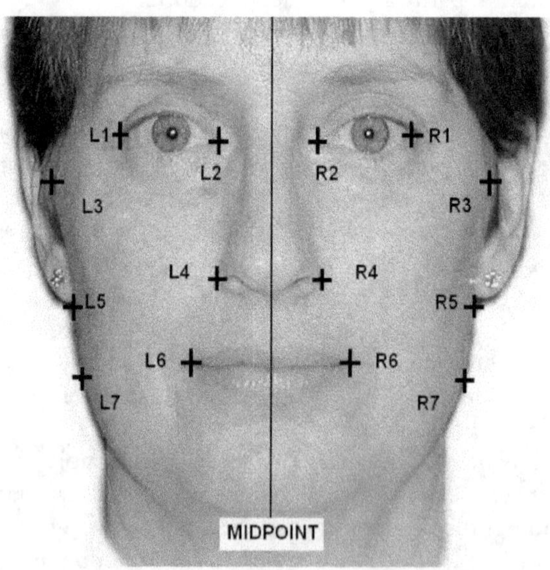

Several studies have examined perception of attractiveness for variations of facial symmetry that occur naturally between individuals (Grammer & Thornhill, 1994; Mealey et al., 1999; Saxton, DeBruine, Jones, Little, & Roberts, 2011; Scheib, Gangestad, & Thornhill, 1999). But there is also experimental evidence of preferences for symmetrical faces created artificially. There are several ways to create artificial symmetry of the face: by mirroring over left and right sides of the face (Perrett et al., 1999), by blending normal and mirror images of a face (Rhodes et al., 1998; 2001), and by remapping the original face to the symmetrical points (Perrett et al., 1999). There are some noted issues when using blending and mirroring techniques to create symmetry because they could produce abnormal features on the facial stimuli (Perrett et al., 1999). For example, mirroring techniques could replicate blemishes that were originally found only on one side of the face and blending normal with mirror images could change skin tone. Controlling for such issues related to skin textures to create perfectly digitized symmetric faces still produced same results though where symmetrical faces were preferred over faces with normal levels of shape asymmetry (Perrett et al., 1999).

It is possible that facial symmetry is not an independent index of fitness but rather simply correlated with other phenotypic expressions. For instance, women still assessed symmetrical male faces as being more attractive even when presented as only a half side of the face, thus removing all cues of actual symmetry (Scheib et al., 1999). So how can this be? Apparently other attractive features that correlated with symmetry such as facial masculinity (i.e., prominent cheekbones and a longer lower face) drove the perception of attractiveness for both the full and half faces alike.

Further investigations have also found reliable associations between facial masculinity and both body and facial FA but only for men, not women (Gangestad & Thornhill, 2003). In a subsequent study examining the relationship between symmetry and sexually dimorphic facial proportions, not only did symmetric men have more masculine facial proportions, but symmetric women had more feminine facial proportions (Little et al., 2008). The features examined for masculinity were ones that tend to be influenced by sex hormones that included jaw breadth, chin length, face length and width, eye height and width as related to brow ridge, and lip fullness. Other investigators that have not been able to confirm the link between masculinity measures of the face and symmetry have suggested that symmetry might be related to other undefined characteristics (e.g., perhaps unblemished complexion) that suggest high developmental quality and are considered attractive (Penton-Voak et al., 2001).

Symmetry in Motion. Most studies that have examined the correlation between symmetry with perceived attractiveness have used still images as stimuli. In our research (Hughes & Aung, 2018), we stressed it is important to realize that the appearance of one's facial symmetry is not always static and may change when there is facial movement, especially while a person is speaking. We found that when we examined video stimuli of persons speaking, the dynamic image of the person had produced a different perception than viewing a static photo of that same person. When facial movements created an appearance of overall greater facial symmetry while a person was speaking in the video, the person was rated as being more attractive than as a still photo. Alternatively, facial movements measured and perceived as less symmetrical while speaking were rated as less attractive in a video clip than in a still photo (Hughes & Aung, 2018).

Sadr et al. (2006) also found symmetry was related to the attractiveness of human gait patterns, and by increasing the symmetry of a person's walking motion, the person was rated as being more attractive. These finding presents a more realistic view of our perceptions of symmetry when assessing others in the real world since we very likely encounter others who are speaking and moving.

Developmental Preferences. Preferences for symmetrical faces do not seem to emerge from birth per se. Rather, the influence of symmetry on attractiveness judgements begins after the age of 5 and matures after the age of 9 (Vingilis-Jaremko & Maurer, 2013). This was evidenced by the fact that 5-year-old children had not rated symmetric faces as more attractive than did 9-year-old children or adults, and the effect was stronger in adults than in 9-yearold children. Those who are age 9 are typically in the end phrase of adrenarche, which is hormonal maturation preceding gonadal maturation (puberty). Researchers concluded that the increased sensitivity to symmetry was either the result of experience with viewing faces over time or was a product of the visual system maturing. From an evolutionary perspective, it seems that the ability to assess symmetry, an important signal of mate quality, would not be necessary until the advent of sexual maturity and actual mate selection.

Changes Across the Cycle. In addition, women's preferences for symmetry also seem to shift across the menstrual cycle. Women prefer more symmetric male faces during peak fertility but only in the context of making judgements for short-term relations or only for women who already had a partner (Little, Jones, Burt, & Perrett, 2007). These shifts in preferences seem to be a quality dependent response to hormones and are an indication that women are seeking potential good genes for offspring when selecting short-term partners or extra-pair (affair) partners. However, risk of conception may not be the sole mechanism explaining for the shifts in symmetry preferences. A woman's own levels of testosterone and progesterone/estrogen ratios also seem to bias her perception of the FA of male faces as suitable long-term partners (Hernández-López, García-

Granados, Chavira-Ramírez, Mondragón-Ceballos, 2017). Interestingly, regardless of hormonal levels, women thought men with symmetrical faces would be more economically successful but also would be poorer fathers as well as a highly unfaithful partners compared to men with more asymmetric faces.

Body Symmetry. As with facial symmetry, the symmetry of bilateral body measures plays a role in the perception of body attractiveness for both men (Gangestad et al., 1994) and women (Hume & Montogomerie, 2001; Tovée, Tasker, & Benson, 2000). Body symmetry can be appraised by taking precise measures of several inconspicuous bilateral features such as ankle width, food breadth, hand and foot breadth, ear length, and finger lengths. Compelling evidence for the negative association between bodily FA with bodily attractiveness comes from a study that examined a composite measure of FA using 360° video stimuli. They removed inherent biases unrelated to body shape such as clothing, hair, skin color, facial appearance and differing viewing angles, and they included more bilateral traits than previous investigations (Brown, Price, Kang, Pound, Zhao, Yu, 2008). Even with these improved methods, they also found that greater symmetry was linked to more sex-typical body shape for both sexes. Thus, just like an attractive face, an attractive body also appears to be a signal of underlying genetic quality.

There is evidence that body symmetry and facial symmetry are positively related to one another for both sexes, however, no relationship was found between body symmetry and ratings of facial attractiveness (Rikowski & Grammer, 1999). The similarity among men's attractiveness judgments of women's faces and nude bodies have also been demonstrated in other studies that utilized cross-cultural data (Thornhill & Grammer, 1999).

The Scent of Symmetry

Beyond visual cues of attractiveness, bilateral symmetry relates to attractiveness in other sensory modalities, as well. For instance, women rate the scent of low FA men as more attractive during ovulation when their sensitivity to the scent of androstenone, one of the first human putative pheromones to be identified, is enhanced (Gangestad & Thornhill, 1998; Thornhill & Gangestad, 1999b). Evidence suggests that the purported steroid pheromone androstenone enhances women's sexual desire and arousal (Verhaeghe, Gheysen, & Enzlin, 2013). The relationship between fertility risk and female preferences for symmetrical men became even stronger when men's showering and fragrance use were controlled for in the analysis (Thornhill & Gangestad, 1999b). One of the proximate mediators thought to be responsible for this mid-cycle preference shift is the level of certain female sex hormones; women's progesterone levels were found to be negatively correlated with the preference for the scent of symmetrical men while estrogen levels were positively related (Garver-Apgar, Gangestad, & Thornhill, 2008).

The Sound of Symmetry

In addition to scent, the human voice conveys symmetry. In our early work, we sought to determine if FA related to perceptions of vocal attractiveness. We took several morphological measures of speakers to determine body symmetry, and we recorded their voices simply counting from one to 10. We then had independent raters assess each voice sample for attractiveness without providing any information about the speaker. Sure enough, both men and women who had less FA (i.e., were more symmetrical) were rated as more sounding more attractive by both sexes (Hughes, Harrison, & Gallup, 2002; Hughes, Pastizzo, & Gallup, 2008). The same relationship seems to hold true when examining facial asymmetry; those with voices rated as more attractive tend to also have lower FA (Hill et al., 2017). Thus, it appears that beyond visual recognition, symmetry measures are related to other sensory traits that can be used to make attractiveness assessments.

Conclusion

Given the host of correlates of symmetry, it is no wonder that individuals use bilateral symmetry as a critical feature for selecting a potential mate. Bilateral symmetry is an important marker of attractiveness, health, and suitability as a mate, and it is one of the few universal traits seen in humans and much of the animal kingdom that predicts reproductive success (Grammer & Thornhill, 1994; Møller & Thornhill, 1998). In terms of the ability to judge a book by its cover, assessing a person's mate value by their symmetrical "cover" confers a host of deep advantages to the perceiver.

References

Baker, R. R., & Bellis, M. A. (1995). *Human sperm competition: Copulation, masturbation and infidelity*. London, UK: Chapman and Hall.

Banks, G. C., Batchelor, J. H., & McDaniel, M. A. (2010). Smarter people are (a bit) more symmetrical: A meta-analysis of the relationship between intelligence and fluctuating asymmetry. *Intelligence, 38,* 393-401.

Bao, A., & Swaab, D. F. (2011). Sexual differentiation of the human brain: Relation to gender identity, sexual orientation, and neuropsychiatric disorders. *Frontiers in Neuroendocrinology, 32*(2), 214-226.

https://doi.org/10.1016/j.yfrne.2011.02.007

Bates, T. C. (2007). Fluctuating asymmetry and intelligence. *Intelligence, 35*(1), 41-46. https://doi.org/10.1016/j.intell.2006.03.013

Borráz-León, J. I., & Cerda-Molina, A. L. (2015). Facial asymmetry is negatively related to assertive personality but unrelated to dominant personality in men. *Personality and Individual Differences, 75*, 94-96. https://doi.org/10.1016/j.paid.2014.11.019

Brown, W. M., & Moore, C. (2003). Fluctuating asymmetry and romantic jealousy. *Evolution and Human Behavior, 24*(2), 113-117. https://doi.org/10.1016/S1090-5138(02)00148-4

Brown, W. M., Price, M. E., Kang, J., Pound, N., Zhao, Y., & Yu, H. (2008). Fluctuating asymmetry and preferences for sex-atypical bodily characteristics. *Proceedings of the National Academy of Sciences of the United States of America, 105*(35), 12938-12943. https://doi.org/10.1073/pnas.0710420105

Cummins, H., & Midlo, C. (1961). *Finger prints, palms and soles.* New York, NY: Dover.

Fink, B., Neave, N., Manning, J. T., & Grammer, K. (2005). Facial symmetry and the "big-five" personality factors. *Personality and Individual Differences, 39*(3),523-529. http://dx.doi.org/10.1016/j.paid.2005.02.002.

Fink, B., Neave, N., Manning, J. T., & Grammer, K. (2006). Facial symmetry and judgements of attractiveness, health and personality. *Personality and Individual Differences, 41*(3), 491-499. doi:10.1016/j.paid.2006.01.017G

Fink, B., & Penton-Voak, I. (2002). Evolutionary psychology of facial attractiveness. *Current Directions in Psychological Science, 11*(5), 154-158. doi:10.1111/1467-8721.00190

Furlow, B. F., Armijo-Prewitt, T., Gangestad, S. W., & Thornhill, R. (1997). Fluctuating asymmetry and psychometric intelligence. *Proceedings of the Royal Society of London B: Biological Sciences, 264*, 823-829.

Furlow, B. F., Gangestad, S. W., & Armijo-Prewitt, T. (1998). Developmental stability and human violence. *Proceedings of the Royal Society of London B: Biological Sciences, 265*, 1-6.

Gangestad, S. W., & Thornhill, R. (1997a). Human sexual selection and developmental stability. In J. A. Simpson & D. T. Kenrick (Eds.). *Evolutionary personality and social psychology,* (pp. 169-195). Hillsdale, NJ: Erlbaum.

Gangestad, S. W., & Thornhill, R. (1997b). The evolutionary psychology of extrapair sex: The role of fluctuating asymmetry. *Evolution and Human Behavior, 18*(2), 69-88. doi:10.1016/S1090-5138(97)00003-2

Gangestad, S. W., & Thornhill, R. (1998). Menstrual cycle variation in women's preference for the scent of symmetrical men. *Proceedings of the Royal Society of London: Biological Sciences, 265*(1399), 927-933.

Gangestad, S. W., & Thornhill, R. (2003). Facial masculinity and fluctuating asymmetry. *Evolution and Human Behavior, 24*(4), 231-241. https://doi.org/10.1016/S1090-5138(03)00017-5

Gangestad, S. W., Thornhill, R., & Yeo, R. A. (1994). Facial attractiveness, developmental stability, and fluctuating asymmetry. *Ethology and*

Sociobiology, 15(2), 73-85. doi:10.1016/0162-3095(94)90018-3

Garver-Apgar, C. E., Gangestad, S. W., & Thornhill, R. (2008). Hormonal correlates of women's mid-cycle preference for the scent of symmetry. *Evolution and Human Behavior, 29*(4), 223-232. doi:10.1016/j.evolhumbehav.2007.12.007

Gerendai, I., & Halász, B. (1997). Neuroendocrine asymmetry. *Frontiers in Neuroendocrinology, 18*(3), 354-381. https://doi.org/10.1006/frne.1997.0154

Grammer, K., & Thornhill, R. (1994). Human (Homo sapiens) facial attractiveness and sexual selection: The role of symmetry and averageness. *Journal of Comparative Psychology, 108*(3), 233-242. doi:10.1037/0735-7036.108.3.233

Hall, J. A., & Kimura, D. (1994). Dermatoglyphic asymmetry and sexual orientation in men. *Behavioral Neuroscience, 108,* 1203-1206.

Hall, P. A., & Schaeff, C. M. (2008). Sexual orientation and fluctuating asymmetry in men and women. *Archives of Sexual Behavior, 37*(1), 158-165. https://doi.org/10.1007/s10508-007-9282-0

Hernández-López, L., García-Granados, D. M., Chavira-Ramírez, R., & Mondragón-Ceballos, R. (2017). Testosterone, the progesterone/estradiol ratio, and female ratings of masculine facial fluctuating asymmetry for a long-term relationship. *Physiology & Behavior, 175,* 66-71. https://doi.org/10.1016/j.physbeh.2017.03.033

Hill, A. K., Cárdenas, R. A., Wheatley, J. R., Welling, L. L. M., Burriss, R. P., Claes, P., ... Puts, D. A. (2017). Are there vocal cues to human developmental stability? Relationships between facial fluctuating asymmetry and voice attractiveness. *Evolution and Human Behavior, 38*(2), 249-258. https://doi.org/10.1016/j.evolhumbehav.2016.10.008

Holt, S. B. (1968). *The genetics of dermal ridges.* Springfield, IL: Charles C. Thomas

Holtzman, N. S., Augustine, A. A., & Senne, A. L. (2011). Are pro-social or socially aversive people more physically symmetrical? Symmetry in relation to over 200 personality variables. *Journal of Research in Personality, 45*(6), 687-691. https://doi.org/10.1016/j.jrp.2011.08.003

Hönekopp, J., Bartholomé, T., & Jansen, G. (2003). Facial attractiveness, symmetry, and physical fitness in young women. *Human Nature, 15*(2), 147-167.

Hope, D., Bates, T., Penke, L., Gow, A. J., Starr, J. M., & Deary, I. J. (2011). Fluctuating asymmetry and personality. *Personality and Individual Differences, 50*(1), 49-52. https://doi.org/10.1016/j.paid.2010.08.020

Hughes, S. M. & Aung, T. (2018). Symmetry in motion: Perception of attractiveness changes with facial movement. *Journal of Nonverbal Behavior.* doi:10.1007/s10919-018-0277-4

Hughes, S. M., & Bremme, R. (2011). The effects of facial symmetry and sexually-dimorphic facial proportions on the assessment of sexual orientation. *Journal of Social, Evolutionary, and Cultural Psychology, 5*(4), 214-230.

Hughes, S. M., Harrison, M. A., & Gallup, G. G., Jr. (2002). The sound of symmetry: Voice as a marker of developmental instability. *Evolution and Human Behavior, 23*(3), 173-180. doi:10.1016/S1090-5138(01)00099-X

Hughes, S. M., Pastizzo, M. J., & Gallup, G. G., Jr. (2008). The sound of symmetry revisited: Subjective and objective analyses of voice. *Journal of Nonverbal*

Behavior, 32(2), 93-108. doi:10.1007/s10919-007-0042-6

Hume, D. K., & Montgomerie, R. (2001). Facial attractiveness signals different aspects of 'quality' in women and men. *Evolution and Human Behavior, 22*(2), 93-112. doi:10.1016/S1090-5138(00)00065-9

Jasienska, G., Lipson, S. F., Ellison, P. T., Thune, I., & Ziomkiewicz, A. (2006). Symmetrical women have higher potential fertility. *Evolution and Human Behavior, 27*, 390-400.

Klingenberg, C. P., Wetherill, L., Rogers, J., Moore, E., Ward, R....(2010). Prenatal alcohol exposure alters patterns of facial asymmetry. *Alcohol, 44*, (7-8), 649-657. https://doi.org/10.1016/j.alcohol.2009.10.016

Knight, C. (2011). "'Most people are simply not designed to eat pasta": Evolutionary explanations for obesity in the low-carbohydrate diet movement', *Public Understanding of Science, 20*(5), 706-719. https://doi.org/10.1177/0963662510391733

Kordsmeyer, T. L., & Penke, L. (2017). The association of three indicators of developmental instability with mating success in humans. *Evolution and Human Behavior, 38*(6), 704-713. https://doi.org/10.1016/j.evolhumbehav.2017.08.002

Kowner, R. (2001). Psychological perspective on human developmental stability and fluctuating asymmetry: Sources, applications and implications. *British Journal of Psychology, 92*(3), 447-469. doi: 10.1348/000712601162284

Koziel, S., Kretschmer, W., & Pawlowski, B. (2010). Tattoo and piercing as signals of biological quality. *Evolution and Human Behavior, 31*(3), 187-192. doi:10.1016/j.evolhumbehav.2009.09.009

Lalumiere, M. L., Blanchard, R., & Zucker, K. J. (2000). Sexual orientation and handedness in men and women: A meta-analysis. *Psychological Bulletin, 126*, 575-592.

Leary, R. F. & Allendorf, F. W. (1989) Fluctuating asymmetry as an indicator of stress: Implications for conservation biology. *Trends in Ecology and Evolution, 4*(7), 214-216.

Lerner, I. M. (1954). *Genetic homeostasis*. Edinburgh, London: Oliver & Boyd.

Little, A. C., Jones, B. C., Burt, D. M., & Perrett, D. I. (2007). Preferences for symmetry in faces change across the menstrual cycle. *Biological Psychology, 76*(3), 209-216. https://doi.org/10.1016/j.biopsycho.2007.08.003

Little, A. C., Jones, B. C., DeBruine, L. M., & Feinberg, D. R. (2008). Symmetry and sexual dimorphism in human faces: Interrelated preferences suggest both signal quality. *Behavioral Ecology, 19*(4), 902-908. https://doi.org/10.1093/beheco/arn049

Little, A. C., Jones, A. C., Waitt, C., Tiddeman, B. P., Feinberg, D. R., Perrett, D. I., Apicella, C. L., & Marlowe, F. W. (2008). Symmetry is related to sexual dimorphism in face: Data across culture and species. *PLoS ONE, 3*(5).

Livshits, G., Davidi, L., Kobyliansky, E., Ben-Amitai, D., Levi, Y., Meriob, P., Optiz, J. M., & Reynolds, J. F. (1998). Decreased developmental stability as assessed by fluctuating asymmetry of morphometric traits in preterm infants. *American Journal of Medical Genetics, 29*(4), 793-805.

Livshits, G. & Kobyliansky, E. (1991). Fluctuating asymmetry as a possible measure of developmental homeostasis in humans: A review. *Human Biology, 63*(4), 441-466.

Luxen, M. F., & Buunk, B. P. (2006). Human intelligence, fluctuating asymmetry and the peacock's tail: General intelligence (g) as an honest signal of fitness. *Personality and Individual Differences, 41*(5), 897-902. https://doi.org/10.1016/j.paid.2006.03.015

Manning, J. T. (1995). Fluctuating asymmetry and body weight in men and women: Implications for sexual selection. *Evolution and Human Behavior, 16*(2), 145-153.

Manning, J. T., Koukourakis, K., & Brodie, D. A. (1997). Fluctuating asymmetry, metabolic rate and sexual selection in human males. *Evolution and Human Behavior, 18*(1), 15-21. doi:10.1016/S1090-5138(96)00072-4

Manning, J. T., Scutt, D., & Lewis-Jones, D. I. (1998). Developmental stability, ejaculate size, and sperm quality in men. *Evolution and Human Behavior, 19*(5). 273-282.

Manning, J. T., Scutt, D., Whitehouse, G. H., & Leinster, S. J. (1997). Breast asymmetry and phenotypic quality in women. *Evolution and Human Behavior, 18*(4), 223–236.

Manning, J. T., Scutt, D., Whitehouse, G. H., Leinster, S. J., & Walton, J. M. (1996). Asymmetry and the menstrual cycle in women. *Ethology and Sociobiology, 17*(2), 129-143.

Manning, J. T., & Wood, D. (1998). Fluctuating asymmetry and aggression in boys. *Human Nature, 9*(1), 53-65. https://doi.org/10.1007/s12110-998-1011-4

Markow, T. A., & Wandler, K. (1986). Fluctuating dermatoglyphic asymmetry and the genetics of liability to schizophrenia. *Psychiatry Research, 19*(4), 323-328.

Martin, J. T., Puts, D. A., & Breedlove, S. M. (2008). Hand asymmetry in heterosexual and homosexual men and women: Relationship to 2D:4D digit ratios and other sexually dimorphic anatomical traits. *Archives of Sexual Behavior, 37,* 119-132.

Martin, S. M., Manning, J. T., & Dowrick, C. F. (1999). Fluctuating asymmetry, relative digit length, and depression in men. *Evolution and Human Behavior, 20*(3), 203-214. doi:10.1016/S1090-5138(99)00006-9

Mealey, L., Bridgstock, R., & Townsend, G. C. (1999). Symmetry and perceived facial attractiveness: A monozygotic co-twin comparison. *Journal of Personality and Social Psychology, 76*(1), 151-158. doi:10.1037/0022-3514.76.1.151

Miller, S. S., Hoffmann, H. L., & Mustanski, B. S. (2008). Fluctuating asymmetry and sexual orientation in men and women. *Archives of Sexual Behavior, 37*(1), 150-157. https://doi.org/10.1007/s10508-007-9256-2

Milne, B. J., Belsky, J., Poulton, R., Thomson, W. M., Caspi, A., & Kieser, J. (2003). Fluctuating asymmetry and physical health among young adults. *Evolution and Human Behavior, 24*(1), 53-63. doi:10.1016/S1090-5138(02)00120-4

Møller, A.P., & Soler, M., Thornhill, R. (1995). Breast asymmetry, sexual selection, and human reproductive success. *Evolution and Human Behavior, 16*(3), 207-219.

Møller, A. P., & Thornhill, R. (1997). A meta-analysis of the heritability of developmental stability. *Journal of Evolutionary Biology, 10*, 1-16.

Møller, A. P., & Thornhill, R. (1998). Bilateral symmetry and sexual selection: A meta-analysis. *American Naturalist, 151*(2), 174-92. doi: 10.1086/286110.

Morrison, E. R., Gralewski, L., Campbell, N., & Penton-Voak, I. S. (2007). Facial movement varies by sex and is related to attractiveness. *Evolution and Human Behavior, 28*(3), 186-192.

Muñoz-Reyes, J. A., Gil-Burmann, C., Fink, B., & Turiegano, E. (2012). Facial asymmetry and aggression in Spanish adolescents. *Personality and Individual Differences, 53*(7), 857-861. https://doi.org/10.1016/j.paid.2012.06.012

Mustanski, B. S., Bailey, J. M., & Kaspar, S. (2002). Dermatoglyphics, handedness, sex, and sexual orientation. *Archives of Sexual Behavior, 31*, 113-122.

Noor, F., & Evans, D. C. (2003). The effect of facial symmetry on perceptions of personality and attractiveness. *Journal of Research in Personality, 37*(4), 339-347. https://doi.org/10.1016/S0092-6566(03)00022-9

Parsons, P. A. (1990). Fluctuating asymmetry: An epigenetic measure of stress. *Biological Review, 65*(2), 131-145.Penton-Voak, I. S. & Chang, H. Y. (2008). Attractiveness judgements of individuals vary across emotional expression and movement conditions. *Journal of Evolutionary Psychology, 6*(2), 89-100.

Penton-Voak, I. S., Jones, B. C., Little, A. C., Baker, S., Tiddeman, B., Burt, D. M, & Perrett, D. I. (2001). Symmetry, sexual dimorphism in facial proportions and male facial attractiveness. *Proceedings of the Royal Society of London B: Biological Sciences, 268*(1476), 1617-1623.

Perrett, D. I., Burt, D. M., Penton-Voak, I. S., Lee, K. J., Rowland, D. A., & Edwards, R. (1999). Symmetry and human facial attractiveness. *Evolution and Human Behavior, 20*(5), 295-307.

Pound, N., Penton-Voak, I. S., & Brown, W. M. (2007). Facial symmetry is positively associated with self-reported extraversion. *Personality and Individual Differences, 43*, 1572-1582. http://dx.doi.org/10.1016/j.paid.2007.04.014.

Prokosch, M. D., Yeo, R. A., & Miller, G. F. (2005). Intelligence tests with higher g-loadings show higher correlations with body symmetry: Evidence for a general fitness factor mediated by developmental stability. *Intelligence, 33*(2), 203-213. doi:10.1016/j.intell.2004.07.007

Rahman, Q. (2005). Fluctuating asymmetry, 2nd to 4th finger length ratios and human sexual orientation. *Psychoneuroendocrinology, 30*, 382-391.

Rahman, Q., & Wilson, G. D. (2003a). Sexual orientation and the 2nd to 4th finger length ratio: Evidence for organizing effects of sex hormones or developmental instability? *Psychoneuroendocrinology, 28*,288–303.

Rahman, Q., & Wilson, G. D. (2003b). Born gay? The psychobiology of sexual orientation. *Personality and Individual Differences, 34*(8), 1337-1382.

Reis, H. T., Wilson, I. M. Monestere, C., Bernstein, S. ... (1990). What is smiling is beautiful and good. *European Journal of Social Psychology, 20*(3), 259-267. https://doi.org/10.1002/ejsp.2420200307

Rhodes, G., Proffitt, F., Grady, J. M., & Sumich, A. (1998). Facial symmetry and the perception of beauty. *Psychonomic Bulletin and Review, 5*(4), 659-669. doi:10.3758/BF03208842

Rhodes, G., Yoshikawa, S., Clark, A., Lee, K., McKay, R., & Akamatsu, S. (2001).

Attractiveness of facial averageness and symmetry in non-Western cultures: In search of biologically based standards of beauty. *Perception, 30*(5), 611–625. https://doi.org/10.1068/p3123

Richman-Abdou, K. (2018). The significance of Leonardo da Vinci's famous "Vitruvian Man" drawing. *My Modern Met.* Retrieved from https://mymodernmet.com/leonardo-da-vinci-vitruvian-man/

Rikowski, A., & Grammer, K. (1999). Human body odour, symmetry and attractiveness. *Proceedings of the Royal Society B, 266*, 869-874

Sadr, J., Troje, N. F., & Nakayama, K. (2006). A pedestrian courtship: Attractiveness and symmetry of humans walking. *Journal of Vision, 6*, 797–798.

Samuels, C. A., Butterworth, G., Roberts, T., Graupner, L., & Hole, G. (1994). Facial aesthetics: Babies prefer attractiveness to symmetry. *Perception, 42*(11), 823-831. doi:10.1068/p230823n

Savic, I., & Lindstrom, P. (2008). PET and MRI show differences in cerebral asymmetry and functional connectivity between homo- and heterosexual subjects. *Proceedings of the National Academy of Sciences of the United States of America 105(27),* 9403-9408.

Saxton, T. K., DeBruine, L. M., Jones, B. C., Little, A. C., & Roberts, S. C. (2011). A longitudinal study of adolescents' judgments of the attractiveness of facial symmetry, averageness and sexual dimorphism. *Journal of Evolutionary Psychology, 9*(1), 43-55. https://doi.org/10.1556/JEP.9.2011.22.1

Scheib, J. E., Gangestad, S. W., & Thornhill, R. (1999). Facial attractiveness, symmetry, and cues of good genes. *Proceedings of the Royal Society of London B: Biological Sciences, 266*(1431), 1913-1917.

Scutt, D., & Manning, J. T. (1996). Symmetry and ovulation in women. *Human Reproduction, 11*(11), 2477-2480.

Simpson, J. A., Gangestad, S. W., Christensen, P. N., & Leck, K. (1999). Fluctuating asymmetry, sociosexuality, and intrasexual competitive tactics. *Journal of Personality and Social Psychology, 76*(1), 159-172. http://dx.doi.org/10.1037/0022-3514.76.1.159

Singh, D. (1995). Female health, attractiveness, and desirability for relationship: Role of breast asymmetry and waist-to-hip ratio. *Evolution and Human Behavior, 16*(6), 465-481.

Swaddle, J. P., & Cuthill, I. C. (1995). Asymmetry and human facial attractiveness: Symmetry may not always be beautiful. *Proceedings of the Royal Society of London B: Biological Sciences, 261*(1360), 111-116.

Thornhill, R., & Gangestad, S. W. (1993). Human facial beauty. *Human Nature, 4*(3), 237-269. doi:10.1111/j.1467-9280.1994.tb00629.x

Thornhill, R., & Gangestad, S. W. (1993). Human facial beauty. *Human Nature, 4*(3), 237-269. https://doi.org/10.1111/j.1467-9280.1994.tb00629.x

Thornhill, R., & Gangestad, S. W. (1994). Human fluctuating asymmetry and sexual behavior. *Psychological Science, 5*(5), 297-302. doi:10.1111/j.1467-9280.1994.tb00629.x

Thornhill, R., & Gangestad, S. W. (1999a). Facial attractiveness. *Trends in Cognitive Science, 3*(12), 452-460. https://doi.org/10.1016/S1364-6613(99)01403-5

Thornhill, R., & Gangestad, S. W. (1999b). The scent of symmetry: A human sex pheromone that signals fitness? *Evolution and Human Behavior, 20,* 175-201.

Thornhill, R., & Gangestad, S. W. (2006). Facial sexual dimorphism, developmental stability, and susceptibility to disease in men and women. *Evolution and Human Behavior, 27*(2), 131-144. https://doi.org/10.1016/j.evolhumbehav.2005.06.001

Thornhill, R., Gangestad, S. W., & Comer, R. (1995). Human female orgasm and mate fluctuating asymmetry. *Animal Behaviour, 50*(6), 1601-1615. doi:10.1016/0003-3472(95)80014-X

Thornhill, R., Gangestad, S. W., Miller, R., Scheyd, G., McCollough, J. K., & Franklin, M. (2003). Major histocompatibility complex genes, symmetry, and body scent attractiveness in men and women. *Behavioral Ecology, 14*(5), 668-678. https://doi.org/10.1093/beheco/arg043

Thornhill, R., & Grammer, K. (1999). The body and face of a woman: One ornament that signals quality? *Evolution and Human Behavior, 20,* 105-120.

Thornhill, R. & Møller, A. P. (1997). Developmental stability, disease and medicine. *Biological Reviews, 72*(4), 497-528.

Tomkinson, G. R., & Olds, T. S. (2000). Physiological correlates of bilateral symmetry in humans. *International Journal of Sports Medicine, 21*, 545-550. https://doi.org/10.1055/s-2000-8479

Tovée, M. J., Tasker, K., & Benson, P. J. (2000). Is symmetry a visual cue to attractiveness in the human female body? *Evolution and Human Behavior, 21*(3), 191-200. doi:10.1016/S1090-5138(00)00040-4

Trivers, R., Fink, B., Russell, M., McCarty, K., James, B., & Palestis, B. G. (2014). The lower body symmetry and running performance in elite Jamaican track and field athletes. *PloS ONE, 9*(11). e113106.

Trivers, R., Palestis, B. G., & Manning, J. T. (2013). The symmetry of children's knees is linked to their adult sprinting speed and their willingness to sprint in a long-term Jamaican study. *PloS ONE, 8*(8). e72244.

Van Valen, L. (1962). A study of fluctuating asymmetry. *Evolution, 16*, 125-142.

Verhaeghe, J., Gheysen, R., & Enzlin, P. (2013). Pheromones and their effect on women's mood and sexuality. *Facts, Views, & Vision in Obgyn, 5*(3), 189-198. https://www.ncbi.nlm.nih.gov/pmc/articles/PMC3987372/

Vingilis-Jaremko, L., & Maurer, D. (2013). The influence of symmetry on children's judgments of facial attractiveness. *Perception, 42*(3), 302-320. https://doi.org/10.1068/p7371

Watson, P. W., & Thornhill, R. (1994). Fluctuating asymmetry and sexual selection. *Trends in Ecology and Evolution, 9*(1), 21-25.

Waynforth, D. (1998). Fluctuating asymmetry and human male life-history traits in rural Belize. *The Royal Society Proceedings of the Royal Society of London B: Biological Sciences, 265*(1405), 1497-1501.

Wisniewski, A. B. (1998). Sexually-dimorphic patterns of cortical asymmetry, and the role for sex steroid hormones in determining cortical patterns of lateralization. *Psychoneuroendocrinology, 23*(5), 519-547. https://doi.org/10.1016/S0306-4530(98)00019-5

Yeo, R. A., Ryman, S. G., Pommy, J., Thoma, R. J., & Jung, R. E. (2016). General cognitive ability and fluctuating asymmetry of brain surface area. *Intelligence, 56*, 93-98. https://doi.org/10.1016/j.intell.2016.03.002

Chapter 4

VOICE

I think the greatest sound in the world is the human voice.

-Miles Davis

The sound of our voice reveals far more than the semantics of the words we speak. The sound of the human voice serves as a powerful medium for transmitting more information than most people probably realize. Consider when you speak on the phone with someone whom you have never met. From the first "Hello," you immediately can determine whether the person is male or female, a child or an adult, whether they have a cold, and if they are crying and upset. In some cases, you can gauge a person's general mood by hearing them speak only a word or two.

In addition to these basic evaluations, voice can reveal quite a lot to a listener, even with minimal exposure of just a few words or even sounds. Evidence from our research, and from the research of others, has shown that by listening to brief voice samples, we can gain accurate information about a speaker's height and weight (Krauss et al., 2002), body configuration (Hughes, Harrison, & Gallup, 2009), sex (Lass, Hughes, Bowyer, Waters, & Bourne, 1976; Lass, Tecca, Mancuso, & Black, 1979), race (Lass et al., 1979; Walton & Orlikoff, 1994), personality traits (Addington, 1968), use of sarcasm (Voyer & Vu, 2016), and even fertility (Bryant & Haselton, 2009). Research has repeatedly shown that a speaker's age can be accurately estimated by hearing the speaker's voice (Hughes & Rhodes, 2010; Krauss, Freyberg, & Morsella, 2002). We found that people were most keen at assessing the exact ages as of children, adolescents, and women in their menopausal years (Hughes & Rhodes, 2010). We attributed this ability to the sex hormonal influences (or lack thereof in the case of children) that help shape the voice during those points in our lifespan. In addition, subjects can accurately match voice samples to a target's facial photograph the majority of the time (Krauss et al., 2002). Voice can also be used in clinical assessment to identify neurological disorders (Gamboa, Jimenez-Jimenez, Mate, & Cobeta, 2001) and to monitor psychoactive drug effects (Scherer & Zei, 1988).

Vocal expressions alone that are independent of any semantic components of speech conveys a wealth of information regarding the emotional state of a speaker (see Scherer, 1986, for review), whether it is derived from spontaneous speech occurring naturally in life situations (Soskin & Kauffman, 1961), or when produced deliberately in experimental settings (Hughes, Mogilski, & Harrison, 2014). A listener does not need a whole sentence or word to appraise a person's emotions, traits and behaviors. You can make judgments about a person just by brief vocal utterances.

Paraverbal cues based on the sound alone (i.e., the tonal qualities of the voice) is appealing to us and tells something more about the speaker. For instance, job candidates are evaluated as being more competent, thoughtful, and intelligent, and consequently, are more likely to be hired when a sample of their voice accompanied their application rather than when evaluators read their credentials only on paper (Schroeder & Epley, 2015).

Why might we have evolved to care about the sound of the human voice? Before the advent of artificial lighting, during our ancestral past we were limited to just the few hours of daylight to communicate and evaluate one another visually. We needed to rely on voice as our main source of communication at night and as the primary means to make assessments about others during the dark. This line of reasoning may explain why the tonal qualities of voice evolved to be a medium that conveys such a considerable amount of information to listeners. In this chapter, we provide an overview of some of the evidence we have uncovered in our research as well as some of the evidence yielded by other research teams about voice psychology.

Voice Attractiveness

The human voice plays a particularly large role in the perception of attractiveness and in providing mate-relevant information to others. Evolutionary psychologists have sought to identify what information the tonal qualities of a human voice can convey to listeners and how the voice can be used as a tool to assess and attract potential mates.

When people think of attractiveness, what typically comes to mind is a person's physical appearance. Because our visual sense is dominant, it stands to reason why physical attributes that can be visibly seen are predominantly used to judge the attractiveness of others. However, our primary mode of communication, speaking, involves our sense of audition (hearing). That is, most of our social interactions do not rely mainly on our sense of vision, but rather our sense of hearing. Evidence from our research, and the research of others, strongly supports the notion that the utterances, tones, intonations, and sounds used in spoken communication provide a wealth of cues that allow us to decipher mate-relevant information. Thus, in addition to physical attractiveness, evidence shows how voice attractiveness plays an integral role in mating psychology.

So, what defines an attractive voice? There is considerable agreement between judges in their subjective ratings as to what constitutes an attractive voice for both male and female voices. Most studies demonstrate a strong interrater reliability for what is perceived as sounding like an attractive voice when made by both same-sex and opposite-sex raters (Babel, McGuire, & King, 2014; Collins & Missing, 2001; Hughes, Harrison, & Gallup, 2002; Zuckerman & Driver, 1989). Some thought it was possible that voice attractiveness ratings were influenced by other knowledge gained about a speaker through social interaction. However, it appears that other social information is not necessary to assess voice attractiveness. Independent female raters who heard a set of unknown male voices in the laboratory judged the voice attractiveness of those voices similarly to women who knew and were acquainted with the male voice donors (Doll, Hill, Rotella, Cardenas, Welling, Wheatley, & Puts 2014).

So, what is driving this consensus in the evaluations of vocal attractiveness? That is, are there specific, identifiable physical parameters that underlie what we find vocally attractive? Because our auditory perception of voice is based upon sound waves, researchers have attempted to examine the exact acoustic properties of the voice to help decipher the physical properties of the sound waves that may be contributing to our perceptions.

There are some commonly measured acoustic parameters that have been investigated when studying the human voice. Software programs such as Praat can be used to measure several of these acoustics (www.pratt.org). Measures of *jitter* reflect perturbations in wave frequency, and measures of *shimmer* are perturbations in wave amplitude, and both contribute to how hoarse a voice sounds (Brockmann, Drinnan, Storck, & Carding, 2011). The *Harmonics-to-noise ratio (HNR)* is a measure of the ratio between periodic components and non-periodic components comprising a segment of voiced speech where the first component arises from the vibration of the vocal cords and the second follows from the glottal noise, expressed in decibels (*dB*), and this contributes to the percept of vocal quality (Teixeira, Oliveira, & Lopes, 2013). *Formants* are the concentration of acoustic energy around a particular frequency in a speech wave. There are several formants, each at a different frequency occurring in 1000 Hz intervals, and each formant corresponds to a resonance in the vocal tract (Boersma & Weenink, 2020). *Pitch* is the rate of vibration of the vocal cords, and as the number of vibrations per second increases, the pitch of the voice sounds higher. The acoustic parameter *fundamental frequency (F₀)*, as measured in hertz, is closely associated with the percept of pitch and can be traced to the mass and size of the vibrating vocal folds of the larynx (Lieberman & Blumstein, 1988). Thus, pitch and fundamental frequency are terms often used synonymously. Whereas individuals can naturally vary their pitch while speaking, researchers can also easily experimentally alter pitch by using spectrographic software while retaining other acoustic parameters of the voice.

Wave form display of voice generated by software

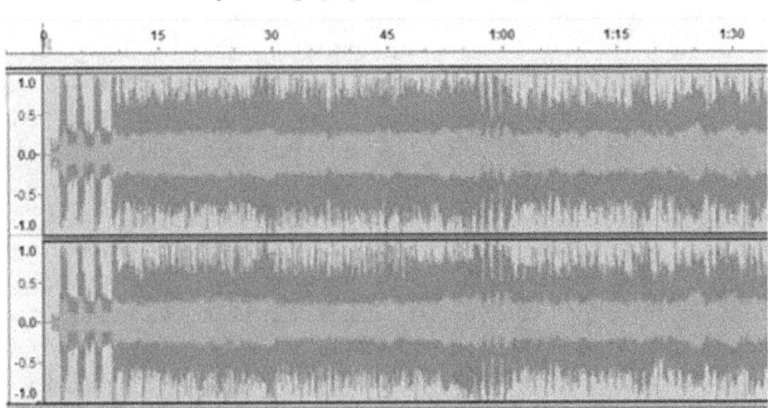

There have been several investigations examining the numerous acoustical aspects described above that can contribute to the tonal qualities of a voice, yet there is no overwhelming consensus in the literature as to which features best define the correlates of what perceivers say is an attractive voice. This may be the case because perceptions of voice attractiveness can be influenced by both the type of stimuli used (e.g., full sentences, vowel utterances, number counts) and stimulus duration (Ferdenzi et al., 2013), which tends to vary across studies. Others argue that it may not be individual characteristics of the voice but rather a unique constellation of acoustic features and the conformity to community speech norms which contribute to the perception of vocal attractiveness (Babel et al., 2014). It may just be that our human auditory system along with neural/biological mechanisms that have evolved to process voices may conduct a different and/or more complicated assessment than what can be captured through current standards of acoustic analyses (Hughes et al., 2008).

Attractive Voice, Attractive Body. Despite not being able to identify which exact properties of a voice allow for the perception of assessing an attractive sounding voice, voice attractiveness appears to be an important mate assessment characteristic and is related to several other traits that signal mate quality. Our research team wanted to evaluate whether voice attractiveness was related to other features of the body associated with attractiveness. We found that people whose voices were rated as sounding attractive by independent raters who had no knowledge of the speaker or study's purpose tended to have greater bilateral body symmetry (bilaterally mirrored morphology), a trait thought to be a marker of developmental fitness and genetic quality (Hughes, Harrison, & Gallup, 2002; Hughes, Pastizzo, & Gallup, 2008), as discussed in Chapter 3 of this book. Our findings regarding the relationship between voice and symmetry have continued to be replicated when examining facial symmetry, as well (Abend, Pflüger, Koppensteiner, Coquerelle, & Grammer, 2015; Hill et al., 2017). Thus, voice may be conveying information about the genetic quality of the speaker.

Further, women with attractive voices tend to have lower waist-to-hip ratios (WHR); i.e., body figures resembling more of an hourglass shape (Hughes, Dispenza, & Gallup, 2004). Men with attractive voices tend to have higher shoulder-to-hip ratios (SHR); i.e., broader shoulders relative to their hips, or a more V-shape body. These sex-specific body configurations are revealing of the influence of sex hormones that shape features that signal our reproductive maturity and potential, with the ideal WHR and SHR reflecting the ideal hormonal milieu for women and men, respectively. In a subsequent study, we also found that listeners were able to match a man's voice with a silhouette approximating his SHR and match a woman's voice with a silhouette approximating her WHR by simply listening to a voice sample (Hughes, Harrison, & Gallup, Jr., 2009). Because both body shape and voice are influenced by sex hormones, especially during pubertal development, then it makes sense that there is a relationship between the two.

Attractive Voice, More Sex. Can you determine someone's sexual history and tendencies just from how their voice sounds? The answer appears to be "yes." Voices convey important information directly related to sexual behavior and mating success. Individuals whose voices were rated to be more attractive have had first sexual intercourse at an earlier age, a greater number of sexual partners, a greater number of affair partners (extra-pair copulations, or EPCs), and a higher number of partners that they had intercourse with that were involved in another committed relationship (i.e., were themselves chosen as an EPC; Hughes et al., 2004). Both heterosexual women and homosexual men agree that men with attractive voices are perceived to have vocal masculinity (Valentova, Roberts, & Havifcek, 2013). As such, men with lower pitched, attractive voices have greater reproductive success and have been documented as having fathered more children (Apicella, Feinberg, & Marlowe, 2007).

The variety of features that correlate with how attractive a voice sounds establishes that the human voice is a salient cue to mate value. Mate value, a major consideration in evolutionary psychology, is defined as, "the total sum of the characteristics an individual possesses at a given moment and within a particular context that impacts their ability to successfully find, attract, and retain a mate" (Fisher, Cox, Bennett, & Gavric, 2008).

Attractive Voice and Fertility. In addition to providing information about mate value, attractive voices provide clues to fertility. Women's voices sound particularly more appealing to men when they are near the fertile part of their menstrual cycle. Voices of women sampled during high fertility were rated as sounding more attractive and had a more feminine, higher pitch than were low fertility voice samples (Bryant & Haselton, 2009; Pipitone & Gallup, 2008). This preference of voices from naturally cycling women at high fertility periods is especially pronounced for men with lower levels of body and vocal masculinity (Pipitone, Gallup, & Bartels, 2016). These lower mate quality men may be more discerning of cues that signal shifts in women's cycle either as a defense against cuckoldry or as an opportunistic mating strategy. Because fertility information about women can be found in the voice, it makes sense why men, in general, respond more favorably towards women's voices during the time when the possibility of conception is greater.

For men, on the other hand, fertility does not seem to be linked to voice attractiveness. Men with lower pitched voices that were rated as sounding more attractive to women did not have better semen quality (Simmons, Peters, & Rhodes, 2011). Rather, men whose voices were rated as more attractive tended to have lower concentrations of sperm in their ejaculate.

These findings are consistent with the idea that there may be a trade-off between sperm production and male investment in competing for and attracting mates, rather than with a phenotype-linked fertility hypothesis. The authors concluded that it was possible that investments in traits that contribute to dominance and attractiveness such as vocal masculinity come at the cost of reduced semen quality. Elevated levels of testosterone associated with male vocal attractiveness and dominance may suppress sperm production and could be the proximate mechanism mediating the negative relationship between these traits.

What-Sounds-Beautiful-Looks-Beautiful Bias

We tend to believe that people who have attractive voices will also have attractive faces (Hughes & Miller, 2015). People certainly seem to become vexed when voice attractiveness and physical attractiveness do not match one another on the same level (Zuckerman & Sinicropi, 2011). There is mixed evidence as to whether voice and face attractiveness *actually do* correlate with one another (for review, see Hughes & Miller, 2015). There is some evidence that the two are in fact related (Abend Pflüger, Koppensteiner, Coquerelle, & Grammer, 2015), even when examining non-Western samples (Wheatley et al., 2014). Nonetheless, there is a stereotypical perception that voice and face attractiveness *should be* associated. This perception can be considered an extension of the what-is-beautiful-is-good stereotype or a "halo effect" whereby people tend to ascribe favorable characteristics to those who are attractive (Dion, Berscheid, & Walster, 1972). As for voice, apparently the bias of "what-sounds-beautiful-looks-beautiful" exists, as well (Hughes & Miller, 2015).

Perceptions Based on Voice Pitch

A considerable amount of research has centered on voice pitch and what this particular acoustic parameter can reveal to listeners, especially regarding perceived voice attractiveness. Evidence suggests that our perception of male and female pitch seems to influence our perception of voice attractiveness for each sex differently. The human voice is a sexually dimorphic trait whose development depends partly upon sex hormone exposure at puberty (Abitbol, Abitbol, & Abitbol, 1999; Dabbs & Mallinger, 1999; Evans, Neave, Wakelin, & Hamilton, 2008), with sex differences seen particularly in measures of pitch. Men typically have lower average pitch than women. Men's vocal folds and vocal tracts are longer than women which results in a lower fundamental frequency (F_0) and closer spacing of formant frequencies (i.e., formant dispersion)(Puts, Hodges, Cárdenas, & Gaulin, 2007), thus creating the percept of a lower voice.

Men's Vocal Pitch. Several studies have found that women generally find lower pitched male voices as more attractive and prefer deeper male voices to higher ones (Apicella, Feinberg, & Marlowe, 2007; Collins, 2000; Feinberg, Jones, Little, Burt, & Perrett, 2005; Karpf, 2006; Riding, Lonsdale, & Brown, 2006; Re, O'Connor, Bennett, & Feinberg, 2012). This preference for a deep male voice is especially evident during the time when a woman is most fertile during her menstrual cycle (Puts, 2005). Women likely prefer deeper male voices because men with lower-pitched voices tend to have larger body sizes (Evans et al., 2006) and higher testosterone levels (Dabbs & Mallinger, 1999), thus making them formidable, viable mates. As such, men with attractive, masculine voices have a greater number of sexual opportunities (Hughes et al., 2004), enjoy greater reproductive success and father more children (Apicella et al. 2007), and have higher fitness markers such as handgrip strength (Atkinson et al., 2012). Women perceived men with lower-pitched male voices to have a higher socioeconomic status than men with higher-pitched voices (O'Connor, Fraccaro, Pisanski, Tigue, O'Donnel, & Feinberg, 2014) and thought they were more capable of acquiring resources (Apicella & Feinberg, 2009).

Women's Vocal Pitch. As for women's voices, some studies have shown that men assess higher pitched female voices as sounding more attractive (Collins & Missing, 2003; Feinberg, DeBruine, Jones, & Perrett, 2008; Jones, Feinberg, DeBruine, Little, & Vukovic, 2008; Re et al., 2012), particularly in short-term mating contexts (i.e., uncommitted sex, or one-night stands) (Puts, Barndt, Welling, Dawood, & Burriss, 2011). However, other studies, have shown that when women lowered the pitch of their voice, men rated their voices as sounding "sexier" (Hughes, Farley, & Rhodes, 2010; Hughes, Mogilski, & Harrison, 2014). Babel and colleagues (2014) also found that female voices with slightly lower than average fundamental frequency (i.e., pitch) were rated as more attractive by listeners. In addition, when we and other investigators asked participants to produce intentionally a "sexy voice," women decreased the pitch of their voices even more than had men and showed greater success in being perceived by independent raters as having sexier voices than their baseline voice (Hughes et al., 2014; Tuomi, & Fisher, 1979).

In addition to a lowered pitch, women projecting their sexy voice also showed greater vocal hoarseness and slowed their speech, and these qualities aided women in being perceived as sounding sexy (Hughes et al., 2014). Female voices with a breathier voice quality were also rated as sounding more attractive and this appears to indicate healthier, younger, more feminine larynges (Babel et al., 2014). Further, Henton and Bladon

(1985) suggested that when a woman displays a breathier, deeper voice, she may be imitating a voice quality associated with arousal. If a woman can manage to sound as though she is sexually aroused, she may be regarded as more desirable by men. Thus, it is possible that raters associated breathy, lower pitched female voices to women who were intentionally showing sexual interest.

In contrast to the above findings, there is also evidence that vocal pitch may not play much of a role in women's vocal attractiveness. Puts and colleagues (2016) examined a large sample of female voices and statistically controlled for several other acoustic parameters and found that pitch had not predicted women's attractiveness for either short- or long-term relationships.

Opposite-Sex Bias. Also of note, there is an opposite-sex bias for preferences of pitch. Men have stronger preferences for women's higher-pitched voices than do women, whereas women have stronger preferences for men's lower-pitched voices than other men (Jones, Feinberg, DeBruine, Little, & Vukovic, 2010). The opposite-sex bias in perception of voices appears to reflect an adaptation for identifying high quality mates rather than a greater sensitivity to pitch manipulations of the opposite sex (Jones et al., 2010).

Pitch Perceptions. Some studies show cross cultural differences regarding pitch and voice attractiveness. For instance, lower pitch was related to voice attractiveness of male voice samples obtained from Cameroon whereas it was not pitch but rather lower mean formants and harmonics-to-noise ratio that were negatively associated with voice attractiveness for a sample of male voices from Namibia (Šebesta et al., 2017). This pattern was attributed to differences in typical physical features such as body mass index between the populations.

Using a Japanese sample, Oguchi and Kikuchi (1997) found that both sexes evaluated a lower-pitched voice with a small pitch range for both sexes as attractive. Oksenberg, Coleman, and Cannell (1986) tested a Western sample and found the opposite, whereby a high pitch with greater variation was associated with voice attractiveness for both sexes. Daniel and McCabe (1992) found that mid-pitched voices for both sexes sounded the "most sexy," suggesting that voices with pitches that deviated too far from the average (within each sex's average voice pitch range) could indicate hormonal abnormalities. In support of this, another study showed that female voices that were raised too high (e.g., above 280 Hz) were rated as sounding less attractive, but these authors attributed their findings to the idea that too high of a pitch sounds "babyish" and is associated with sexual immaturity (Borkowska & Pawlowski, 2011). Yet another study showed that when voices were exaggerated in an atypical way (i.e., raising a male pitch voice and lowering a female pitch voice), this did decrease voice attractiveness (Fraccaro, O'Connor, Re, Jones, DeBruine, & Feinberg, 2013). In turn, when voices were experimentally manipulated to exaggerate the sex-typical voice (i.e., lowering a male pitch voice and raising a female pitch voice), it did not seem to increase ratings of voice attractiveness. Given the lack of consensus in the literature regarding pitch and voice attractiveness, clearly, more research should be conducted to attempt to clarify these phenomena.

Voice Context and Pitch Preferences. The interplay between context and tone of voice not only influences the interpretation of what is said (Voyer & Vu, 2016), but also the evaluation of the voice attractiveness. Interestingly, there is an overall low pitch preference for men regardless of context of what is being said, whereas context or situation seems to override pitch preferences for female voices (Tsantani, Belin, Paterson, & McAleer, 2016). Jones, Feinberg, DeBruine, Little, and Vukovic (2008) first tested this idea and found that their male participants generally rated higher pitched women's voices sounding more attractive than lower pitched voices. However, when the content of the female voice samples were manipulated to express interest or not (i.e., using the phrases "I really like you" or "I don't really like you"), men rated the female voices as sounding more attractive only when hearing the phrase expressing interest regardless of pitch. In a similar study, women who were presented with male voices showed a preference for those who had masculinized (lower pitched) voices regardless of whether or not the vocal content was expressing interest or not (Vukovic, Feinberg, Jones, DeBruine, Welling, Little & Smith, 2008). Thus, unlike the male raters from the previous study, the vocal content of what was said by the men (i.e., either expressed interest or not) seemed to have no impact on women's attractiveness ratings of men as it did for men evaluating women's vocal attractiveness.

Individual Differences Affect Pitch Preferences. Whereas context appears to influence men's evaluation of women's voices, women's preferences for male voices seems to be influenced by several personal factors. For instance, the strength of women's preferences for masculine, lower pitch voices tend to depend upon the sound of her own voice. Women who have higher-pitched, attractive voices have an even stronger preference for attractive, lower-pitched, masculine voices (Vukovic et al., 2010). It appears that if women realize that their mate value is high because they, themselves have attractive voices, their standards for desiring a mate with an attractive voice is greater. They may recognize that they are in a better position to attract and retain high quality mates who also have attractive voices. Along these lines of realizing one's own mate value when selecting mates, homosexual men describing themselves as relatively masculine also show a greater preference for lower-pitched male voices, especially if they are single (Valentova, Roberts, & Havifcek, 2013).

Women's preferences for more masculine male voices are also contingent upon their desire and openness toward engaging in short-term relationships. Women with more positive attitudes toward uncommitted sex and who scored higher on sexual desire inventories had stronger preferences for vocal masculinity regardless if it was judged for short- or long-term relationships (O'Connor, Jones, Fraccaro, Tigue, Pisanski, & Feinberg, 2014). In particular, older women who reported strong preferences for short-term relationships tended to demonstrate even stronger attraction to masculine male voices (Jones, Boothroyd, Feinberg, & DeBruine, 2010). Further, the extent to which women select masculine men as short-term partners appears to be tied to the increased risk of infidelity associated with male masculinity (O'Connor, Pisanski, Tigue, Fraccaro, & Feinberg, 2014). The more often women rated men with lower-pitched voices as likely to commit infidelity, the greater their preference for lower-pitched men's voices in a short-term relative to a long-term relationship context. It is believed women often display a mating strategy that entails seeking genetically superior men as extra-pair partners while concurrently having another in-pair partner willing to invest in the long-term (Thornhill & Gangestad, 2003), so it makes sense that women would perceive men with masculine voices as viable short-term mates.

Women's preferences for low pitch males' voices particular as short-term partners as opposed to long-term partners is also dependent upon the extent to which a woman attributes masculine voices as a sign of the speaker possessing negative personality attributes such as being physically dominant and untrustworthy (Vukovic, Jones, Feinberg, DeBruine, Smith, Welling, & Little, 2011). Women who had a strong tendency to perceive masculine voices as more dominant demonstrated a greater preference for those men to be short-term partners as compared to long-term partners. Women perceive men with more feminized, higher-pitched voices as being more likely to invest time and effort in romantic relationships and be more financially generous with their partners (O'Connor, Fraccaro, & Feinberg, 2012), thus making them desirable long-term partners. As follows, higher pitched voices are related to lower testosterone levels, (Dabbs & Mallinger, 1999; Evans Neave, Wakelin, & Hamilton, 2008) and lower testosterone is associated with marriage and fatherhood in men (Gray, Kahlenberg, Barrett,

Lipson, & Ellison, 2002). In addition, women who were currently breastfeeding had stronger preferences for higher pitched male voices, further suggesting that women's preferences for male voices may reflect a trade-off between securing good genes versus obtaining paternal investment (Apicella & Feinberg, 2009).

Women who experience menarche (i.e., first menses) at a younger age also show stronger preferences for masculinized lowered pitch male voices than those who had later menarche (Jones, Boothroyd, Feinberg, & DeBruine, 2010). The authors of this study explained that as adolescents, women who experienced early puberty may have been targeted more by older men who possessed more masculine traits than their peers. Therefore, women who reported early puberty could have learned to associate desirable mates with those that possess more masculine characteristics.

Women's voice preferences are also linked to their hormone levels. Specifically, higher estradiol levels collected from salivary assays strongly predicted women's preferences for vocal masculinity (Pisanski, Hahn, Fisher, DeBruine, Feinberg, & Jones, 2014). As such, women's preferences for masculinized voices (i.e., those that have lower voice pitches and larger vocal tract lengths) are heightened during their fertile (late-follicular) part of their menstrual cycle (Feinberg et al., 2006). However, preference shifts for masculine male voices during fertility was more pronounced in women who had low estrogen levels, not higher levels. It was speculated that because more masculinized women (low estrogen) cannot attain masculinized men as easily as their feminine counterparts, it is necessary for those women to change their mating strategy across the cycle to capitalize on attaining a high-quality mate during fertility.

Mate-Relevant Pitch Memory. Women are so sensitive to the male voice pitch that it can affect their memory. Women's memory was enhanced in a visual object memory task when an object's name was spoken in a masculinized (i.e., lower-pitch) versus feminized (i.e., higher-pitch) male voice during encoding (Smith, Jones, Feinberg, & Allan, 2012). No such effect occurred when women listen to other women's voices. This finding suggests that human memory is attuned to information that has adaptive value in selecting a favorable mate.

Voice and Perceived Traits

Voice, and specifically voice pitch, plays a pivotal role in impression formation of a speaker. Some of the most extensively studied traits influenced by voice are leadership, body size and shape, dominance, trustworthiness, and other realms of personality. Below we highlight some of these research findings.

The Sound of Leadership. There is evidence to suggest that men and women with lower-pitched voices have greater success in obtaining leadership positions. Leaders with lower voices are perceived as more competent than those with higher pitched voices (Oleszkiewicz, Pisanski, Lachowicz-Tabaczek, & Sorokowska, 2017). People prefer to vote for male politicians with lower-pitched voices and ascribe more favorable personality traits to those candidates such as intelligence, honesty, trustworthiness, dominance, leadership, and attractiveness (Tigue, Borak, O'Connor, Schandl, & Feinberg 2012). Especially in a wartime voting scenario, voters were sensitive to vocal cues of dominance for elected leaders and thought candidates with a lower voice pitch had greater physical prowess and integrity, traits especially needed during wartime era.

Even when considering female political candidates, there is a preference of lower pitch voices. For instance, when recordings of mock candidates' voices were manipulated for pitch, both men and women were more likely to vote for the male and female candidates when the lower-pitched version of their voice was played than the higher-pitched version (Klofstad, Anderson, & Peters, 2012). The authors of that study even went so far as to speculate that because women tend to have higher pitched voices than men, it may contribute to why fewer women hold leadership positions.

A U.S. Military Staff Sergeant, an authority figure, yells orders to soldiers.

Photo by Staff Sgt. D. Love, U.S. Department of Defense. Public domain.

Another study evaluated how the interaction between voice pitch and candidate age affects electoral success. Flofstad, Anderson, and Nowicki (2015) found that not only can voters discriminate age based on voice pitch alone, but voters preferred candidates at ages when voice pitch is lowest (i.e., during a candidate's 40s and 50s as opposed to ages 30s, 60s, or 70s). Nonetheless, the perception of age played less of a role in determining the preference for candidates than had the overall pitch of the candidates' voices.

So why would people believe that lower-pitched-voiced individuals would be better leaders? The preference for leaders with lower pitched voices may not be indicative of the fact that they are more competent leaders per se. But because low pitch voices are linked to higher testosterone levels (Dabbs & Mallinger, 1999), voters may feel that those candidates could be more assertive in pursuing the interests of their constituents, thus possessing qualities that are related to good leadership. Further, it has been speculated that because women show higher sensitivity to vocal dominance cues than men do (Borkowska & Pawlowski, 2011), this sensitivity may explain why women still show greater approval of male leaders, even if it is not in the best interest for the professional advancement of their own gender (Michael & Crawford, 1927).

Not only do men with lower pitch voices seem to have an advantage in political elections, but Mayew, Parsons, and Venkatachalam (2013) found that a common factor among CEOs of the most successful companies have deeper voices, as well as they enjoy longer tenures at their position. Women with deeper voices also experience some benefits, too. Female teachers who have lower pitch voices tend to have less voice complaints from their students (Rantala & Vilkman, 1999). It appears that positive perceptions of deeper voices contribute to success seen among those with lower-pitched voices in leadership positions.

The Sound of Body Size and Shape. Voice pitch can also be used to glean information about body size. There is evidence that larger women tend to have lower voices (Collins & Missing, 2001). Not only is F_0 (i.e., mean pitch) related to weight and BMI in women, but women with higher BMI tend to present more irregularities in their voice pitch (Gonzalez, 2007). As women's average speaking voice pitch gets lower, various body measures increase such as weight, body mass index, body fat percentage, waist and hip circumferences, and waist-to-hip ratios (Vukovic, Feinberg, DeBruine, Smith, & Jones, 2010). Because these traits have been known to predict long-term health outcomes in women, voice pitch is thought to also be a cue to women's long-term health.

Higher pitched female voices were assessed as being more attractive and belonging to younger women (Collins & Missing, 2001) and men rated smaller and more feminine-sounding women as being more attractive (Pisanski, Mishra, & Rendall, 2012). Alternatively, women with lower voices are judged as having less attractive voices and faces (Collins & Missing, 2001), and women rated as sounding larger were also rated as being more masculine (Pisanski et al., 2012). Further, taller women display more of a glottal fry to their voice than shorter women (Gonzalez, 2007) and also have narrower formant dispersion (Collins & Missing, 2001).

As for men's voices, there is a significant negative relationship between fundamental frequency and body size and shape (Evans et al., 2006). Higher levels of circulating testosterone indicate lower fundamental frequency (Evans et al., 2008). Male speakers who were taller and had higher salivary testosterone levels also had lower fundamental frequency (i.e., mean pitch) and were, in turn, rated by women as more masculine (Cartei, Bond, Reby, 2014). In addition, women judge men with voices with low-frequency harmonics as being more attractive, older and heavier, more likely to have a hairy chest, and of a more muscular body type (Collins, 2000). However, weight was the only measure that could be reliably estimated from males' voices, whereas a man's age, height, and hairiness of chest could not (Collins, 2000). In addition to pitch, heavier men and those with larger body surface area were found to have more breathiness to their voices (Gonzalez, 2007). From a perceptual standpoint, men whose voices were rated by women as sounding larger were rated as being more masculine (Pisanski et al., 2012), so clearly there is a perceptual link between voice and body size for men irrespective of whether this relationship may be real.

Listeners seem to attend to sexually dimorphic voice cues to assess not only size of the speaker's body, but also their body shape. In our research, we found that women who had lower waist-to-hip ratios(WHR), or a more hour-glass figure, and men who had higher shoulder-to-hip ratios (SHR), or more v-shaped figure with broader shoulders, had voices that were rated consistently as more attractive (Hughes et al., 2004). In a follow-up study, we investigated whether participants could infer the actual WHR or SHR of a speaker based solely from hearing their voice by selecting from an array of line-drawn figures that depicted variation in WHR and SHR (Hughes et al., 2009). We found that participants could estimate the actual measurements of the WHR of female speakers and the SHR of male speakers simply by hearing their voice.

This evidence underscores the interdependence of the physiological, acoustic, and perceptual dimensions of voice (Cartei, Bond, Reby, 2014).

The connection between voice and body is so prominent that visual experience is not necessary to make accurate body size and shape estimations. Both blind and sighted listeners estimated women's height with the same degree of accuracy and error patterns by using low auditory frequencies to gauge larger body sizes (Pisanski, Feinberg, Oleszkiewicz, & Sorokowska, 2017).

The Sound of Dominance and Competition. Lower pitched voices are judged to be more dominant than higher pitched voices for both men (Puts, Gaulin & Verdolini, 2006; Puts, Hodges, Cárdenas, & Gaulin, 2007; Tsantani, Belin, Paterson, & McAleer, 2016) and women (Borkowska & Pawlowski, 2011; Jones, Feinberg, DeBruine, Little, Vukovic 2010), although some have been unable to demonstrate this relationship with women's voices (Tsantani, Belin, Paterson, & McAleer, 2016). For men, a masculine, low-pitch voice increased ratings of both physical and social dominance, but the manipulation of pitch in male voices had a stronger influence on the judgment of physical dominance than it did on the judgment of social dominance (Puts, Gaulin & Verdolini, 2006; Puts, Hodges, Cárdenas, & Gaulin, 2007). Although not tested, some argue that it is possible that female dominance is more closely associated with social than physical dominance. This may explain why the influence of vocal pitch on judgments of dominance could be weaker across studies for female voices compared with male voices when just testing the overarching construct of "dominance" (Tsantani, Belin, Paterson, & McAleer, 2016). There is also the possibility that prenatal androgen exposure may influence the development of women's vocal dominance. In our own work, we found that women, but not men, with lower second digit to fourth digit (2D:4D) ratios (as described in Chapter 5 is an indirect measure of greater prenatal hormone exposure within each sex), have voices that are rated as sounding mature and dominant when they were adults (Hughes, Pastizzo, Gallup, 2008).

Whereas men's normal speaking voices are typically rated as sounding more dominant than women's normal speaking voice, when asked to deliberately portray a dominant-sounding voice, both sexes were fully capable of doing so as assessed by independent raters who heard both their projected dominant voice compared to their normal speaking voice (Hughes, Mogilski, & Harrison, 2014). This ability to modify one's voice to sound more dominant could be useful in terms of competition. Indeed, it was shown that when men were placed into an experimental competitive dating task, they lowered their voices when they were near another man who appeared to be more dominant (Puts, Gaulin, & Verdolini, 2006).

Along these lines of vocal dominance subserving a competitive edge, it is thought that certain acoustic features (e.g., fundamental frequency, formant position) of men's voices are honest signals of threat potential, such that there are relationships between these acoustic parameters and men's body size, strength, testosterone, and physical aggressiveness in both industrialized and forager societies (see Puts, Apicella & Cárdenas, 2012). Both sexes can accurately predict the physical strength of other individuals, especially men, based only on hearing the sound of their voices, and such estimates of strength are thought to be used to assess fighting ability (Sell et al., 2010). Further, both men and women in a hunting and gathering society viewed lower pitched voices in the opposite sex as being better at acquiring resources than their higher-pitched counterparts (Apicella & Feinberg, 2009).

Women seem to be more sensitive to dominance cues in other women's voices than are men, further suggesting some intra-competitive awareness (Borkowska & Pawlowski, 2011). Likewise, men may have an increased sensitivity to dominance cues in other men's voices as evidenced by their enhanced implicit memory for sentences when spoken by musicalized male voice (Albert et al., 2018). Men's own self-perceived dominance and formidability does not seem to impact their attentiveness to vocal masculinity of other men, and men who considered themselves to be very dominant tend to rate other men's voices as sounding less dominant (Wolff & Puts, 2010). Thus, vocal dominance appears to play an important role in competition and rivalry.

The Sound of Trustworthiness. Several studies have examined how voice pitch is important in the perception of trustworthiness. Typically, low pitched voices of both genders were perceived as more trustworthy than high pitched voices (Tsantani, Belin, Paterson, & McAleer, 2016). However, there is an interesting interaction between semantic content and voice pitch that influences the perception of credibility of male speakers. Lower pitched male voices were perceived by women as more trustworthy and attractive only under the context of prosocial speech; for antisocial speech, higher male voice pitch was preferred presumably because it counteracted the negative effects of the antisocial content (O'Connor & Barclay, 2018). This finding can be impactful in several realms such as when delivering news reports, advertising marketing messages, and giving political speeches. Audiences may perceive antisocial semantic content more negatively if given by a lower-pitched male speaker.

Both voice pitch and the sex of the speaker affects perceived trustworthiness when considering different contexts in which trust is of concern. In general, listeners trusted women with lower-pitched voices and men with higher-pitched voices, however, higher pitched male and female voices were perceived as more trusting in economic and in mating-related contexts (e.g., infidelity, mate stealing; O'Connor & Barclay, 2017). Particularly with economic decisions, it appears that people do not trust men with masculine voices to divide financial resources equitably and it is therefore a wonder why we entrust our leaders to have lower-pitch voices to lead our governments (Montano, Tigue, Isenstein, Barclay, & Feinberg, 2017).

The Pitch of Personality. Several other personality traits have been assessed based on pitch perception. For instance, lowered-pitched voices of both men and women are judged as being more competent (Oleszkiewics, Pisanski, Lachowics-Tabaczek, & Sorokowska, 2017). Observers attribute confidence to those who spoke with a higher pitch (in certain conditions) along with increased loudness, shorter pauses, and a rapid rate of speech (Scherer, London, & Wolf, 1973). Higher-pitch voices are also perceived as sounding warmer, but only for women's voices and not men's (Oleszkiewics, Pisanski, Lachowics-Tabaczek, & Sorokowska, 2017). Those with feminine-pitch traits were found to be more cooperative than those with more masculinized voices perhaps because they were perceived as more friendly and less threatening (Knowles & Little, 2016). Alternatively, masculine-sounding voices were perceived as less cooperative. This is likely due to the fact that masculinized voices are more so associated with prestige and social and physical dominance (Puts, Gaulin, & Verdolini, 2006).

Salient Sounds. It is important to point out that perceptual association between voice pitch and social and personal dimensions of a speaker can develop without visual input as evidenced by studies showing only small differences in personal assessments via voice between blind and sighted individuals (Oleszkiewics, Pisanski, Lachowics-Tabaczek, & Sorokowska, 2017). Further, listeners across different languages form very similar personality impressions regardless of whether a speaker's voice belongs to the native or the foreign language of the listener (Baus, McAleer, Marcoux, Belin, & Costa, 2019). It is just the acoustical properties that listeners pay attention to when judging other's personality that varies across languages. Baus et al. (2019) showed that across different cultures and languages, the two main components of voice from which we form social impressions are trust and strength, two categories in which low voices rate high (Baus et al., 2019).

Manipulating How We Sound

People often change the sound of their voices to convey certain emotions, motives, and directives. But are people any good at it? We tested to see if people were able to deliberately and effectively modulate the sound of their voice to convey particularly traits, and we aimed to determine whether it was possible for others to detect those changes (Hughes, Mogilski, & Harrison, 2014). We found that, with little instruction on how to do so, both women and men could modulate their voices to sound more dominant and more intelligent, as judged by independent raters. However, when they were asked to speak in a "sexier" voice, men were unable to make their voices sound more attractive when compared to their normal speaking voices, whereas women were able to make their voices sound more attractive. In contrast, women were unable to portray a more confident voice, but men were. We interpreted these results through an evolutionary lens. Men, compared to women, emphasize attractiveness more when looking for mates (Buss, 1989). Therefore, it would be beneficial for a woman to manipulate the sound of her voice effectively to enhance her overall sex appeal to men, and for men to be sensitive to detect this. Alternatively, women, compared to men, prioritize the earning potential and financial resources of potential mates (Sprecher, 1989). Evidence suggests that confidence is related to a man's earning potential, power in society, and other personality characteristics related to success (Buss, 1989). Therefore, it would be advantageous for men to have the ability to project a voice of confidence, and for women to be adept at detecting this trait in a potential mate.

Vocal manipulation tends to occur in context when attraction is involved, whether or not we are consciously aware that we make such changes. Voice can be a striking feature that signals a person's attraction to another and there is evidence to support the idea that attraction and/or romantic interest can be easily distinguished through vocal tones alone. In an experimental setting, we (Hughes, Farley, & Rhodes, 2010) asked participants to speak on the phone with an opposite-sex person whose picture (a confederate) was shown to them. Independent raters had previously judged these target photos to be to either highly attractive or unattractive. We recorded participants' voice and had independent raters review the scripted voice messages they left for the person that they thought they were calling.

We found that both men and women lowered the pitch of their voices when communicating with the attractive person of the opposite-sex as opposed to the unattractive target. Further, listeners who were blind as to the context of the speaking thought the samples directed toward the attractive persons sounded more pleasant. We presumed that participants lowered their voice as a likely attempt to sound more seductive or appealing to the attractive target (whether they were consciously aware of this or not), and voice was likely serving as a signal of romantic interest. In support of this reasoning, Anolli and Ciceri (2002) documented that men who exercised greater vocal modulation and gradually deepened their voices during conversations with unfamiliar women were more successful at getting future dates in a simulated dating scenario.

It was interesting to see how easy it was for others to discern the vocal changes when speaking to attractive individuals. Indeed, this perceptual ability to detect romantic interest via the voice may be adaptive for identifying interested potential mates, detecting partner interest in others, and even detection of a partner's attraction to a rival.

Even under more natural conditions, vocal changes tend to occur in the exchanges between mates. We recorded phone conversations between heterosexual participants and their newly in-love romantic partner and a same-sex friend and presented clips of these recordings to independent raters but obscured the content of the conversation to using software to create paralanguage vocalizations (Farley, Hughes, & LaFayette, 2013). Paralanguage is a vocal technique where certain voice qualities such as prosody, pitch, volume, intonation, etc. are retained but the sounds of the words are muddled, sounding similar to the adult characters *Charlie Brown* cartoons ("Wah wah wah wah…"). We found that voice samples directed toward romantic partners were judged by independent raters as sounding more pleasant, sexier, and reflecting greater romantic interest than those directed toward same-sex friends. Raters were also able to determine whether the brief voice samples were spoken to a romantic partner or to a friend.

In a similar study, female speakers were perceived by raters as sounding more approachable, sincere, submissive, and scatterbrained when their speech was directed toward intimate male partners than when directed to just male friends during phone conversations (Monepare & Vega, 1988). Other studies have also shown that romantic partners tend to use prosodic exaggeration, or "loverese," when speaking to one another (Chang & Garcia, 2011). These findings point to the effectiveness of vocal change as a mechanism for communicating relationship status.

According to affection exchange theory, the successful use of nonverbal cues to detect and signal affection and connectedness to others offers individuals a survival advantage (Floyd et al., 2008). It may be adaptive to attend to vocal cues of romantic interest to either avoid or engage in expending energy on individuals who may or may not be interested or available.

In addition to the realm of mating, intentional voice manipulation is observed in a variety of other social contexts. For instance, individuals tend to raise the pitch of their voice when attempting to deceive another person (Ekman et al. 1976; Streeter et al. 1977) and individuals who are confident in what they are saying tend to speak faster and louder (Kimble and Seidel 1991). Professionals tend to lower their voice when giving their expert advice, with women lowering their pitch even more than men (Sorokowski et al., 2019). In this study, they were able mask cues of vocal content because English speaking voice samples were judged by foreign-speaking listeners. Despite the language barrier, voices of professionals giving advice were rated sounding more competent and authoritative. These findings suggest that people are capable of modulating their voice to elicit certain desired outcomes, and the nonverbal aspects of the voice are effective in altering perceptions.

Speakers also tend to modify their voice depending upon their audience. For instance, when people speak to infants, they tend to use exaggerated vocal intonation, having a higher pitch, broader pitch range, slower rate, and longer pauses (Burnham, Kitamura, & Vollmer-Conna, 2002; Cooper & Aslin, 1994). This exaggerated prosodic profile is known as infant-directed speech (Cooper & Aslin 1994), formerly referred to as "motherese" (e.g., Fernald & Kuhl, 1987). People also tend to speak to their pets in a similar manner, termed pet-directed speech (Burnham, Kitamura, & Vollmer-Conna, 2002). People speak differently to men versus women. Speech directed towards men, regardless of the speaker's own gender, is perceived as sounding more dominant and formal than when directed towards women (Hall & Braunwald, 1981).

Further, people seem to modulate their voices according to their perception of the social status of the listener relative to their own social status. For instance, in a study that entailed simulated job interviews, participants increased their mean pitch in response to dominant and prestigious employers as compared to those who were not, especially for those who had self-perception of having low dominance themselves (Leongómez, Mileva, Little, & Roberts, 2017). Voice manipulation even comes into play in mating competitions. Men who believed they were physically dominant to their competitor in a dating game scenario lowered their voice pitch when addressing their rival, whereas men who believed they are less dominant raised their pitch when confronted with a male competitor (Puts, Gaulin, & Verdolini, 2006).

There are sex differences when it comes to modulating one's voice relative to the listener's status. Women sound more competent when speaking to their bosses than when speaking to their subordinates or peers, whereas men sound more competent when speaking to their peers (Steckler & Rosenthal, 1985). Burnham et al. (2002) suggested that speakers have an intuitive sense of the emotional needs of their listeners and will adjust their speech accordingly.

It may be assumed that we can simply change our voices to deceive others of our level of attractiveness. However, we would equate transient vocal modulation to a woman wearing make-up. Making such changes certainly could enhance a person's attractive appearance, but it will not drastically transform someone into a new person. We are all constrained to an extent by our genes and biology, and our vocal development is under the influence of sex hormone exposure, particularly during pubertal changes (Abitbol, Abitbol, & Abitbol, 1999). Further, sustaining a deceptive appearance interminably (i.e., keeping the make-up on or constantly modifying one's voice) would not be very feasible. Our voices are also a byproduct of our environments and our cultures as reflected by our accents, local dialects, education, and other experiences (e.g., age, years of smoking, exposure to diseases affecting speech). These environmental influences can contribute to the perception of how we speak. Interestingly, vocal coaching and training is readily available to modify one's speech patterns in order to speak in a desired manner. It has been long documented that those in certain occupations such as actors, politicians, and other public figures frequently take advantage of these professional vocal training services (Karpf, 2006).

Perception of Our Own Voices

Did you ever hear a recording of your own voice, either from a voicemail or video, and think, wow, is that me? I sound terrible! It has long been known that people will frequently express some disdain when hearing a recording of their own voice. Listeners tend to react negatively when made aware that they are hearing a recording of their own voices, yet they do not seem to have this reaction when hearing recordings of others' voices (Holzman & Rousey 1966). This reaction may be due to the fact that we do not hear our live, spoken voice as others hear it. Our perception of our live speaking voice is distorted because we hear it through bone and air conduction, while others hear our voices through air conduction alone (Reinfeldt, Östli,

Håkansson, & Stenfelt, 2010). Therefore, we believe our recorded voice should sound more like it does when we hear it live in our own head. Because of this, we may not be able to evaluate our own vocal attractiveness, or interpret our own vocal profile, as others perceive it (Hughes & Harrison, 2013).

Despite the anticipation that a recording of one's own voice may sound differently than what is expected, when tested experimentally, we (Hughes & Harrison, 2013) found a preference for the sound of a person's own voice recordings. When participants were given an array of voice recordings of different individuals and were not told that their own recorded voices were included in the presentation, they rated their own voices as sounding more attractive than others rated their voices (Hughes & Harrison, 2013). Participants also rated their own voices as sounding more attractive than they rated the voices of others. We pointedly called this paper, "I like my voice better." Our findings suggest that people may engage in vocal implicit egotism, a nonconscious form of self-enhancement (Pelham, Mirenberg, & Jones, 2002). In other words, people have an unconscious tendency to react more favorably to anything marginally related to oneself. For instance, we even like the letters in our names and the numbers in our birthdates better than other numbers and letters. This preference for one's own voice can be further explained by a mere exposure effect (Bornstein & D'Agostino, 1992). Even if our recorded voice does not sound exactly like we thought it would, we have consistent exposure to our voice and hear every single word we say. The voice in our head and our recorded voice are going to sound a lot more alike than our voice in comparison to someone else's voice. Some level of similarity or familiarity must come into play when we evaluate recordings of our own voice.

Voice, Jealousy, and Infidelity

Those who have more attractive voices that are within the ideal sex-specific pitch range seem to elicit jealous reactions from the same-sex. For instance, participants were asked to rate how jealous they felt if their romantic partners were accompanied by someone of the opposite-sex on a weekend trip where they had to imagine flirting had occurred. After hearing same-sex voices samples that represented this potential rival, men with masculine male voices (i.e., lower pitch) and women with feminine female voices (i.e., higher pitch) had conjured greater feelings of jealousy than those with pitches outside the ideal ranges (O'Connor & Feinberg, 2012). Because these audible cues reflect underlying mate quality, they seem to be triggering feelings of intrasexual competition and mate guarding practices.

It appears that listeners are also unconsciously tuning into voice pitch to ascribe infidelity risk to speakers. O'Connor, Re, and Feinberg (2011) manipulated the pitch of men's and women's voices and found that listeners would make cheating ascriptions based on voice pitch alone. So, can you actually detect a cheater based solely on their voice? While O'Connor and colleagues' study showed how manipulating pitch plays a role in appraising a speaker's proclivity to be unfaithful, we conducted a follow-up study that demonstrated that perceptions of a speaker's actual history of infidelity could, in fact, be determined through voice alone (Hughes & Harrison, 2017). We found that participants rated the voices of those who had a history of cheating as more likely to cheat than those who reported never having cheated. We controlled for aspects that may clue a listener to the speaker's mate value such as voice attractiveness, age, voice pitch, and other acoustic measures to assure that greater attractiveness was not driving this effect. We were unable to exactly pinpoint all the acoustic features of a voice that allow our perceptual system to make this assessment. Voice pitch played a role but did not represent the entire picture.

Further, we found that for both sexes, voices manipulated to have a lower pitch were also thought to be more likely to have cheated than those with higher pitches. When people are asked to intentionally display a "sexy voice," they tend to lower their pitch of their (Hughes et al., 2014; Tuomi, & Fisher, 1979). Women especially tend to speak with deeper voices when conveying sexual interest to men (Hughes et al., 2010; Karpf, 2006). Therefore, it is possible that raters associated a lower pitched voice with those who were intentionally trying to sound sexy and who are seeking casual sexual encounters such as affairs. Also, because higher levels of testosterone contribute to a lower pitch voice (Abitbol et al., 1999; Evans et al., 2008), as well as a higher sex drive (Abitbol et al., 1999; Davis, 2000), we may come to associate the two together when hearing a speaker and think a lower pitched individual is more likely to stray.

These findings demonstrate the validity of the "thin slice theory" which stipulates that one can make accurate assessments of another based on merely brief observation (Ambady & Rosenthal, 1992). In the case of vocal information, only very brief voice samples are needed to predict a variety of physical and behavioral elements. Collectively, these data suggest that cognitive strategies have evolved to facilitate wise mate choices, holding true even when only the auditory sensory modality is operating. As a society that is becoming increasingly reliant on written, electronic communication, versus vocal communication, it will be fascinating to see what effects this will have on human mate choices in the millennia to come.

People have entire relationships via text message now, but I am not partial to texting. I need context, nuance, and the warmth and tone that can only come from a human voice.

-Author Danielle Steel

Conclusion

The sound of the human voice reveals much more information than we may understand. People respond to subtle cues within the voice in order to decipher a considerable amount of information about the speaker, and tonal qualities can enhance understanding and communication. Beyond the semantic content of the spoken word, the sound of the human voice unequivocally provides a substantial amount of information that we use to assess one another, particularly in mating contexts. Our physical appearance may be at the forefront of others' evaluations and interactions with us, but we cannot overlook the impact that our voice has upon others, particularly within the realm of mate attraction and assessment. As the poet Maya Angelou once said, "Words mean more than what is set down on paper. It takes the human voice to infuse them with deeper meaning."

References

Abend, P., Pflüger, L. S., Koppensteiner, M., Coquerelle, M., & Grammer, K. (2015). The sound of female shape: a redundant signal of vocal and facial attractiveness. *Evolution and Human Behavior, 36*(3), 174–181.

Abitbol, J., Abitbol, P., & Abitbol, B. (1999). Sex hormones and the female voice. *Journal of Voice, 13*, 424–446.

Addington, D. W. (1968). The relationship of selected vocal characteristics to personality perception. *Speech Monographs, 35*, 492–503. doi:10.1080/03637756809375599

Albert, G., Pearson, M., Arnocky, S., Wachowiak, M., Nicol, J., & Murphy, D. R. (2018). Effects of masculinized and feminized male voices on men and women's distractibility and implicit memory. *Journal of Individual Differences, 39*(3), 151–165. https://doi.org/10.1027/1614-0001/a000259

Ambady, N., & Rosenthal, R. (1992). Thin slices of expressive behavior as predictors of interpersonal consequences: A meta-analysis. *Psychological Bulletin, 111*, 256–274.

Apicella, C. L, & Feinberg D. R. (2009). Voice pitch alters mate-choice-relevant perception in hunter-gatherers. *Proceedings of the Royal Society of London B, 276*, 1077–1082. https://doi.org/10.1098/rspb.2008.1542

Apicella, C. L., Feinberg, D. R., & Marlowe, F. W. (2007). Voice pitch predicts reproductive success in male hunter-gatherers. *Biology Letters, 3*, 682–684. doi:10.1098/rsbl.2007.0410

Atkinson, J., Pipitone, R. N., Sorokowski, A., Sorokowski, P., Mberira, M., Bartels, A., & Gallup, G. G. Jr. (2012). Voice and handgrip strength predict reproductive success in a group of indigenous African females. *PLOS One.* doi: 10.1371/journal.pone.0041811

Babel, M., McGuire, G., & King, J. (2014). Towards a more nuanced view of vocal attractiveness. *PLOS One, 9,* e88616.

Baus, C., McAleer, P., Marcoux, K., Belin, P., & Costa, A. (2019). Forming social impressions from voices in native and foreign languages. *Scientific Reports, 9*(1), 1-414. doi:10.1038/s41598-018-36518-6

Boersma, Paul & Weenink, David (2020). Praat: Doing phonetics by computer [Computer program]. Version 6.1.09, retrieved from http://www.praat.org/

Borkowska, B., & Pawlowski, B. (2011). Female voice frequency in the context of dominance and attractiveness perception. *Animal Behaviour, 82*(1), 55–59. https://doi.org/10.1016/j.anbehav.2011.03.024

Bornstein R. F., & D'Agostino P. R. (1992). Stimulus recognition and the mere exposure effect. *Journal of Personality and Social Psychology, 63,* 545–552.

Brockman, M. Drinnan, M. J., Storck, C. & Carding, P. N. (2011). Reliable jitter and shimmer measurements in voice clinics: The relevance of vowel, gender, vocal intensity, and fundamental frequency effects in a typical clinical task. *Journal of Voice, 25*(1) , 44-53.

Bryant, G. A., & Haselton, M. G. (2009). Vocal cues of ovulation in human females. *Biology Letters, 5,* 12–15. doi:10.1098/rsbl.2008.0507

Burnham, D., Kitamura, C., & Vollmer-Conna, U. (2002). What's new, pussycat? Talking to babies and animals. *Science, 296*(5572), 1435.

Buss, D. M. (1989). Sex differences in human mate preferences: Evolutionary hypotheses tested in 37 cultures. *Behavior and Brain Sciences, 12,* 1–14. doi:10.1017/S0140525X00023992

Cartei, V., Bond, R., & Reby, D. (2014). What makes a voice masculine: Physiological and acoustical correlates of women's ratings of men's vocal masculinity. *Hormones and Behavior, 66*(4), 569–576. https://doi.org/10.1016/j.yhbeh.2014.08.006

Chang, R. S., & Garcia, J. R. (2011). *Behind closed doors: On the use of loverese and pet-names between romantic partners.* Poster session presented at the Annual Conferences of the Northeast Evolutionary Society, Binghamton, NY.

Collins, S. A. (2000). Men's voices and women's choices. *Animal Behaviour, 60,* 773–780.

Collins, S. A., & Missing, C. (2003). Vocal and visual attractiveness are related in women. *Animal Behaviour, 65,* 997–1004.

Cooper, R. P., & Aslin, R. N. (1994). Developmental differences in infant attention to the spectral properties of infant-directed speech. *Child Development, 65,* 1663–1677.

Dabbs, Jr., J. M., & Mallinger, A. (1999). High testosterone levels predict low voice pitch among men. *Personality and Individual Differences, 27,* 801–804.

Daniel, H. J., & McCabe, R. B. (1992). The nature of the sexes: The sociobiology of sex differences and the "battle of the sexes." In J. M. G. van der Dennen (Ed.), *Gender differences in the perception of vocal sexiness* (p. 55). The Netherlands: Origin Press.

Davis, S. (2000). Testosterone and sexual desire in women. *Journal of Sex Education and Therapy, 25,* 25–32.

Dion, K. Berscheid, E., & Walster, E. (1972). What is beautiful is good. *Journal of Personality and Social Psychology, 24,* 285–290. doi:10.1037/h0033731

Doll, L. M., Hill, A. K., Rotella, M. A., Cárdenas, R. A., Welling, L. L. M., Wheatley, J. R., & Puts, D. A. (2014). How well do men's faces and voices index mate quality and dominance? *Human Nature, 25*(2), 200–212. https://doi.org/10.1007/s12110-014-9194-3

Ekman, P., Friesen, W. V., & Scherer, K. (1976). Body movements and voice pitch in deceptive interaction. *Semiotica, 16,* 23–27.

Evans, S. N., Neave, N., & Wakelin, D. (2006). Relationship between vocal characteristics and body size and shape in human males: an evolutionary explanation for a deep male voice. *Biological Psychology, 72,* 160–163.

Evans, S., Neave, N., Wakelin, D., & Hamilton, C. (2008). The relationship between testosterone and vocal frequencies in human males. *Physiology and Behavior, 93,* 783–788.

Farley, S. D., Hughes, S. M., & LaFayette, J. N. (2013). People will know we are in love: Evidence of differences between vocal samples directed toward lovers and friends. *Journal of Nonverbal Behavior, 37,* 123–138. doi:10.1007/s10919-013-0151-3

Feinberg, D. R., DeBruine, L. M., Jones, B. C., & Perrett, D. I. (2008). The role of femininity and averageness of voice pitch in aesthetic judgments of women's voices. *Perception, 37,* 615–623.

Feinberg, D. R., Jones, B. C., Little, A. C., Burt, D. M., & Perrett, D. (2005). Manipulations of fundamental and formant frequencies influence the attractiveness of human male voices. *Animal Behaviour, 69,* 561–568.

Feinberg, D. R., Jones, B. C., Smith, M. J. L., Moore, F. R., DeBruine, L. M., Cornwell, R. E., Hillier, S. G., & Perrett, D. I. (2006). Menstrual cycle, trait estrogen level, and masculinity preferences in the human voice. *Hormones and Behavior, 49*(2), 215–222. https://doi.org/10.1016/j.yhbeh.2005.07.004

Ferdenzi, C., Patel, S.,Mehu-Blantar, I., Khidasheli, M., Sander, D., & Delplanque, S. (2013). Voice attractiveness: Influence of stimulus duration and type. Behavior Research Methods, 45, 405–413. doi:10.3758/s13428-012-0275-0

Fernald, A., & Kuhl, P. (1987). Acoustic determinants of infant preference for motherese speech. *Infant Behavior and Development, 10*(3), 279–293.

Fisher, M., Cox, A., Bennett, S., & Gavric, D. (2008). Components of self-perceived mate value. *Journal of Social, Evolutionary, and Cultural Psychology, 2,* 156–168.

Floyd, K., Judd, J., & Hesse, C. (2008). Affection exchange theory. In L. A. Baxter, D. O. Braithewaite, L. A. Baxter, & D. O. Braithewaite (Eds.), *Engaging theories in interpersonal communication: Multiple perspectives* (pp. 285–293). Thousand Oaks, CA: Sage.

Fraccaro, P. J., Jones, B. C., Vukovic, J., Smith, F. G., Watkins, C. D., Feinberg, D. R., … DeBruine, L. M. (2011). Experimental evidence that women speak in a higher voice pitch to men they find attractive. *Journal of Evolutionary Psychology, 9*(1), 57–67. https://doi.org/10.1556/JEP.9.2011.33.1

Fraccaro, P. J., O'Connor, J. J. M., Re, D. E., Jones, B. C., DeBruine, L. M., & Feinberg, D. R. (2013). Faking it: Deliberately altered voice pitch and vocal attractiveness. *Animal Behaviour, 85*(1), 127–136. https://doi.org/10.1016/j.anbehav.2012.10.016

Gamboa, J., Jimenez-Jimenez, F. J., Mate, M. A., & Cobeta, I. (2001). Voice disorders caused by neurological diseases. *Review of Neurology, 33*(2), 153–168.

Gray, P. B., Kahlenberg, S. M.., Barrett, E. S., Lipson, S. F., & Ellison, P. T. (2002). Marriage and fatherhood are associated with lower testosterone in males. *Evolution and Human Behavior, 23*(3) 193-201. https://doi.org/10.1016/S1090-5138(01)00101-5

Hall, J. A., & Braunwald, K. G. (1981). Gender cues in conversations. *Journal of Personality and Social Psychology, 40*, 99–110.

Hill, A. K., Cárdenas, R. A., Wheatley, J. R., Welling, L. L. M., Burriss, R. P., Claes, P., … Puts, D. A. (2017). Are there vocal cues to human developmental stability? Relationships between facial fluctuating asymmetry and voice attractiveness. *Evolution and Human Behavior, 38*(2), 249–258. https://doi.org/10.1016/j.evolhumbehav.2016.10.008

Holzman, P. S., & Rousey, C. (1966). The voice as a percept. *Journal of Personality and Social Psychology*, 4, 79–86. doi:10.1037/h0023518

Hughes, S. M., Dispenza, F., & Gallup, G. G., Jr. (2004). Ratings of voice attractiveness predict sexual behavior and body configuration. *Evolution and Human Behavior, 25*, 295–304. doi:10.1016/j.evolhumbehav.2004.06.001

Hughes, S. M., Farley S. D., & Rhodes, B. C. (2010). Vocal and physiological changes in response to the physical attractiveness of conversational partners. *Journal of Nonverbal Behavior, 34*, 155–167. doi:10.1007/s10919-010-0087-9

Hughes, S. M. & Harrison, M. A. (2017). Your cheatin' voice will tell on you: Detection of past infidelity from voice. *Evolutionary Psychology*. doi: 10.1177/1474704917711513

Hughes, S. M., & Harrison, M. A. (2013). I like my voice better: Self-enhancement bias in perceptions of voice attractiveness. *Perception, 42*, 941–949. doi:10.1068/p7526

Hughes, S. M., Harrison, M. A., & Gallup, G. G., Jr. (2002). The sound of symmetry: Voice as a marker of developmental instability. *Evolution and Human Behavior, 23*, 173–180. doi:10.1016/S1090-5138(01)00099-X

Hughes, S. M., Harrison, M. A., & Gallup, G. G., Jr. (2009). Sex-specific body configurations can be estimated from voice samples. *Journal of Social, Evolutionary, and Cultural Psychology, 3*, 343–355. http://dx.doi.org/10.1037/h0099311

Hughes, S. M., & Miller, N. E. (2015). What sounds beautiful looks beautiful stereotype: The matching of attractiveness of voices and faces. *Journal of Social and Personal Relationships*. Advance online publication. doi:10.1177/0265407515612445

Hughes, S. M., Mogilski, J. K., & Harrison, M. A. (2014). The perception and parameters of intentional voice manipulation. *Journal of Nonverbal*

Behavior, 38(1), 107–127. https://doi.org/10.1007/s10919-013-0163-z

Hughes, S. M., Pastizzo, M. J., & Gallup, G. G. Jr. (2008). The sound of symmetry revisited: Subjective and objective analyses of voice. *Journal of Nonverbal Behavior, 33,* 93–108. doi:10.1007/s10919-007-0042-6

Hughes, S. M., & Rhodes, B. C. (2010). Making age assessments based on voice: The impact of the reproductive viability of the speaker. *Journal of Social, Evolutionary, and Cultural Psychology, 4,* 290–304. http://dx.doi.org/10.1037/h0099282

Jones, B. C., Boothroyd, L., Feinberg, D. R., & DeBruine, L. M. (2010). Age at menarche predicts individual differences in women's preferences for masculinized male voices in adulthood. *Personality and Individual Differences, 48*(7), 860–863. https://doi.org/10.1016/j.paid.2010.02.007

Jones, B. C., Feinberg, D. R., DeBruine, L. M., Little, A. C., & Vukovic, J. (2008). Integrating cues of social interest and voice pitch in men's preferences for women's voices. *Biology Letters, 4,* 192-194.

Jones, B. C., Feinberg, D. R., DeBruine, L. M., Little, A. C., & Vukovic, J. (2010). A domain-specific opposite-sex bias in human preferences for manipulated voice pitch. *Animal Behaviour, 79*(1), 57–62. https://doi.org/10.1016/j.anbehav.2009.10.003

Karpf, A. (2006). *The human voice.* New York, NY: Bloombury.

Klofstad, C. A., Anderson, R. C., & Nowicki, S. (2015). Perceptions of competence, strength, and age influence voters to select leaders with lower-pitched voices. *PLoS ONE, 10*(8). https://doi.org/10.1371/journal.pone.0133779

Klofstad, C. A., Anderson, R. C., & Peters, S. (2012). Sounds like a winner: Voice pitch influences perception of leadership capacity in both men and women. *Proceedings of the Royal Society B: Biological Sciences,* 1-7. https://doi.org/10.1098/rspb.2012.0311

Knowles, K. K., & Little, A. C. (2016). Vocal fundamental and formant frequencies affect perceptions of speaker cooperativeness. *The Quarterly Journal of Experimental Psychology, 69*(9), 1657–1675. https://doi.org/10.1080/17470218.2015.1091484

Krauss, R. M., Freyberg, R., & Morsella, E. (2002). Inferring speakers' physical attributes from their voices. *Journal of Experimental Social Psychology, 38,* 618–625. doi:10.1016/S0022-1031(02)00510-3

Lass, N. J., Hughes, K. R., Bowyer, M. D., Waters, L. T., & Bourne, V. T. (1976). Speaker sex identification from voiced, whispered, and filtered isolated vowels. *Journal of the Acoustical Society of America, 59,* 675–678. doi:10.1121/1.380917

Lass, N. J., Tecca, J. E., Mancuso, R. A., & Black, W. I. (1979). The effect of phonetic complexity on speaker race and sex identification. *Journal of Phonetics, 7,* 105–118.

Leongómez, J. D., Mileva, V. R., Little, A. C., & Roberts, S. C. (2017). Perceived differences in social status between speaker and listener affect the speaker's vocal characteristics. *PLoS ONE, 12*(6). https://doi.org/10.1371/journal.pone.0179407

Lieberman, P., & Blumstein, S. E. (1988). *Speech physiology, speech perception, and acoustic phonetics.* Cambridge, MA: Cambridge University Press.

Mayew, W. J., Parsons, C. A., & Venkatachalam, M. (2013). Voice pitch and the labor market success of male chief executive officers. *Evolution and Human Behavior, 34,* 243-248. 10.1016/j.evolhumbehav.2013.03.001

Michael, W., & Crawford, C. C. (1927). An experiment in judging intelligence by the voice. *Journal of Educational Psychology, 18*(2), 107-114.

Montano, K. J., Tigue, C. C., Isenstein, S. G. E., Barclay, P., & Feinberg, D. R. (2017). Men's voice pitch influences women's trusting behavior. *Evolution and Human Behavior, 38*(3), 293–297. https://doi.org/10.1016/j.evolhumbehav.2016.10.010

O'Connor, J. J. M., & Barclay, P. (2017). The influence of voice pitch on perceptions of trustworthiness across social contexts. *Evolution and Human Behavior, 38*(4), 506–512. https://doi.org/10.1016/j.evolhumbehav.2017.03.001

O'Connor, J. M., & Barclay, P. (2018). High voice pitch mitigates the aversiveness of antisocial cues in men's speech. *British Journal of Psychology.* https://doi.org/10.1111/bjop.12310

O'Connor, J. J. M., & Feinberg, D. R. (2012). The influence of facial masculinity and voice pitch on jealousy and perceptions of intrasexual rivalry. *Personality and Individual Differences, 52*(3), 369–373. https://doi.org/10.1016/j.paid.2011.10.036

O'Connor, J. J. M., Fraccaro, P. J., & Feinberg, D. R. (2012). The influence of male voice pitch on women's perceptions of relationship investment. *Journal of Evolutionary Psychology, 10*(1), 1–13. https://doi.org/10.1556/JEP.10.2012.1.1

O'Connor, J. J. M., Fraccaro, P. J., Pisanski, K., Tigue, C. C., O'Donnell, T. J., & Feinberg, D. R. (2014). Social dialect and men's voice pitch influence women's mate preferences. *Evolution and Human Behavior, 35*(5), 368–375. https://doi.org/10.1016/j.evolhumbehav.2014.05.001

O'Connor, J. J. M., Jones, B. C., Fraccaro, P. J., Tigue, C. C., Pisanski, K., & Feinberg, D. R. (2014). Sociosexual attitudes and dyadic sexual desire independently predict women's preferences for male vocal masculinity. *Archives of Sexual Behavior, 43*(7), 1343–1353. https://doi.org/10.1007/s10508-014-0298-y

O'Connor, J. J. M., Pisanski, K., Tigue, C. C., Fraccaro, P. J., & Feinberg, D. R. (2014). Perceptions of infidelity risk predict women's preferences for low male voice pitch in short-term over long-term relationship contexts. *Personality and Individual Differences, 56,* 73–77. https://doi.org/10.1016/j.paid.2013.08.029

O'Connor, J. J. M., Re, D. E., & Feinberg, D. R. (2011). Voice pitch influences perceptions of sexual infidelity. *Evolutionary Psychology, 9*(1), 64–78. https://doi.org/10.1177/147470491100900109

Oguchi, T., & Kikuchi, H. (1997). Voice and interpersonal attraction. *Japanese Psychological Research, 39,* 56–61.

Oksenberg, L., Coleman, L., & Cannell, C. F. (1986). Interviewers' voice and refusal rates in telephone surveys. *Public Opinion Quarterly, 50,* 97–111.

Oleszkiewicz, A., Pisanski, K., Lachowicz-Tabaczek, K., & Sorokowska, A. (2017).

Voice-based assessments of trustworthiness, competence, and warmth in blind and sighted adults. *Psychonomic Bulletin & Review, 24*(3), 856–862. https://doi.org/10.3758/s13423-016-1146-y

Pelham, B., Mirenberg, M. C., & Jones, J. T. (2002). Why Susie sells seashells by the seashore: Implicit egotism and major life decisions. *Journal of Personality and Social Psychology, 82,* 469–487. doi:10.1037/0022-3514.82.4.469

Pipitone, R.N., & Gallup, G.G., Jr. (2008).Women's voice attractiveness varies across the menstrual cycle. Evolution and *Human Behavior, 29,* 268–274. https://doi.org 10.1016/j.evolhumbehav.2008.02.001

Pipitone, R. N., Gallup, G. G., Jr., & Bartels, A. (2016). Variation in men's masculinity affects preferences for women's voices at different points in the menstrual cycle. *Evolutionary Behavioral Sciences, 10*(3), 188–201. https://doi.org/10.1037/ebs0000073

Pisanski, K., Feinberg, D., Oleszkiewicz, A., & Sorokowska, A. (2017). Voice cues are used in a similar way by blind and sighted adults when assessing women's body size. *Scientific Reports, 7*(1), 10329. https://doi.org/ 10.1038/s41598-017-10470-3.

Pisanski, K., Hahn, A. C., Fisher, C. I., DeBruine, L. M., Feinberg, D. R., & Jones, B. C. (2014). Changes in salivary estradiol predict changes in women's preferences for vocal masculinity. *Hormones and Behavior, 66*(3), 493–497. https://doi.org/10.1016/j.yhbeh.2014.07.006

Pisanski, K., Mishra, S., & Rendall, D. (2012). The evolved psychology of voice: Evaluating interrelationships in listeners' assessments of the size, masculinity, and attractiveness of unseen speakers. *Evolution and Human Behavior, 33*(5), 509–519. https://doi.org/10.1016/j.evolhumbehav.2012.01.004

Puts, D. A. (2005). Mating context and menstrual phase affect women's preferences for male voice pitch. *Evolution and Human Behavior, 26*(5), 388–397. https://doi.org/10.1016/j.evolhumbehav.2005.03.001

Puts, D. A., Apicella C.L., & Cárdenas, R.A. (2012). Masculine voices signal men's threat potential in forager and industrial societies. *Proceedings of the Royal Society of London B.* https://doi.org/10.1098/rspb.2011.0829.

Puts, D. A., Gaulin, S. J. C., & Verdolini, K. (2006). Dominance and the evolution of sexual dimorphism in human voice pitch. *Evolution and Human Behavior, 27*(4), 283–296. https://doi.org/10.1016/j.evolhumbehav.2005.11.003

Puts, D. A., Hill, A. K., Bailey, D. H., Walker, R. S., Rendall, D., Wheatley, J. R., . . . Ramos-Fernandez, G. (2016). Sexual selection on male vocal fundamental frequency in humans and other anthropoids. *Proceedings of the Royal Society B: Biological Sciences, 283,* pii: 20152830. https://doi.org/10.1098/rspb.2015.2830Puts, D. A., Hodges, C. R., Cárdenas, R.A., & Gaulin, S. J. C., (2007) Men's voices as dominance signals: vocal fundamental and formant frequencies influence dominance attributions among men. *Evolution and Human Behavior 28*(5), 340–344. https://doi.org/10.1016/j.evolhumbehav.2007.05.002

Puts, D. A., Hodges, C. R., Cardenas, R. A., & Gaulin, S. J. C. (2007). Men's voices as dominance signals: Vocal fundamental and formant frequencies influence dominance attributions among men. *Evolution and Human Behavior, 28*, 340–344.

Rantala, L., & Vilkman, E. (1999). Relationship between subjective voice complaints and acoustic parameters in female teachers' voices. *Journal of Voice, 13*(4), 484-495. https://doi.org/10.1016/S0892-1997(99)80004-6

Reinfeldt, S., Östli, P., Håkansson, B., & Stenfelt, S. (2010). Hearing one's own voice during phoneme vocalization: Transmission of air and bone conduction. *Journal of the Acoustic Society of America, 128*, 751–762. doi:10.1121/1.3458855

Riding, D., Lonsdale, D., & Brown, B. (2006). The effects of average fundamental frequency and variance of fundamental frequency on male vocal attractiveness to women. *Journal of Nonverbal Behavior, 30*, 55–61.

Scherer, K. R. (1986). Vocal affect expression: A review and a model for future research. *Psychological Bulletin, 99*, 143–165.

Scherer, K. R., London, H., & Wolf, J. J. (1973). The voice of confidence: Paralinguistic cues and audience evaluation. *Journal of Research in Personality, 7*(1)31-44. https://doi.org/10.1016/0092-6566(73)90030-5

Scherer, K. R., & Zei, B. (1988). Vocal indicators of affective disorders. *Psychotherapy and Psychosomatics, 49*, 179–186. doi:10.1159/000288082

Schroeder, J., & Epley, N. (2015). The sound of intellect: Speech reveals a thoughtful mind, increasing a job candidate's appeal. *Psychological Science, 26*(6), 877-891. https://doi.org/10.1177/0956797615572906

Šebesta, P., Kleisner, K., Tureček, P., Kočnar, T., Akoko, R. M., Třebický, V., & Havlíček, J. (2017). Voices of Africa: Acoustic predictors of human male vocal attractiveness. *Animal Behaviour, 127*, 205–211. https://doi.org/10.1016/j.anbehav.2017.03.014

Sell, A. Bryant, G. A., Cosmides, L. Tooby, J., Sznycer, D., von Rueden, C., Krauss, A., & Gurven. M. (2010). Adaptations in humans for assessing physical strength from voice. *Proceedings of the Royal Society B, 277*(1699). https://doi.org/10.1098/rspb.2010.0769

Simmons, L. W., Peters, M., & Rhodes, G. (2011). Low pitched voices are perceived as masculine and attractive but do they predict semen quality in men? *PLoS ONE, 6*(12). https://doi.org/10.1371/journal.pone.0029271

Smith, D. S., Jones, B. C., Feinberg, D. R., & Allan, K. (2012). A modulatory effect of male voice pitch on long-term memory in women: Evidence of adaptation for mate choice? *Memory and Cognition, 40*(1), 135–144. https://doi.org/10.3758/s13421-011-0136-6

Sorokowski, P., Puts, D., Johnson, J., Żółkiewicz, O., Oleszkiewicz, A., Sorokowska, A. ... Pisanski, K. (2019). Voice of authority: Professionals lower their vocal frequencies when giving expert advice. *Journal of Nonverbal Behavior.* https://doi-org.felix.albright.edu/10.1007/s10919-019-00307-0

Soskin, W. F., & Kauffman, P. E. (1961). Judgment of emotion in word-free voice samples. *Journal of Communication, 11*, 73-80. http://dx.doi.org/10.1111/j.1460-2466.1961.tb00331.x

Sprecher, S. (1989). The importance to males and females of physical attractiveness, earning potential, and expressiveness in initial attraction. *Sex Roles, 21*,

591–607. doi:10.1007/BF00289173

Steckler, N. A., & Rosenthal, R. (1985). Sex differences in nonverbal and verbal communication with bosses, peers, and subordinates. *Journal of Applied Psychology, 70*, 157–163.

Streeter, L. A., Krauss, R. M., Geller, V. J., Olson, C. T., & Apple, W. (1977). Pitch changes during attempted deception. *Journal of Personality and Social Psychology, 35*, 345–350.

Teixeira, J. P., Oliveira, C., & Lopes, C. (2013). Vocal acoustic analysis: Jitter, shimmer, and HNR parameters. *Procedia Technology, 9*, 1112 –

Tigue, C. C., Borak, D. J., O'Connor, J. J. M., Schandl, C., & Feinberg, D. R. (2012). Voice pitch influences voting behavior. *Evolution and Human Behavior, 33*(3), 210–216. https://doi.org/10.1016/j.evolhumbehav.2011.09.004

Tuomi, S. K., & Fisher, J. E. (1979). Characteristics of a simulated sexy voice. *Folia Phoniatrica, 31*, 242–249.

Tsantani, M. S., Belin, P., Paterson, H. M., & McAleer, P. (2016). Low vocal pitch preference drives first impressions irrespective of context in male voices but not in female voices. *Perception, 45*(8), 946–963. https://doi.org/10.1177/0301006616643675

Valentová, J., Roberts, S. C., & Havífček, J. (2013). Preferences for facial and vocal masculinity in homosexual men: The role of relationship status, sexual restrictiveness, and self-perceived masculinity. *Perception, 42*(2), 187–197.

Voyer, D., & Vu, J. P. (2016). Using sarcasm to compliment: Context, intonation, and the perception of statements with a negative literal meaning. *Journal of Psycholinguistic Research, 45*(3), 615–624. https://doi.org/10.1007/s10936-015-9363-5

Vukovic, J., Feinberg, D. R., DeBruine, L., Smith, F. G., & Jones, B. C. (2010). Women's voice pitch is negatively correlated with health risk factors. *Journal of Evolutionary Psychology, 8*(3), 217–225.

Vukovic, J., Jones, B. C., DeBruine, L., Feinberg, D. R., Smith, F. G., Little, A. C., Welling, L. L. M., & Main, J. (2010). Women's own voice pitch predicts their preferences for masculinity in men's voices. *Behavioral Ecology, 21*(4), 767–772. https://doi.org/10.1093/beheco/arq051

Vukovic, J., Jones, B. C., Feinberg, D. R., DeBruine, L. M., Smith, F. G., Welling, L. L. M., & Little, A. C. (2011). Variation in perceptions of physical dominance and trustworthiness predicts individual differences in the effect of relationship context on women's preferences for masculine pitch in men's voices. *British Journal of Psychology, 102*(1), 37–48.

Walton, J. H., & Orlikoff, R. F. (1994). Speaker race identification from acoustic cues in the vocal signal. *Journal of Speech and Hearing Research, 37*, 738–45.

Wheatley, J. R., Apicella, C. A., Burriss, R. P., Cárdenas, R. A., Bailey, D. H., Welling, L. L. M., & Puts, D. A. (2014). Women's faces and voices are cues to reproductive potential in industrial and forager societies. *Evolution and Human Behavior, 35*(4), 264–271. https://doi.org/10.1016/j.evolhumbehav.2014.02.006

Wolff, S., & Puts, D. (2010). Vocal masculinity is a robust dominance signal in men. *Behavioral Ecology and Sociobiology, 64*, 1673–1683.

https://doi.org/10.1007/s00265-010-0981-5

Zuckerman, M., & Driver, R. (1989). What sounds beautiful is good: The vocal attractiveness stereotype. *Journal of Nonverbal Behavior, 13*, 67–82.

Zuckerman, M., & Sinicropi, V. (2011). When physical and vocal attractiveness differ: Effects on favorability of interpersonal impressions. *Journal of Nonverbal Behavior, 35,* 75-86. http://dx.doi.org/10.1007/s10919-011-0106-5

Chapter 5

FINGERS

Your fingers cannot be of the same length.

-Chinese proverb

Do you have the fingers of a criminal?

Roman and Egyptian traditions held belief that there was a special vein running from the fourth finger to the heart. The placement of an engagement ring or wedding band on the fourth finger, therefore, represented the heart's devotion (Kuntz, 1917). Is there truth to this belief? Is there something about our digits that reveals cues to our behaviors and motivations? In this chapter we will discuss the relation between digits and behavior, posited to be moderated by a common prenatal hormonal milieu. We focus on fingers here and on toes in the next chapter. We review some key evidence yielded by this intriguing research, and we note limitations and shortcomings to these assertions.

In this chapter we do not purport to present a systematic review of all existing literature on the topic of digit ratios, as the sum of these efforts to date would fill volumes. As of this writing, a PsycINFO literature search on the topic of "2D:4D" (second digit to fourth digit ratio) yields nearly 500 results, and a PubMed search shows well over 600 results. Instead, we offer a selection of articles that we feel represents the current body of knowledge and that will intrigue the reader.

Do fingers provide a window into behavior and mental processes?

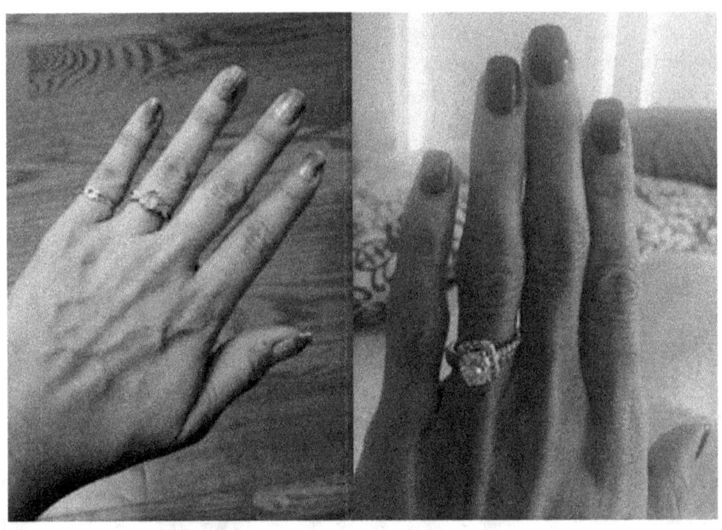

Many years ago, V. Rae Phelps (1952) conducted analyses of finger length ratios, reported in *American Journal of Human Genetics*. She based her work on theory and observations dating back to the 19th century. Phelps classified three patterns of digit ratios: 1. "index finger shorter than ring finger (2<4)"; 2. "index finger equal in length to ring finger (2=4)"; and 3. "index finger longer than ring finger (2<4)" (p. 74). She documented that, whereas men and women display all three of these patterns, men display the "short index finger formula" most frequently, and women display the "long index finger formula" most frequently. With this noted sex difference, it is logical that hormones are involved in the development of this characteristic. Phelps called it "a sex influenced trait."

Indeed, Manning and colleagues (1998; 2002) and many other psychological scientists have contended for decades that finger lengths—in particular, finger ratios—offer a window into prenatal development. The ratio of the second finger ("index finger") relative to the fourth ("ring finger") (2D:4D), formed by about the seventh week in utero (Phelps, 1952), is a proxy for ascertaining fetal hormone exposure. The 2D:4D ratio, typically measured on the ventral (palm) surface of the hand from basal crease to fingertip (Manning, 2002; Jeevanandam & Muthu, 2016), is thought to be influenced particularly by prenatal androgen (testosterone) and estrogen exposure. The development of digit formation coincides with the surge of prenatal sex hormones during the first trimester and remains fixed in utero (Garn, Burdi, Babler, & Stinson, 1975). Men typically have more prenatal androgens than women, and thus, tend to have a shorter second finger compared to the fourth (a lower 2D:4D), and women tend to have a longer second finger compared to the fourth (a higher 2D:4D). Since this ratio is sexually dimorphic, it is purported to inform our understanding of sexuality, competitiveness, and many other sexually dimorphic behaviors and traits (Manning, 2002; Manning, Kilduff, Cook, Crewther, & Fink, 2014). In fact, the constancy of this sex difference has led to the suggestion that the 2D:4D ratio be used as a forensic tool to identify the sex of mutilated remains (Dey & Kapoor, 2016).

What can fingers tell us about behavior and mental processes?

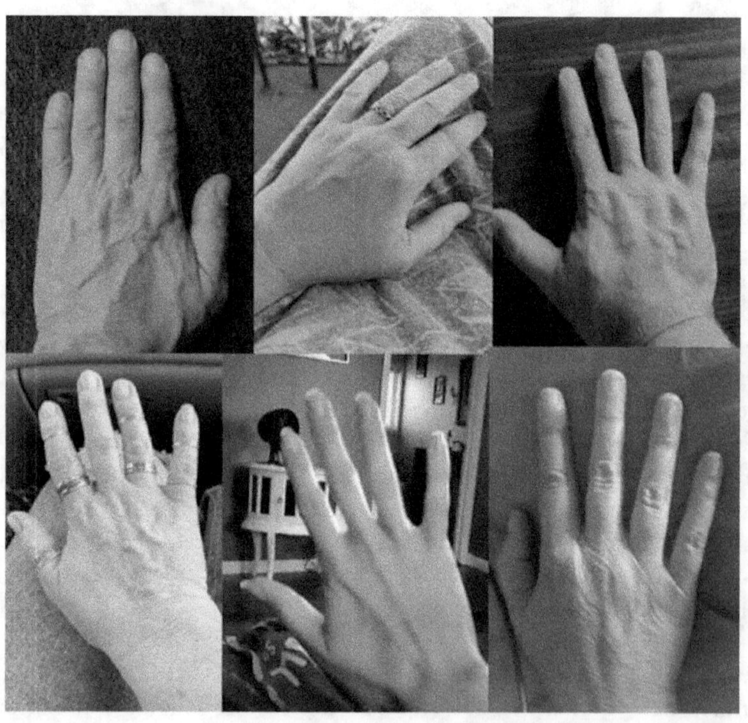

This assertion about fetal formation of digit ratios was corroborated with subsequent examinations. Malas, Dogan, Evcil, and Desdicioglu (2006) studied deceased human fetuses and documented a higher 2D:4D ratio in females compared to males. Similarly, Galis, Ten Broek, Vam Dongen, and Wijnaendts (2010) studied a large sample of deceased human fetuses and found sexual dimorphism, albeit to a lesser extent than adult samples, with female fetuses having the expected higher 2D:4D. The fetal ratios were smaller than those observed in living children and adults (Manning, Scutt,

Wilson, & Lewis-Jones, 1998; Puts, Gaulin, Sporter, & McBurney, 2004), suggesting that 2D:4D ratios slowly increase over the life span vis-à-vis more pronounced second-digit growth after birth, as asserted earlier by Trivers, Manning, and Jacobson (2006), Manning et al. (2014), and others.

Amniotic fluid analysis corroborates that low right-hand 2D:4D is related to high fetal testosterone (T), an androgen, and low fetal estrogen (E), as measured in children at age 2 years (Lutchmaya, Baron-Cohen, Raggatt, Knickmeyer, & Manning, 2004). Moreover, experiments decreasing androgen and increasing estrogen exposure in utero can feminize 2D:4D, whereas increasing androgen and decreasing estrogen exposure in utero can masculinize 2D:4D (Zheng & Cohn, 2011).

In addition, both the formation of digits (fingers and toes) and the urinogenital system are mediated by the action of a common *Hox* gene which contributes to sexual differentiation during early pregnancy. Specifically, *HoxA* and *HoxD* are both involved in digit and genital development. Researchers have identified that *HoxD13* is associated with distal limb development (Brison, Debeer, & Tylzanowski, 2013; Archambeault, Taylor, & Crow, 2014) and with mammalian genital formation (Kondo, Zákány, Innis, & Duboule, 1997). Manipulation of *Hox* function leads to digit and genital malformation or absence (Kondo et al., 1997). Kondo et al. (1997) suggested that the clitoris, the penis, and digits share a common phylogeny that may have emerged during a transition to terrestrial living, an adaptation that facilitates internal fertilization and is conducive to locomotion.

Finger Psychology?

First, we describe the *organizational hypothesis* of the role of steroid hormones during development. Behavioral neuroendocrinologists assert that during fetal development, the nervous system undergoes permanent organization, with androgens (sex steroids) sexually differentiating the genitalia, brain, and behaviors (Phoenix, Goy, Gerall, & Young, 1959; Arnold, 2009). As genitals are being differentiated early in development, fingers and toes are also forming. Indeed, researchers have noted that androgens exert most of their effects between week 7 and week 12 in utero (Rommerts, 1998).

Additionally, limbs and genitals are subject to the same developmental genetic regulation. As an example, Sonic hedgehog (Shh) is one gene that has been identified as common to finger, toes, and formation of the penis and clitoris (Blaschko, Cunha, & Baskin, 2012; Perriton et al., 2002)

In studies of finger ratios, researchers typically measure fingers on the ventral hand from basal crease to fingertip.

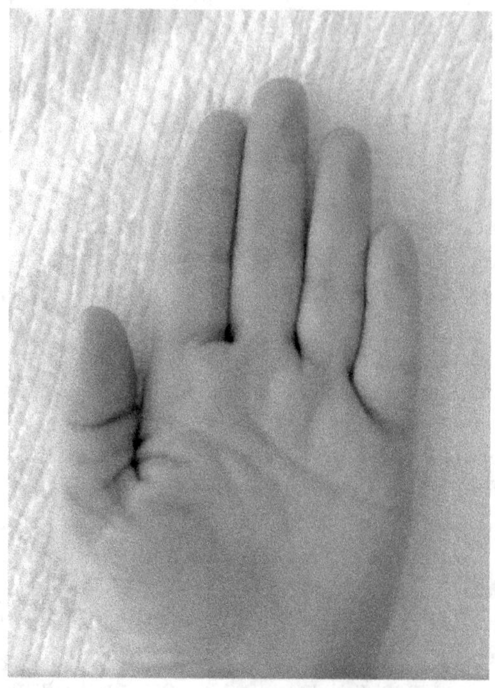

Logically, then, since the same genetic and hormonal processes moderate finger, toe, and genital development, and we understand that androgens influence genital formation during this embryonic period, it makes sense that androgens affect finger and toe development (Manning, 1998; Brown, Hines, Fane, & Breedlove, 2002). Further, we have an understanding that these same sex steroids influence behavior, so can we make predictions about behavior from how finger and toes appear? There is evidence to suggest that indeed finger-length and toe-length ratios can predict sexually dimorphic behaviors, as we discuss in this chapter.

As a caveat, the evidence is not without controversy and criticism, which we also acknowledge where appropriate. Caveats include different operational definitions of 2D:4D and inconsistent measurement techniques. Pratt, Turanovic, and Cullen (2016) wisely cautioned against putting too much credence in any one study to determine the relationship of 2D:4D to behaviors and mental processes. Nonetheless, we present some intriguing research studies below.

In the Beginning

As noted above, V. Rae Phelps (1952) published one of the foundational papers on sex differences in digit ratios. Years later, J. T. Manning and colleagues conducted what can be considered the seminal work connecting 2D:4D to various behaviors and mental processes. Manning, Scutt, Wilson, and Lewis-Jones (1998) were among the first psychological scientists known to us to connect 2D:4D with behaviors and traits. Considering the long-documented sex difference in 2D:4D with men having a lower ratio, Manning et al. presented the argument that during fetal organization, a balance of sex steroid hormones testosterone (T) and estrogen (E) mediate digit ratios. Male fetuses typically have higher testosterone (Manning et al., 2014), and so high T and low E yield a masculine lower 2D:4D (Manning, 2002; Manning et al., 1998, 2014; Puts et al., 2004). Therefore, behaviors associated with increased androgens/testosterone should be associated with lower 2D:4D. Many works have followed to document, and disprove, the connection between 2D:4D and various behaviors and mental processes.

Clinical Syndromes

Research involving atypical sexual differentiation models has offered some support to prenatal affixation of 2D:4D. We underscore that the approaches to definition and measurement varies, and the evidence yielded by these studies is mixed.

Congenital Adrenal Hyperplasia (CAH). Brown and colleagues (2002) examined 2D:4D in in people with congenital adrenal hyperplasia (CAH), a condition marked by increased fetal androgens. Measures of digit length were taken using photocopies of the ventral side of hands, and they found lower (more masculinized) right-hand 2D:4D in CAH females and in left-hand 2D:4D in CAH males compared to controls. Similarly, Öktena, Kalyoncu, and Yariş (2002) measured 2D:4D from photocopies and X-rays and found a lower 2D:4D in those with 21-hydroxylase deficiency-related CAH compared to those without CAH, but only in soft tissue ratios, and not in phalangeal bone length ratio. Using measurement of X-rays, Buck, Williams, Hughes, and Acerini (2003) did not find 2D:4D difference between people with CAH and those without the condition.

Complete Androgen Insensitivity Syndrome (CAIS). Berenbaum, Bryk, Nowak, Quigley, and Berenbaum (2009) studied 2D:4D in individuals with complete androgen insensitivity syndrome (CAIS). This is a condition marked by a male chromosome karyotype (46, XY) and the presence of testes. However, the individual experiences no androgen effects in utero because of androgen receptor dysfunction or absence. (If a target organ or structure lacks receptors for a particular hormone, that hormone will not exert direct effects on it.) This results in external female genitalia, and individuals typically identify as women and are reared as girls. Berenbaum et al. had independent raters measure photocopies of subjects' hands from proximal crease to fingertip. As predicted, with no prenatal androgen exposure, CAIS individuals had a higher 2D:4D (feminized) compared to typically developing men and equivalent to typically developing women.

Klinefelter Syndrome (KS). Men with Klinefelter syndrome (KS) have an extra X chromosome (47, XXY karyotype). These men typically have hypogonadism with resulting disrupted mechanisms of sperm production, smaller penises, and smaller testes, thereby leading to infertility. Those with KS have low testosterone, even during fetal development and childhood (Ross, Samango-Sprouse, Lahlou, Kowal, Elder, & Zinn, 2005). With decreased androgen exposure in utero, Manning, Kilduff, and Trivers (2012) posited that those with KS would have more feminized (higher) 2D:4D compared to unaffected men. Measured by photocopies of hands, men with KS indeed had higher right-hand and left-hand 2D:4D than male controls and their unaffected fathers, and higher left-hand 2D:4D than their mothers.

Polycystic Ovary Syndrome (PCOS). Women with the hyperandrogenic disorder, polycystic ovary syndrome (PCOS), have increased androgen production (Udhane & Flück, 2016). Results from animal studies show that increased prenatal androgen exposure contributes to PCOS (Abbott, Dumesic, Eisner, Colman, & Kemnitz, 1998). Cattrall, Vollenhoven, and Weston (2005) took digital caliper measures of finger lengths and showed that women with PCOS had lower 2D:4D than women without PCOS. The difference, they reported, was small yet statistically significant.

Based on the above evidence, it seems that 2D:4D has potential as a diagnostic tool, as suggested by many of the authors cited above. Of course, we cannot stress enough that finger morphology <u>does not cause</u> the aforementioned conditions, and these conditions do not lead to alterations in finger morphology. Rather, there is likely some prenatal or other early developmental morphogenetic event that influences both.

Mental Health

Are finger ratios a window into mental health? Evidence also suggests that 2D:4D is associated with several clinical psychological phenomena.

Schizophrenia. Arnold (2009) and others have posited that prenatal gonadal androgens play a role in cell migration and the formation of new synapses and dendrites. Disruption of androgens, therefore, may have deleterious effects on brain development. Based on this rationale, Qian and colleagues (2016) examined 2D:4D ratios is individuals with schizophrenia, a mental illness associated with neural maldevelopment. Analyzing digital photos, they determined that patients with schizophrenia had a higher (more feminized) right-hand and mean 2D:4D than controls. Women with schizophrenia also had higher left-hand 2D:4D than did controls. Qian and colleagues posited that people with schizophrenia are more likely to experience decreased prenatal testosterone exposure and increased prenatal estrogen exposure compared to controls. Stated another way, if androgens are required for brain cells to get where they need to go during development and function normally, then a lack of androgen in schizophrenia may be interfering with normal brain development. Additionally, Zhu and colleagues (2014) found that higher right-hand 2D:4D was related to a higher number of schizotypal personality traits in unaffected men and women. However, Zhu et al. did not find a difference in 2D:4D between people with schizophrenia and healthy controls.

Autism. With a high male-to-female ratio of autism (about 4:1), some researchers believe that testosterone plays a role in its etiology, as males typically have more testosterone than do females. Baron-Cohen (2002) put forth the "extreme male brain" hypothesis of autism. He posited that testosterone contributes to exaggerated growth of the right hemisphere of the brain, predisposing the individual to have exaggerated "systemized" thinking (i.e., following rules and order, attention to detail) and decreasing social and empathic thinking (Baron-Cohen, 2002; Baron-Cohen, Auyeung, Ashwin, Knickmeyer, Lombardo, & Chakrabarti, 2012). If increased prenatal testosterone is a factor in autism, it makes sense that 2D:4D would be markedly lower in those with autism. As expected, Manning et al. (2001) found a lower 2D:4D in children with autism, their parents, and their siblings compared to the unaffected population. Further, children with Asperger syndrome, considered less severe on the autism spectrum, had higher 2D:4D ratios (more feminized) than children with autism, but lower (more masculinized) than population controls.

Similar results have emerged cross-culturally. Researchers reported a lower 2D:4D in boys with autism compared to controls in Saudi and Slovak samples, and several research groups have actually suggested the ratio may be used as a diagnostic screening tool for autism (Al-Zaid, Alhader, & Al-Ayadhi, 2015; Krajmer, Spajdel, Kubranska, & Ostatnikova, 2011).

Mackus and colleagues (2017) did not replicate this finding in a sample of students from the Netherlands, failing to find a relation between 2D:4D ratio and Autism Spectrum Quotient scores. However, this was a non-clinical sample, and the authors noted it would be informative to repeat this protocol with patients who have a diagnosis of autism.

Depression. Depression is sexually dimorphic, with women's risk for the disorder being nearly twice as high as men's risk globally (Whiteford et al., 2013). Animal studies, and studies of perimenopausal women, provide evidence for a role of female hormones, such as estrogen, in protecting against the development of depression (Albert, 2015). It is puzzling, then, why women, who have more estrogen overall, are more prone to depression than are men. Nonetheless, women with depressive symptoms are reported to have increased blood serum testosterone (Baischer, Koinig, Hartmann, & Langer, 1995). It seems, then, that lower 2D:4D (i.e., less prenatal E, more prenatal T) should be associated with depression. However, research results are mixed.

Bailey and Hurd (2005a) measured right-hand 2D:4D and administered the NEO-PI trait depression subscale. Male and female participants had equivalent trait depression subscale scores. Men with lower 2D:4D had higher depression scores, suggesting that men with prenatal exposure to less testosterone and more estrogen had increased risk of developing depression. There was no relation for women. Smedley, McKain, and McKain (2014) found different results. They measured ratios using hand scans and measured depression using the Beck Depression Inventory-II. They found a positive correlation between 2D:4D and BDI-II scores for women but no significant results for men. It may be the case that too much estrogen exposure is deleterious to female brain development. It can also be the case that organizing steroid hormones (prenatal T and E) and activational hormones (those working in the endocrine system later in life to exert temporary and cyclical effects) may promote different processes.

Anxiety. Evardone and Alexander (2009) explored the relationship between anxiety and 2D:4D. They noted that lower 2D:4D appears to be related to male-linked disorders, such as autism, and higher 2D:4D appears to be related to female-linked disorders, such as depression. Since anxiety is occurs more often in women, it stands to reason there would be a positive relationship with 2D:4D. Using measures of right-hand scans, they found that men, but not women, with more feminine 2D:4D ratios experienced greater trait anxiety. The authors did underscore the complexity of anxiety development and the limitations to studying anxiety in a sub-clinical sample.

*Can you judge someone's mental and behavioral health
from the appearance of their fingers?*

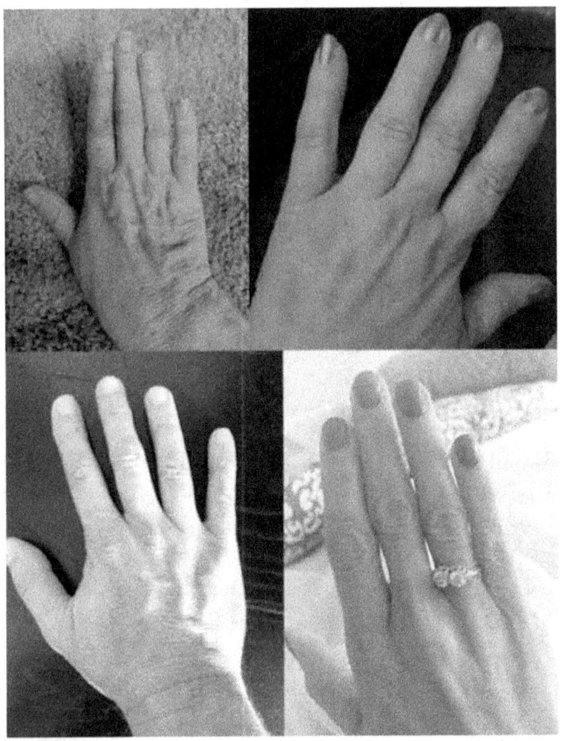

Substance Abuse. Evidence suggests that increased organizational androgens and manipulation of androgen receptors can predispose the brain to addiction pathology. Further, prenatal antagonists (blockers) of androgens can decrease adult alcohol consumption, vis-à-vis alterations in the brain's reward circuitry and monoamine function (Huber et al., 2018, Siegmann, Bouna, Pyrrou, Lenz, & Kornhuber, 2019). It makes sense, then, that those with a lower 2D:4D (more androgens in utero) may exhibit substance abuse and other addictions. Siegmann and colleagues (2019) conducted a sophisticated meta-analysis to examine the relationships between 2D:4D and substance abuse, and 2D:4D and computer dependency (arguably another addiction). They examined research from 1983 to 2018 and used strict criteria for inclusion of data, thereby selecting 19 studies for the meta-analysis that represented data collected in Europe, the United States, Asia, and online. They documented a lower 2D:4D in participants with substance use and computer dependency, with a stronger effect seen in men.

Sex and Reproduction

As started earlier, fingers, toes, and genitals share the same *HoxA* and *HoxD* gene control (Archambeault et al. 2014). It makes sense, then, that finger and toe morphology would relate to genital morphology. The authors of this book have been studying human sexuality for over 20 years, so the literature linking 2D:4D to sexual behavior has made its way into our studies, writing, and teaching. Students are usually intrigued to learn about finger ratios and their relation to sexuality, competitiveness, musical ability, etc. We see them looking at the ventral side of their own hands, wondering about their own developmental milieu. We remind them, of course, no one is likely going to approach you in a night club and drop a pick-up line that incorporates how attractive finger ratios are. If they do, they should have a digital caliper ready, as these physical indexes are minute.

The subtle differences in digit ratio, likely not discernible with the naked eye, have not stopped those with some knowledge of this topic from attempting sensationalizing the ratio. McQuade (2011) has described "sexy ratio" advertisements. She pointed to a blog titled, *"Your Hands Give Away Your Hotness"* (Barribeau, 2011). Hot or not, below we review evidence from several 2D:4D studies that show that the ratio can be predictive of sexual behaviors and traits related to gonadal steroid hormones.

Fertility. There is some interesting evidence linking 2D:4D to male reproductive functioning. Using direct finger measurements, and semen and scrotum analyses, Auger and Eustache (2011) found that, in fertile men, right 2D:4D was negatively related to testicle volume, sperm count, and decreased time to impregnate a partner from first conception attempt. That is, the lower his 2D:4D (higher T), the more reproductive assets he had.

This relationship is not always straightforward. In a large study of Danish men, Bang et al. (2005) traced right hand 2D:4D and examined several parameters of testis functioning. Using linear regression, in men with a 2D:4D greater than 1.0, they found a negative relation between the ratio and follicle-stimulating hormone (FSH), a pituitary hormone responsible for spermatogenesis. Interestingly, FSH targets Sertoli cells. These cells create substances that maintain architecture and nutrition of testis. Sertoli cells form at about 8 weeks during gestation, which is about the same developmental window for finger and toe formation (see Plant & Marshall, 2001, for review). In men with a 2D:4D less than 1.0, they found a positive relation between the ratio and sperm count.

Firman, Simmons, Cummins, and Matson (2003) conducted a similar study. Using direct measures of both hands, they found no relationship between 2D:4D and sperm count, sperm motility, sperm head length, and sperm tail length. They contrasted their results to those from Manning et al. (1998) who did find a negative relation between right 2D:4D and sperm per ejaculate, sperm swimming speed, and sperm motility. Curiously, Firman et al.'s sample had comparable mean 2D:4D, but their results did not yield similar relationships to sperm parameters. Firman and colleagues suggested that since Manning and colleagues took their sample from a fertility clinic, men with oligozoospermia likely reduced sperm mean numbers, thereby contributing to the statistical significance of Manning's results.

What about female fertility? Evidence emerging from the same laboratory using large samples have found that high 2D:4D (a more feminized pattern) was related to reproductive success in women, across several countries (Manning et al., 2000; Manning & Fink, 2008). In married English heterosexual couples, a higher wife than husband 2D:4D predicted more reproductive success (Manning et al., 2000).

Speaking to this phenomenon, Vehmas, Solovieva, and Leino-Arjas (2006) did not bury the lead in a paper they published in the Journal of Negative Results in Biomedicine. Using radiography to study 2D:4D in nearly 500 women, their study title says it all: *"Radiographic 2D:4D index in females: No relation to anthropometric, behavioural, nutritional, health-related, occupational or fertility variables."* Stated another way, there was no relation between 2D:4D and female fertility, or female anything. Vehmas et al. (2006) stated, "It can therefore be questioned whether any real associations between the bony 2D:4D index in adult life and (direct or indirect) hormone dependent effects exist" (p. 6). Vehmas and colleagues posited that there is a publication bias regarding 2D:4D wherein the significant results that are actually reported, versus the null results that are not, make it seem there is a clearly established link between 2D:4D and various behaviors. They further suggested that if such a connection exists, it is due to tissue and not bone characteristics.

Attractiveness. Early in the history of this research, Neave, Laing, Fink, and Manning (2003) hypothesized a significant, negative association between 2D:4D and attractiveness, dominance, and masculinity. Since low 2D:4D is associated with higher testosterone, it makes sense that low 2D:4D would be associated with ratings of male attractiveness, perhaps because the masculinization of features would signify dominance. They measured left- and right-hand fingers directly, and then they measured photocopies to ensure measurement reliability. As predicted, lower left and right 2D:4D (so, high organizational T) was related to women's ratings of perceived male dominance and masculinity. However, 2D:4D had no relation to attractiveness ratings. Interestingly, too, there was no relation between right or left 2D:4D with ratings of dominance, masculinity, or attractiveness, or with measured salivary testosterone in men.

Ferdenzi et al. (2011) found that right 2D:4D and R-L difference were negative predictors (thus high testosterone) of men's attractiveness as rated as short-term and long-term partners. Similarly, Roney and Maestripieri (2004) examined women's perceptions of male attractiveness in a laboratory interaction. They found through measuring photocopies of hands that lower 2D:4D was associated with increased female ratings of male attractiveness, increased ratings of the men as a desirable partner, and perceptions of men displaying more courtship. The latter was operationalized by the researchers using social interaction parameters such as showing polite interest, trying to impress, being talkative, and demonstrating arousal signs (p. 275).

Hönekopp (2013) measured young men's 2D:4D from digital photographs taken from a sample of 115 secondary school students with a mean age of about 17 years, and a community sample with a mean age of about 22 years. Women raters judged the participants' attractiveness or masculinity from photographs. Although attractiveness and masculinity were correlated ($r = .58$), there was no statistical relation between 2D:4D and either of these characteristics.

Further, Bogaert, Fawcett, and Jamieson (2009) studied the relation between 2D:4D and attractiveness in men, controlling for body size and personality in a relatively large study of university students. They measured the ventral side of hands and found that a low right 2D:4D had a small but significant relation to physical attractiveness as rated by one's self and by others. The authors, noting the weak relationship even with a larger sample than most other studies, the use of aggregate attractiveness ratings, and direct measures, gave several interpretations. They suggested that 2D:4D may not be a precise indicator of prenatal hormonal milieu. Instead, it makes sense that masculinity, if a product of prenatal androgen exposure, is not the only factor in determining attractiveness, and that women's ovulatory status should be considered when using their attraction preferences. Speaking to the latter, again, convincing evidence exists that women prefer more masculine faces near ovulation (Little et al., 2007).

As for women, there is relatively scarce literature on the relationship between 2D:4D and female attractiveness. Manning and Quinton (2007) obtained data from over 250,000 participants through self-reported measures of 2D:4D. They also asked participants to rate how attractive they found their own faces and bodies. Reports from both women and men showed evidence of a negative correlation between 2D:4D (more testosterone) and their self-ratings of face and body attractiveness. However, since testosterone is related to posturing (Dabbs & Morris, 1990), it is possible these data merely reflect "showing off." Also, there is obvious concern with respect to having participants take and report their own finger measurements, ostensibly with one hand, and with evaluating their own physical attractiveness.

Voice Attractiveness. We add null results of 2D:4D relationship with other traits from our own research experience here. Knowing the keen interest in digit ratios in psychology at the time of our research, we (Hughes, Harrison, & Gallup, 2002) included 2D:4D measures in our original study that examined the relationship between voice attractiveness and fluctuating asymmetry (FA), *"The sound of symmetry: Voice as a marker of developmental instability."* Because fluctuating asymmetry, deviations from perfect bilateral symmetry, (see Chapters 3 and 4 and also Graham et al., 2010, for review) is thought to be influenced by prenatal conditions (Thornhill & Gangestad, 1994, 1999), and digit ratios are thought to be influenced by prenatal sex steroids (Manning et al., 1998, 2000), we explored whether there was a relation between the two.

We measured fingers directly with a digital caliper, and we calculated a mean 2D:4D for both hands. Although there was a negative correlation (r = -.46) between FA and voice attractiveness (less asymmetry, higher attractiveness ratings), we were surprised to find no correlation between 2D:4D and voice attractiveness, and no correlation between 2D:4D and FA, in men or women. J. T. Manning (personal communication) suggested that we try right-only 2D:4D or L-R difference. Taking his advice, our post-hoc analyses still showed no relationship with 2D:4D and vocal attractiveness. In a later investigation, the only relationship we found between voice and 2D:4D was that women who had lower 2D:4D had voices that were perceived as sounding more dominant and mature by independent raters (Hughes, Pastizzo, & Gallup, 2008). Our finding is consistent with evidence showing that dominance and sexual maturity are often linked to increased testosterone levels (Mazur & Booth, 1998) and studies suggesting that 2D:4D is a stronger correlate of personality traits in women than in men (Fink, Manning, & Neave, 2004). Yet, we still could not find a relationship between voice attractiveness and 2D:4D for either sex.

Others have replicated these null results. Ferdenzi, Lemaître, Leongómez, and Roberts (2011) used direct finger measures and found no relationship between ratings of voice attractiveness and 2D:4D. There were no associations between 2D:4D measures of left, right, and difference ratios and voice attractiveness or voice frequency. Manning and Quinton (2007) also failed to find an association between 2D:4D and vocal attractiveness. Again, these null results convey evidence of a convoluted, yet intriguing phenomenon that needs increasingly sophisticated research to untangle.

Someone Went There: Genital Size. If fingers, toes, and genitals are all forming at the same time and are subject to the same androgenic and *Hox* gene influences in utero, it makes sense that there is a relationship between finger and genital morphology. Choi et al. (2011) recruited and obtained informed consent from a sample of 144 Korean men hospitalized for urological surgery. As penis length has been documented to vary between ethnicities, this study kept ethnicity constant. Choi's team studied the relationship between flaccid penis size and 2D:4D, and between stretched penis size and 2D:4D, positing that lower 2D:4D (more androgens) would be associated with longer penis length. They measured fingers directly on the ventral side of the right hand, from basal crease to fingertip. Using a rigid ruler, as the subject was anesthetized, penis length was measured from the dorsal pubic-penile skin junction to the penis tip. They found that stretched penis length was indeed negatively related to 2D:4D. In their study, only height predicted flaccid penis length. It is worth noting that the patients all presented for urological concerns, and this may have affected the distribution of penis size observed in the study.

Is penis size, then, something you can judge by finger appearances? This has a sound ontogenetic rationale (maybe not "junk" science?) and certainly an attention-getting concept. Time Magazine even picked up on Choi et al.'s (2011) work with a piece entitled, *"Penis size: It may be written in the length of his fingers"* (Szalavitz, 2011).

Davarci and colleagues (2012) conducted a similar study with children and found contrasting results. In a sample of 1,028 male elementary school students from Turkey, researchers measured flaccid penis length with a straight-edge ruler from the penopubic skin junction to the glans tip, and they measured stretched penis length from the penopubic junction to the glans by gently applying traction to the penis to the point of organ resistance, what they called "an easily appreciated end point" (p. 540). They took 2D:4D measurements directly from hands. They found weak but significant positive relationships between the length of the second digit and both flaccid and stretched penis length, and between the length of the fourth digit and both flaccid and stretched penis length. However, they did not find 2D:4D relationships with penis length. The authors cautioned that child penis length may not correlate to adult penis length.

High T: Size Matters? Whether or not size matters, a lower 2D:4D in men may not always signify a satisfying sexual partner. Bolat and colleagues (2017) found than men with lower digit ratios, assumed as a marker of higher prenatal testosterone exposure, had a greater risk of premature ejaculation, as measured by intravaginal ejaculatory latency. Interestingly, however, they found no relationship between 2D:4D and serum (blood) T levels.

Gender Identity. Gender identity is the internal perception of one's own gender, be it on a feminine/masculine continuum, or non-binary. In the case of a cisgender person, gender identity is congruent with sex assigned at birth. For those who are transgender, however, this is not a match. Whereas gender identity it is not the same concept as sexual orientation (discussed below), evidence suggests that both are under some genetic and hormonal influence early in prenatal development (Bao & Swaab, 2011). Leinung and Wu (2017) showed that those who were female-to male (FTM) transgender (assigned female at birth but have a male gender identity) had a lower dominant hand 2D:4D compared to cisgender women. This ratio was statistically comparable to those of cisgender men. However, those who were male-to-female (MTF) transgender (assigned male at birth but have a female gender identity) had ratios comparable to cisgender male controls. Kraemer et al. (2009) reported mixed results. They documented that although right 2D:4D was higher (more feminized) in MTF trans persons compared to cisgender male controls, they found no difference between 2D:4D of FTM trans persons compared to cisgender female controls. Kraemer's sample was of individuals with gender identity disorder, so the caveat exists that these digit ratios may reflect different or extreme prenatal hormonal values, but this seems doubtful. Still, these results provide evidence of prenatal hormonal correlates of gender identity development.

However, as Bao and Swaab (2011) pointed out in their review, genital differentiation takes place before sexual differentiation of the brain in utero. We should note, then, that because fingers are forming at the same time as genitals, we may not see a clear relationship between gender identity and 2D:4D.

"Pride" in your fingers? Sexual Orientation. Can you determine someone's sexual orientation from their fingers? Evidence from the literature suggests that is dubiously unclear. One's sexual orientation speaks to whom one is attracted in a romantic and physical sense, be it men, women, both, or neither. Sexual orientation also appears to be a product of early developmental genetic and hormonal milieu. One of the first papers known to us to address 2D:4D and sexual orientation was that from Robinson and Manning (2000). They reported that homosexual men had a lower (more masculinized) 2D:4D than controls (participants not selected based on sexual orientation) and bisexual men had an even lower 2D:4D.

Watts et al. (2018) examined photographs of digit ratios in identical co-twins discordant for sexual orientation. Their sample consisted of 18 female and 14 male pairs around 30 years old. Although men had more masculinized ratios overall, in women, they found that homosexual twins had lower (more masculinized) 2D:4D than their heterosexual twins. They found no differences for men. They had included participants with mixed ethnicities which may have affected the results, but it is remarkably difficult to recruit identical twins, let alone those discordant for sexual orientation, for a research study.

Controlling for ethnicity, Lippa (2003) found no differences in 2D:4D between heterosexual and lesbian women but did find that heterosexual men had lower 2D:4D than did gay men. However, using a large community sample of 409 participants, Kraemer et al. (2006) found a negative relation between 2D:4D and homosexual orientation in women, but not in men (i.e., lower 2D:4D confers an increased likelihood of nonheterosexuality).

Similarly, Brown and colleagues (2002) found that women who reported having a lesbian "butch" orientation (consider themselves more masculine) had a lower 2D:4D than women who reported having a lesbian "femme" orientation. However, it is unclear the overlap here of sexual orientation and gender identity.

Competitiveness and Aggressiveness

Higher testosterone levels have long been associated with increased competitiveness and aggression (e.g., Eisenegger et al., 2017; see Fuxjager, Trainor, & Marler, 2017, for review). It makes sense, then, that several studies have examined the relation between 2D:4D and sports and other competitive scenarios.

Manning and Taylor (2001) found a lower 2D:4D (marker of higher testosterone) in men who played professional football (soccer) than controls. They also found an even lower 2D:4D in first squad players compared to reserve players. Later, Mailhos and colleagues (2016) could not replicate the significant association between 2D:4D and soccer performance, although they did find that more aggressive players (i.e., those who received one or more red cards, indications of penalty game dismissal) had lower 2D:4D than those who did not. Similarly, Tamiya, Lee, and Ohtake (2012) studied 2D:4D in sumo wrestlers. They showed that male sumo wrestlers with more wins had lower 2D:4D. Longman, Stock, and Wells (2011) took direct finger measurements and showed that men with a lower right and left 2D:4D had faster rowing (crew) times. However, this was not true for women rowers.

Hönekopp and colleagues (2006) found a negative relationship between right 2D:4D and physical education class grades in teen boys, and similarly, between right and left 2D:4D and physical education class grades in teen girls. They also found a negative relationship between right 2D:4D and physical fitness in young men, and left 2D:4D and physical fitness in young women. They operationalized their physical fitness measure by using a composite score of achievement on gym exercises such as pushups and hurdle jumping.

Later, Hönekopp and Schuster (2010) conduced a meta-analysis of 24 samples of right 2D:4D and 22 samples of left 2D:4D studies. They found that both right and left 2D:4D are reliably, negatively associated with athletic prowess. They noted that 2D:4D accounted for between 1% and 16% of the variance in athletic prowess in research studies and concluded that 2D:4D is "probably not a very accurate measure of prenatal T" (p. 8).

Competitiveness is not the same construct as aggression, as the latter conveys a violent and pugnacious disposition. Bailey and Hurd (2005b) found a negative relation between 2D:4D and trait aggression in men, but not in women. Ribeiro and colleagues (2016) presented evidence that the relationship is more complex. They studied a sample of 89 men by taking direct measures of 2D:4D. They found a negative relation (thus more testosterone) between left 2D:4D and handgrip strength in men who witnessed videos of aggression, or what they termed challenge conditions, and found an increase in salivary testosterone. Testosterone, it seems, may prepare you for battle. These researchers found no relation between 2D:4D and handgrip strength in control conditions and emphasized the necessity of studying traits under ecologically valid conditions.

Spatial and Numerical Abilities

Spatial ability has long been associated with increased androgens. Fink and colleagues (2006) found a lower left and right 2D:4D in boys, but not girls, with greater number knowledge, counting abilities, and visual representation of numbers. On the other hand, a meta-analysis by Puts and colleagues (2008) revealed a negligible relation between 2D:4D and spatial ability. Again, it seems more research is needed on this topic.

Fingered for the Crime?

Are there "criminal" fingers? Could prenatal testosterone exposure predict aggressive, risky, and criminal behavior later in life? Pratt et al. (2016) reminded us that the search for a link between crime and behavior started with fallacious phrenology (the pseudoscience of cranial shape indicators of behavior) and continues. They conducted an impressive meta-analysis of 660 effect sizes from 47 different studies on the relationship between 2D:4D and criminal behaviors and crime analogs. They found a small (.047) but significant overall effect of the relationship between 2D:4D and aggression, crime, and risk/impulsivity. For gender-specific and outcome-specific analyses, there was no relationship between 2D:4D and aggression for men or women.

Pratt and colleagues (2016) emphasized that their analysis was of a bivariate relationship only, and they did not account for individualistic, social, or context criminological influences. They asserted that 2D:4D cannot be considered a central index of criminal or other wayward behavior and is "dwarfed in magnitude" by other factors such as self-control, family systems, and antisocial attitudes (p. 607).

Pointing Out the Not-So-Obvious: What Does This All Mean?

The 2D:4D ratio may reflect a prenatal hormonal milieu, but do prenatal sex hormones correlate with adult hormone levels? Puts and colleagues (2004) provided an eloquent and thorough review of literature regarding the mixed evidence in support of this phenomenon at that time. Later, Hönekopp et al. (2007) reported that there was actually no relationship between adult hormone levels and 2D:4D. What does this mean for the utility of 2D:4D as a psychological index? Should you prepare to bring a digital caliper on your next date to measure finger ratios? It would be useful to have an app for instant and accurate digit ratio assessment. (You heard it here first, so we require royalties if you decide to develop one!). Social ramifications aside, the scientific answer to this is not clear. Whereas the results are fascinating, and the 2D:4D ratio would be a noninvasive diagnostic tool, there is too much inconsistency in research results to warrant the acceptance of the ratio as psychological law. What we see in the literature is that there is no crystal-clear approach to, or interpretation of, the connection to 2D:4D and psychological mechanisms. Nonetheless, 2D:4D remains a fascinating indirect measure of the possible hormonal occurrences of our prenatal past.

Measurement Issues and Other Limitations

Hönekopp and Watson (2010) conducted a random-effects meta-analysis on 116 samples, which involved data from 13,260 females and 11,789 males. They substantiated the long-known lower 2D:4D in males, with a larger right 2D:4D sex difference. However, they underscored that sex differences may be driven by how digit measurements are taken and whether it is a measure of the right or left hand. For example, they estimated the reliability of Manning et al.'s large BBC Internet study of self-reported finger measurements to only 46% of those measured by experts.

It cannot be emphasized enough that operationalizing digit ratios, particularly 2D:4D, is seldom consistent across studies. As Jeevanandam and Muthu (2016) pointed out, there are advantages and disadvantages to the various approaches to measuring 2D:4D. Researchers have measured finger lengths with digital calipers or computer analyses, using photographs, photocopies, scans, direct hand measurements. Researchers have also studied both living and deceased subjects. As Puts and colleagues (2004) reported, calculations have included left-hand 2D:4D, right-hand 2D:4D, mean 2D:4D, and the difference between right and left 2D:4D (DR-L). Creating an even more complex picture, Loehlin, Medland, and Martin (2009) presented the argument that rel2, calculated as 2D/(2D+3D+4D+5D), is a more accurate representation of prenatal androgen exposure than is 2D:4D. Burriss, Little, and Nelson (2007) also reported on consistency issues with various approaches to measuring 2D:4D. It seems that the field is consistent in presenting the argument that inconsistent measurement techniques confuse our understanding of the value of digit ratios as indexes of psychological phenomena.

Puts and colleagues noted (2004) the failure to replicate many 2D:4D studies, and they attributed this, at least in part, to wide methodological variation. Manning, Fink, Neave, and Caswell (2005) reported that measurements taken from photocopies produce lower 2D:4D ratios than do measurements directly taken from fingers. Ribeiro and colleagues (2016) reviewed the literature, asserting, "It is difficult to successfully navigate through the world of direct versus indirect 2D:4D measurement" (p. 5). Manning and others have offered that caveat that mixed measures (i.e., using both direct and photocopy measures) should not be combined in single paradigm. Further, as Ribeiro et al. stated, there are statistical power issues with many existing studies, and a publication bias may contribute to our inability to decipher this mystery with certainty.

Some researchers report measuring fingers via photocopies.

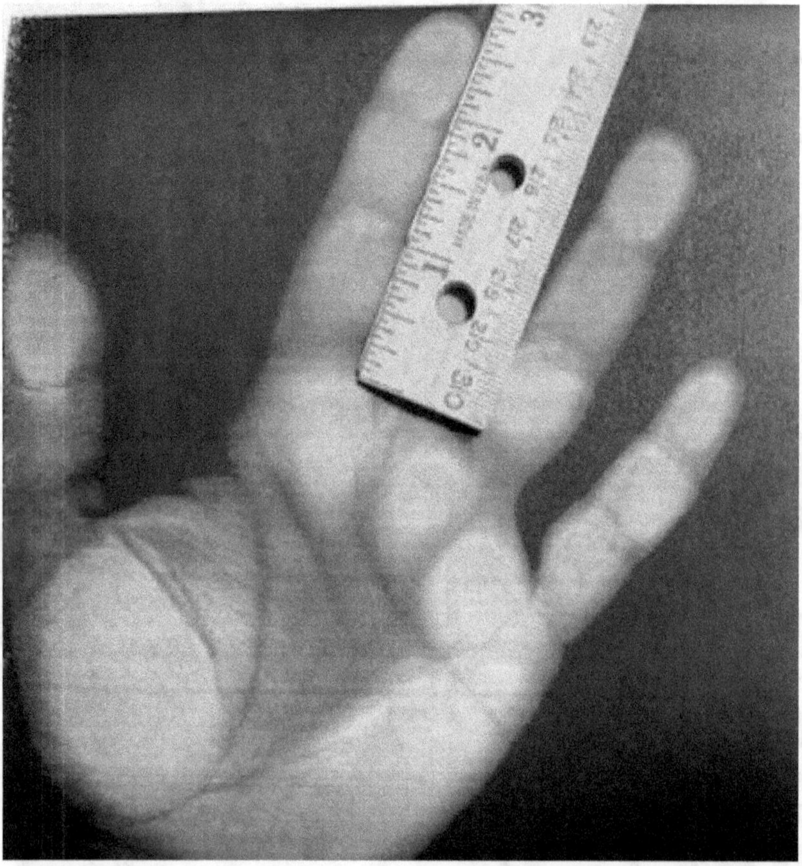

In addition, ethnicity should be considered in 2D:4D studies, and it is not always. In a large Internet sample ($N = 255, 116$), Manning, Churchill, and Peters (2007) asked participants to measure and report their own finger lengths. While researchers found the expected male-female differences, they also noted differences across ethnicities. People who reported as White, Non-Chinese Asian, and Middle Eastern had higher 2D:4D than people who were Chinese and Black. In addition, the caveats of self-report and self-measurement are evident in this type of Internet research study.

Conclusion

We have presented evidence from the literature that appears to support some connection between digit ratios and behaviors. However, there does not seem to be a universal law generated to understand the connection between finger 2D:4D and behavior, nor does not seem to be a unified approach for determining a definitive, reliable, sex-based relationship between 2D:4D and various behaviors and mental processes. Even after decades of research, the picture remains unclear. Again, we stress we did not provide an exhaustive review and incorporate evidence from every research study conducted on this topic including all the studies on animal digit ratio morphology that substantiate much of the work with humans. Be that as it may, we leave this chapter with the assertion that the evidence suggests it may be possible to judge behaviors and mental processes from digit lengths. With more sophisticated means of investigation continuously emerging, perhaps future research on digit ratios may point us in a different direction and we may be able to better gauge this relationship. So, until then, it is unwise to use digit ratios as a definitive index of ability, mental state, or character.

References

Abbott, D. H., Dumesic, D. A., Eisner, J. R., Colman, R. J., & Kemnitz, J. W. (1998). Insights into the development of polycystic ovary syndrome (PCOS) from studies of prenatally androgenized female Rhesus monkeys. *Trends in Endocrinology and Metabolism, 9*(2), 62-67. https://doi.org/10.1016/S1043-2760(98)00019-8

Al-Zaid, F. S., Alhader, A. A., & Al-Ayadhi, L. Y. (2015). The second to fourth digit ratio (2D:4D) in Saudi boys with autism: A potential screening tool. *Early Human Development, 91*(7), 413-415. https://doi.org/10.1016/j.earlhumdev.2015.04.007

Archambeault, S., Taylor, J. A., & Crow, K. D. (2014). HoxA and HoxD expression in a variety of vertebrate body plan features reveals an ancient origin for the distal Hox program. *EvoDevo, 5*(44), 1-10. doi: 10.1186/2041-9139-5-44.

Arnold, A. P. (2009). The organizational–activational hypothesis as the foundation for a unified theory of sexual differentiation of all mammalian tissues. *Hormones and Behavior, 55*(5), 570-578. doi:10.1016/j.yhbeh.2009.03.011.

Auger, J., & Eustache, F. (2010). Second to fourth digit ratios, male genital development and reproductive health: A clinical study among fertile men and testis cancer patients. *International Journal of Andrology, 34*(4 pt. 2), e49-e58. https://doi.org/10.1111/j.1365-2605.2010.01124.x

Bailey, A. A., & Hurd, P. L. (2005a). Depression in men is associated with more feminine finger length ratios. *Personality and Individual Differences, 39*(4), 829-836. https://doi.org/10.1016/j.paid.2004.12.017

Bailey, A. A., & Hurd, P. L. (2005b). Finger length ratio (2D:4D) correlates with physical aggression in men but not in women. *Biological Psychology, 68*(3), 215-222. https://doi.org/10.1016/j.biopsycho.2004.05.001

Baischer, W., Konig, G., Hartmann, B., & Langer, G. (1995). Hypothalamic-pituitary-gonadal axis in depressed premenopausal women: Elevated blood testosterone concentrations compared to normal controls. *Psychoneuroendocrinology, 20*(5), 553-559.

Bang, A. K., Carlsen, E., Holm, M., Petersen, J. H., Skakkebæk, N. E., & Jørgensen, N. (2005). A study of finger lengths, semen quality and sex hormones in 360 young men from the general Danish population. *Human Reproduction, 20*(11), 3109-3113. https://doi.org/10.1093/humrep/dei170

Bao, A., & Swaab, D. F. (2011). Sexual differentiation of the human brain: Relation to gender identity, sexual orientation and neuropsychiatric disorders. *Frontiers in Neuroendocrinology, 32*(2), 214-226. https://doi.org/10.1016/j.yfrne.2011.02.007

Baron-Cohen, S. (2002). The extreme male brain theory of autism. *Trends in Cognitive Sciences, 6*(6), 248-254. https://doi.org/10.1016/S1364-6613(02)01904-6

Baron-Cohen, S., Auyeung, B., Ashwin, E., Knickmeyer, R., Lombardo, M. & Chakrabarti, B. (2012). The extreme male brain theory of autism: The role of fetal androgens. In D. Amaral, D. Geschwind, & G. Dawson (Eds.) *Autism spectrum disorders*, pp. 991-998. New York, NY: Oxford University Press. doi: 10.1093/med/9780195371826.001.0001

Barribeau, T. (2011). *Your hands give away your hotness.* Retrieved from https://www.gizmodo.com.au/2011/04/your-hands-give-away-your-hotness/

Berenbaum, S. A., Bryk, K. K., Nowak, N., Quigley, C. A., & Moffat, S. (2009). Fingers as markers of prenatal androgen exposure. *Endocrinology, 150*(11), 5119-5124. doi: 10.1210/en.2009-0774

Blaschko, S. D., Cunha, G. R., & Baskin, L. S. (2012). Molecular mechanisms of external genital development. *Differentiation, 83*(3), 261-268. doi: 10.1016/j.diff.2012.06.003

Bogaert, A. F., Fawcett, C. C., & Jamieson, L. K. (2009). Attractiveness, body size, masculine sex roles and 2D:4D ratios in men. *Personality and Individual Differences, 47*(4), 273-278. https://doi.org/10.1016/j.paid.2009.03.011

Bolat, D., Kocabas, G. U., Kose, T., Degirmenci, T., Aydin, M. E., & Dincel, C. (2017). The relationship between the second-to-fourth digit ratios and lifelong premature ejaculation: A prospective, comparative study. *Andrology, 5*(3), 535-540. https://doi.org/10.1111/andr.12318

Brison, N., Debeer, P., & Tylzanowski, P. (2013). Joining the fingers: A *HOXD13* story. *Developmental Dynamics, 243*(1), 37-48. https://doi.org/10.1002/dvdy.24037

Brown, W. M., Finn, C. J., Cooke, B. M., & Breedlove, S. M. (2002). Differences in finger length ratios between self-identified "butch" and "femme" lesbians. *Archives of Sexual Behavior, 31*(1), 117-121. doi: 10.1023/A:1014091420590

Brown, W. M., Hines, M., Fane, B. A., & Breedlove, S. M. (2002). Masculinized finger length patterns in human males and females with congenital adrenal hyperplasia. *Hormones and Behavior, 42*(4), 380-386.

Buck, J. J., Williams, R. M., Hughes, I. A., Acerini, C. L. (2003). In-utero androgen exposure and 2nd to 4th digit length ratio—comparisons between healthy controls and females with classical congenital adrenal hyperplasia. *Human Reproduction, 18*(5), 976-979. https://doi.org/10.1093/humrep/deg198

Burriss, R. P., Little, A. C., Nelson, E. C. (2007). 2D:4D and sexually dimorphic facial characteristics. *Archives of Sexual Behavior, 36*, 377-384. doi: 10.1007/s10508-006-9136-1

Cattrall, F. R., Vollenhoven, B. J., & Weston, G. C. (2005). Anatomical evidence for in utero androgen exposure in women with polycystic ovary syndrome. *Fertility and Sterility, 84*(6), 1689-1692. https://doi.org/10.1016/j.fertnstert.2005.05.061

Choi, I. H., Kim, K. H., Jung, H., Yoon, S. J., Kim, S. W., & Kim, T. B. (2011). Second to fourth digit ratio: A predictor of adult penile length. *Asian Journal of Andrology, 13*(5), 710-714. doi:10.1038/aja.2011.75

Dabbs, J. M., & Morris, R. (1990). Testosterone, social class, and antisocial behavior in a sample of 4,462 men. *Psychological Science, 1*(3), 209-211. http://dx.doi.org/10.1111/j.1467-9280.1990.tb00200.x

Davarci, M. et al. (2012). A new anthropometric measurement of penile length and its relation to second and fourth digital lengths. *Turkish Journal of Medical Sciences, 42*(3), 539-544. doi:10.3906/sag-1103-32

Dey, S., & Kapoor, A. K. (2016). Digit ratio (2D:4D) – A forensic marker for sexual dimorphism in North Indian population. *Egyptian Journal of Forensic Sciences, 6*(4), 422-428. https://doi.org/10.1016/j.ejfs.2016.09.003

Eisenegger, C., et al. (2017). Testosterone and androgen receptor gene polymorphism are associated with confidence and competitiveness in men. *Hormones and Behavior, 92*, 93-102. https://doi.org/10.1016/j.yhbeh.2016.09.011

Evardone, M., & Alexander, G. M. (2009). Anxiety, sex-linked behaviors, and digit ratios (2D:4D). *Archives of Sexual Behavior, 38*(3), 442-455. doi: 10.1007/s10508-007-9260-6

Ferdenzi, C., Lemaître, J., Leongómez, J. D., & Roberts, S. C. (2011). Digit ratio (2D:4D) predicts facial, but not voice or body odour, attractiveness in men. *Proceedings of the Royal Society of London B, 278*(1724), 3551-3557. doi: 10.1098/rspb.2011.0544

Firman, R. C., Simmons, L. W., Cummins, J. M., & Matson, P. L. (2003). Are body fluctuating asymmetry and the ratio of 2nd to 4th digit length reliable predictors of semen quality? *Human Reproduction, 18*(4), 808-812. https://doi.org/10.1093/humrep/deg174

Fink, B. et al. (2006). Second to fourth digit ratio and numerical competence in children. *Brain and Cognition, 61*(2), 211-218. doi: 10.1016/j.bandc.2006.01.001

Fink, B., Manning, J. T., & Neave, N. (2004). Second to forth digit ratio and the "big five" personality factors. *Personality and Individual Differences, 37*, 495–503.

Fuxjager, M. J., Trainor, B. C., & Marler, C. A. (2017). What can animal research tell us about the link between androgens and social competition in

humans? *Hormones and Behavior, 92*, 182-189.
https://doi.org/10.1016/j.yhbeh.2016.11.014

Galis, F., Ten Broek, C. M. A., Van Dongen, S., & Wijnaendts, L. C. D. (2010). Sexual dimorphism in the prenatal digit ratio (2D:4D). *Archives of Sexual Behavior, 39*(1), 57-62. doi:10.1007/s10508-009-9485-7

Garn, S. M., Burdi, A. R., Babler. W. J., & Stinson, S. (1975). Early prenatal attainment of adult metacarpal-phalangeal rankings and proportions. American *Journal of Physical Anthropology, 43*(3), https://doi.org/10.1002/ajpa.1330430305

Graham, J. H., Raz, S., Hel-Or, H., Nevo, E. (2010). Fluctuating asymmetry: Methods, theory, and applications. *Symmetry, 2*(2), 466-540. https://doi.org/10.3390/sym2020466

Hönekopp, J. (2013). Digit ratio (2D:4D) and male facial attractiveness: New data and a meta-analysis. *Evolutionary Psychology, 11*(5), 944-952.

Hönekopp J., Bartholdt, L., Beier, L., & Liebert, A. (2007) Second to fourth digit length ratio (2D:4D) and adult sex hormone levels: New data and a meta-analytic review. *Psychoneuroendocrinology, 32*(4), 313-321. 10.1016/j.psyneuen.2007.01.007

Hönekopp, J., Manning, J. T., & Müller, C. (2006). Digit ratio (2D:4D) and physical fitness in males and females: Evidence for effects of prenatal androgens on sexually selected traits. *Hormones and Behavior, 49*, 545-549. doi: 10.1016/j.yhbeh.2005.11.006

Hönekopp, J., & Schuster, M. (2010). A meta-analysis on 2D:4D and athletic prowess: Substantial relationships but neither hand out-predicts the other. *Personality and Individual Differences, 48*(1), 4-10. https://doi.org/10.1016/j.paid.2009.08.009

Hönekopp, J., & Watson, S. (2010). Meta-analysis of digit ratio 2D:4D shows greater sex difference in the right hand. *American Journal of Human Biology, 22*(5), 619-630. doi: 10.1002/ajhb.21054.

Huber, S. E. et al. (2018). Prenatal androgen receptor activation determines adult alcohol and water drinking in a sex-specific way. *Addiction Biology, 23*(3), 904-920. https://doi.org/10.1111/adb.12540

Hughes, S. M., Harrison, M. A., & Gallup, G. G. Jr. (2002). The sound of symmetry: Voice as a marker of developmental instability. *Evolution and Human Behavior, 23*(3), 173-180. doi:10.1016/S1090-5138(01)00099-X

Hughes, S. M., Pastizzo, M. J., & Gallup, G. G., Jr. (2008). The sound of symmetry revisited: Subjective and objective analyses of voice. *Journal of Nonverbal Behavior, 32*(2), 93-108. doi:10.1007/s10919-007-0042-6

Jeevanandam, S., & Muthu, P. K. (2016). 2D:4D ratio and its implications in medicine. *Journal of Clinical and Diagnostic Research, 10*(12), CM01-CM03. doi: 10.7860/JCDR/2016/21952.9000

Kondo, T., Zákány, J., Innis, J. W., & Duboule, D. (1997). Of fingers, toes, and penises. *Nature, 390*(6655), 29. http://dx.doi.org/10.1038/36234

Kraemer, B., Noll, T., Delsigore, A., Milos, G., Schnyder, U., Hepp, U. (2006). Finger length ratio (2D:4D) and dimensions of sexual orientation. *Neuropsychobiology, 53*, 210-214. https://doi.org/10.1159/000094730

Kraemer, B., Noll, T., Delsigore, A., Milos, G., Schnyder, U., & Hepp, U. (2009).

Finger length ratio (2D:4D) in adults with gender identity disorder. *Archives of Sexual Behavior, 38*, 359-363. doi:10.1007/s10508-007-9262-4

Krajmer, P., Spajdel, M., Kubranska, A., & Ostatnokova, D. (2011). 2D:4D finger ratio in Slovak autism spectrum population. *Bratislava Medical Journal (Bratislavske Lekarske Listy), 112*(7), 377-379.

Kuntz, G. F. (1917). *Rings for the finger.* Philadelphia, PA: J. B. Lippincott Company.

Leinung, M., & Wu, C. (2017). The biological basis of transgender identity: 2D:4D finger length ratios implicate a role for prenatal androgen activity. *Endocrine Practice, 23*(6), 669-671.   doi: 10.4158/EP161528

Lippa, R. A. (2003). Are 2D:4D finger-length ratios related to sexual orientation? Yes for men, no for women. *Journal of Personality and Social Psychology, 85*(1), 179-188. http://dx.doi.org/10.1037/0022-3514.85.1.179

Little, A. C., Jones, B. C., Burriss, R. P. (2007). Preferences for masculinity in male bodies change across the menstrual cycle. *Hormones and Behavior, 51*(5), 633-639. doi: 10.1016/j.yhbeh.2007.03.006

Loehlin, J.C., Medland, S.E., & Martin, N.G. (2009). Relative finger lengths, sex differences, and psychological traits. *Archives of Sexual Behavior, 38*, 298-305. http://dx.doi.org/10.1007/s10508-007-9303-z

Longman, D., Stock, J. T., & Wells, J. C. K. (2011). Digit ratio and rowing ergometer performance in males and females. *American Journal of Physical Anthropology*, 144, 337-341.

Mailhos, A., Buunk, A. P., del Arca, D., & Tutte, V. (2016). Soccer players awarded one or more red cards exhibit lower 2D:4D ratios. *Aggressive Behavior, 42*(5), 417-426. doi: 10.1002/ab.21638

Malas, M. A., Dogan, S., Evcil, E. H., & Desdicioglu, K. (2006). Fetal development of the hand, digits and digit ratio (2D:4D). *Early Human Development, 82*(7), 469-475. doi: 10.1016/j.earlhumdev.2005.12.002

Mackus, M., de Kruijff, D., Otten, L. S., Kraneveld, A. D., Garssen, J., & Verster, J. C. (2017). The 2D:4D digit ratio as a biomarker for autism. *Autism Research and Treatment, 2017*, 1-5. https://doi.org/10.1155/2017/1048302

Manning, J. T. (2002). *Digit ratio: A pointer to fertility, behavior, and health.* New Brunswick, NJ: Rutgers University Press.

Manning, J. T., Barley, L., Walton, J., Lewis-Jones, D. I., Trivers, R. L., Singh, D., Thornhill, R....Szwed, A. (2000). The 2nd:4th digit ratio, sexual dimorphism, population differences, reproductive success: Evidence for sexually antagonistic genes? *Evolution and Human Behavior, 21*(3), 163-183.

Manning, J. T., Baron-Cohen, S., Wheelwright, S., & Sanders, G. (2001). The 2nd to 4th digit ratio and autism. *Developmental Medicine and Child Neurology, 43*(3), 160-164. https://doi.org/10.1017/S0012162201000317

Manning, J. T., Churchill, A. J., & Peters, M. (2007). The effects of sex, ethnicity, and sexual orientation on self-measured digit ratio (2D:4D). *Archives of Sexual Behavior, 36*(2), 223-233. doi: 10.1007/s10508-007-9171-6

Manning, J. T., & Fink, B. (2008). Digit ratio (2D:4D), dominance, reproductive success, asymmetry, and sociosexuality in the BBC Internet Study. *American Journal of Human Biology, 20*(4), 451-461. https://doi.org/10.1002/ajhb.20767.

Manning, J. T., Fink, B., Neave, N., & Caswell, N. (2005). Photocopies yield lower digit ratios (2D:4D) than direct finger measurements. *Archives of Sexual Behavior, 34*(3), 329-333. doi: 10.1007/s10508-005-3121-y

Manning, J. T., Kilduff, L., Cook, C., Crewther, B., & Fink, B. (2014). Digit ratio (2D:4D): A biomarker for prenatal sex steroids and adult sex steroids in challenge situations. *Frontiers in Endocrinology, 5*(9), 1-5. doi: 10.3389/fendo.2014.00009

Manning, J. T., Kilduff, L. P., & Trivers, R. (2012). Digit ratio (2D:4D) in Klinefelter's syndrome. *Andrology, 1*(1), 64-99. doi: 10.1111/j.2047-2927.2012.00013.x.

Manning, J. T., & Quinton, S. (2007). Association of digit ratio (2D:4D) with self-reported attractiveness in men and women. *Journal of Individual Differences, 28*, 73-77. https://doi.org/10.1027/1614-0001.28.2.73

Manning, J. T., Scutt, D., Wilson, J., Lewis-Jones, D. I. (1998). The ratio of 2nd to 4th digit length, a predictor of sperm numbers and concentrations of testosterone, luteinizing hormone and oestrogen. *Human Reproduction, 13*(11), 3000-3004. doi: 10.1093/humrep/13.11.3000

Manning, J. T., & Taylor, R. P. (2001). Second to fourth digit ratio and male ability in sport: implications for sexual selection in humans. *Evolution and Human Behavior, 22*(1), 61-69.

Mazur, A., & Booth, S. (1998). Testosterone and dominance in men. *Behavioral and Brain Sciences, 21,* 353–397.

McQuade, D. B. (2011). Does digit ratio (2D:4D) predict penile length? *Asian Journal of Andrology, 13*(5), 667-668. doi:10.1038/aja.2011.81

Neave, N., Laing, S., Fink, B., & Manning, J. T. (2003). Second to fourth digit ratio, testosterone, and perceived male dominance. *Proceedings of the Royal Society of London B, 270*(1529), 2167-2172. doi:10.1098/rspb.2003.2502

Ökten, A., Kalyonc, M., & Yariş, N. (2002). The ratio of second- and fourth-digit lengths and congenital adrenal hyperplasia due to 21-hydroxylase deficiency. *Early Human Development, 70*(1-2), 47-54. https://doi.org/10.1016/S0378-3782(02)00073-7

Penton-Voak, I. S., Perrett, D. I., Castles, D. L., Kobayashi, T., Burt, D. M., Murray, L. K., & Minamisawa, R. (1999). Menstrual cycle alters face preference. *Nature, 399(6738),* 741-742. doi:10.1038/21557

Perriton, C. L., Powles, N., Chiang, C., Maconochie, M. K., and Cohn, M. J. (2002). Sonic hedgehog signaling from the urethral epithelium controls external genital development. *Developmental Biology, 247*(1), 26-46. doi: 10.1006/dbio.2002.0668

Phelps, V. R. (1952). Relative index finger length as a sex-influenced trait in man. *American Journal of Human Genetics, 4*, 72-89.

Phoenix, C. H., Goy, R. W., Gerall, A .A., & Young, W. C. (1959) . Organizing action of prenatally administered testosterone propionate on the tissues mediating mating behavior in the female guinea pig. *Endocrinology 65*(3), 369–382. doi: 10.1210/endo-65-3-369

Plant, T. M., & Marshall, G. R. (2001), The functional significance of FSH in spermatogenesis and the control of its secretion in make primates. *Endocrine Reviews, 22*(6), 764-786. https://doi.org/10.1210/edrv.22.6.0446

Pratt, T. C., Turanovic, J. J., & Cullen, F. T. (2016). Revisiting the criminological consequences of exposure to fetal testosterone: A meta-analysis of the 2D:4D ratio. *Criminology, 54*(4), 587-620. https://doi.org/10.1111/1745-9125.12115

Puts, D. A., Gaulin, S. J. C., Sporter, R. J., McBurney, D. H. (2004). Sex hormones and finger length: What does 2D:4D indicate? *Evolution and Human Behavior, 25*, 182-199. doi: 10.1016/j.evolhumbehav.2004.03.005.

Qian, W., Huo, Z., Lu, H., Sheng, Y., Geng, Z., & Ma, Z. (2016). Digit ratio (2D:4D) in a Chinese population with schizophrenia. *Early Human Development, 98*, 45-48. https://doi.org/10.1016/j.earlhumdev.2016.05.003

Ribeiro, E., Neave, N., Morais, R. N., & Manning, J. T. (2016). Direct versus indirect measurement of digit ratio (2D:4D): A critical review of the literature and new data. *Evolutionary Psychology, 14*(1), 1-8. doi: 10.1177/1474704916632536

Robinson, S. J., & Manning, J. T. (2000). The ratio of 2nd to 4th digit length and male homosexuality. *Evolution and Human Behavior, 21*(5), 333-345. https://doi.org/10.1016/S1090-5138(00)00052-0

Rommerts, F. F. G. (1998). Testosterone: An overview of biosynthesis, transport, metabolism and nongenomic actions. In E. Nieschlag & H. M. Behre (Eds.) *Testosterone*. pp. 1-31. Berlin, Heidelberg: Springer-Verlag.

Roney, J. R., & Maestripieri, D. (2004). Relative digit lengths predict men's behavior and attractiveness during social interactions with women. *Human Nature, 15*(3), 271-282.

Ross, J. L., Samango-Sprouse, C., Lahlou, N., Kowal, K., Elder, F. F., & Zinn, A. (2005). Early androgen deficiency in infants and young boys with 47,XXY Klinefelter syndrome. *Hormone Research in Paediatrics, 64*, 39-45. https://doi.org/10.1159/000087313

Siegmann, E., Bouna-Pyrrou, P., Lenz, B., Kornhuber, J. (2019). Digit ratio (2D:4D) in relation to substance and computer use: A meta-analysis. *Journal of Neural Transmission, 126*, 623-636. https://doi.org/10.1007/s00702-019-02002-2

Smedley, K. D., McKain, K. J., & McKain, D. N. (2014). 2D:4D digit ratio predicts depression severity for females but not for males. *Personality and Individual Differences, 70*, 136-139. https://doi.org/10.1016/j.paid.2014.06.039

Szalavitz, M. (2011). Penis size: It may be written in the length of his finger. *Time Magazine*, retrieved from http://healthland.time.com/2011/07/06/penis-size-it-may-be-written-in-the-length-of-his-fingers/

Tamiya, R., Lee, S. Y., & Ohtake, F. (2012). Second to fourth digit ratio and the sporting success of sumo wrestlers. *Evolution and Human Behavior, 33*(2), 130-136. doi: 10.1016/j.evolhumbehav.2011.07.003

Thornhill, R., & Gangestad, S. W. (1994). Human fluctuating asymmetry and sexual behavior. *Psychological Science, 5*(5), 297-302. https://www.jstor.org/stable/40063121

Thornhill, R., & Gangestad, S. W. (1999). The scent of symmetry: A human sex pheromone that signals fitness? *Evolution and Human Behavior, 20*(3), 175-201. http://dx.doi.org/10.1016/S1090-5138(99)00005-7

Trivers, R., Manning, J. T., Jacobson, A. (2006). A longitudinal study of digit ratio (2D:4D) and other finger ratios in Jamaican children. *Hormones and*

Behavior, 49(2), 150-156. doi: 10.1016/j.yhbeh.2005.05.023

Udhane, S. S., & Flück, C. E. (2016). Regulation of human (adrenal) androgen biosynthesis—New insights from novel throughput technology studies. *Biochemical Pharmacology, 102*(15), 20-33. https://doi.org/10.1016/j.bcp.2015.10.010

Vehmas, T., Solovieva, S., & Leino-Arjas, P. (2006). Radiographic 2D:4D index in females: No relation to anthropometric, behavioural, nutritional, health-related, occupational or fertility variables. *Journal of Negative Results in BioMedicine, 5*(12), 1-7. doi:10.1186/1477-5751-5-12

Watts, T. M., Holmes, L., Raines, J., Orbell, S., & Rieger, G. (2018). Finger length ratios of identical twins with discordant sexual orientation. *Archives of Sexual Behavior, 47*(8), 2435-2444. https://doi.org/10.1007/s10508-018-1369-2

Whiteford, H. A. (2013). Global burden of disease attributable to mental and substance use disorders: findings from the Global Burden of Disease Study 2010. *Lancet, 382*(9904), 1575-1586. doi: 10.1016/S0140-6736(13)61611-6

Zheng, Z., & Cohn, M. J. (2011). Developmental basis of the sexually dimorphic digit ratio. *PNAS, 108*(39), 16289-16294. doi: 10.1073/pnas.1108312108

Zhu, Y., Li, C., Jin, J., Wang, J., Lachmann, B., Sariyska, R., & Montag, C. (2014). The 2D:4D ratio of the hand and schizotypal personality traits in schizophrenia patients and healthy control persons. *Asian Journal of Psychiatry, 9*, 67-72. https://doi.org/10.1016/j.ajp.2014.01.005

Chapter 6

TOES

The human foot is a masterpiece of engineering and a work of art.

-Leonardo da Vinci

Do you have competitive toes?

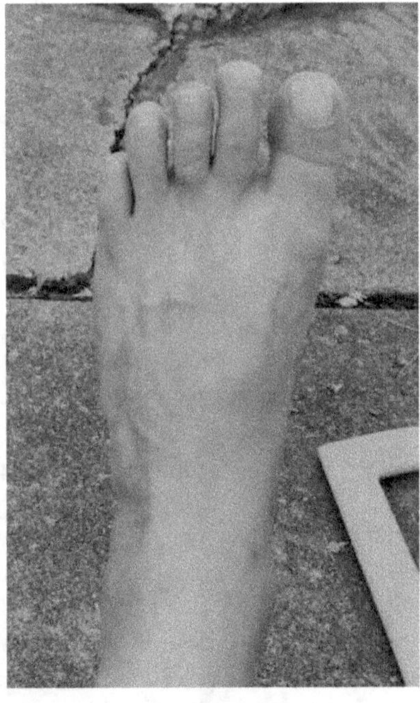

In the previous chapter we discussed the connection between fingers and behaviors. The prevailing theory is that there is a connection between genital development and finger and toe development, vis-à-vis a shared hormonal milieu in utero (Manning, 2002). There are hundreds of published research papers devoted to studying the connection between finger ratios and various behaviors related to androgens. Has anyone studied digit ratios vis-à-vis toes and psychology? It turns out very few research teams have examined this association, with our team being one of the few included on that list.

With 2D:4D finger digit research populating the field, it is intriguing to examine if toe 2D:4D, or any toe configurations, are related to behavior and mental processes as well. Not only are fingers, toes, and genitals purported to be substantially influenced by exposure to androgens, and likely estrogens (Manning et al., 2000; Manning 2002), but they also have common *HoxA* and *HoxD* gene foundations (Brison, Debeer, & Tylzanowski, 2013). In fact, there are several syndromes that involve both urogenital and limb defects, such as in the case of hand-foot-genital (HFG) syndrome. A *HoxA* mutation has been associated with HFG syndrome (Mortlock & Innis, 1997; Tas et al., 2017). It makes sense, then, that behaviors related to androgens can somehow be related to toe morphology.

McFadden and Shubel (2002) were among the first, and among the only, authors known to us to attempt to address the relation between toes and psychological processes in humans. Based on previous evidence of sex differences in toe lengths in mice, gorillas, and baboons (see McFadden & Shubel, 2002, for a good review), they sought to elucidate associations between finger and toe lengths and several behaviors. They examined finger and toe lengths of 186 college students using a digital scanner for image capture and measurement. Although they aimed to determine if there were differences in individuals' toe configurations, they encountered difficulty obtaining toe measures from scans because foot anatomy and toe articulation obscure creases from which measurements were to be made. For this reason, they ended up discontinuing the toe part of their study. From what they were able to gauge, it is typical to have a 1D>2D>3D>4D>5D toe length configuration, with men generally having larger toes than women.

McFadden and Shubel (2002) reported that they calculated 10 theoretically possible toe ratios but did not report these values. Results showed that men had larger toe ratios than did women, with small to medium effect sizes. There were also small correlations between finger and toe lengths for corresponding sides of the body, but they did not report these; rather, they stated that most were under 0.35. Nonetheless, these researchers appear to be the first team to establish a connection between finger and toe ratios.

Our research team understood the challenge of measuring toes accurately. In fact, there were weekends we coaxed our fellow graduate students (now esteemed professors) into our research lab so we could try to measure their toes through a plexiglass contraption that Harrison built. This was markedly unsuccessful, leaving a failed heap of wood and plastic scientific sadness ripe for the recycling. We also attempted to measure toes by using a flexible string placed on the underside of the toe as our measurement device to account for the natural curvature of the toes that could ultimately compromise the appearance of its length when using a straight-edge ruler; but that also was a failing endeavor. Despite our unsuccessful efforts, we still found toe ratios as a potential index of behavior to be thought-provoking. We decided to try again, starting with the obvious. Most people may have noticed that some of us have a longer second toe relative to all our other toes. Although 2D:4D finger lengths are measured with sophisticated tools because of the subtlety of differences, it seems pretty obvious if someone has a second toe that is longer than the others (i.e., the toe next to the hallux or "big toe"), because you can easily observe this pattern when looking down at your feet.

We delved into the embryological literature to trace toe ontogeny and found that there is indeed some evidence to suggest that the second toe may be androgenized. Chondrogenesis of the second toe (the second metatarsal) begins at about seven weeks in utero, even before great toe/hallux formation. The second toe is typically longer in fetuses (Minami, 1952). By about eight weeks, human limb buds rotate in different directions. The upper limb rotates laterally so that elbows are caudal (down). The lower limb rotates ventrally so that knees are oriented cranially (see Larsen, 2002). In other words, your knees bend the opposite way from your elbows, so your second toe, as appearing from above, would be fourth when looking at you from the bottom of your feet. Manning (2002) and others have suggested that the fourth finger digit is particularly vulnerable to androgen effects. Might this be true of the second toe?

About eight weeks in utero there is a 2>3>1>4>5 toe length formula (Bareither, 1995). This is the same time that androgens are known to be exerting their effects on the urogenital tract as well as the fingers and toes. With the second toe longest during this critical embryological period, it could be more prone to androgenization (Harrison, 2010) as in the fourth finger (Manning, 2002). We decided to focus our research on the connection between second toe and various behaviors related to androgen exposure. A longer second toe is called Morton's toe, or Greek foot, and has been of interest in art (Decherchi, 2005) and dance science (Ogilvie-Harris et al., 1995).

Again, McFadden and Shubel (2002) underscored the difficulty of measuring toes, and we had more than one major fail with respect to apparatus construction attempts. We therefore decided to pursue self-report methodology. In Harrison (2010), we expressed faith that college student participants could easily look down at their own toes and report if their second toe is longer than all their other toes. We asked, "Is your second toe longer than all your other toes (does it extend beyond your other toes)?" and we provided an illustration of a foot with its second toe extended. We stated that we were "operating on the premise that college students are capable of examining their own toes to make a crude categorization of whether their second toes extend beyond their other toes" (p. 249).

We certainly acknowledge a gross characterization foregoes the subtlety captured in traditional finger-length measurements, but we felt this was a good starting point down a research avenue heretofore unexplored.

Presupposing college student participants can look down at their feet with marked success, we used a similar illustration and asked, "Is your second toe longer than all your other toes (does it extend beyond your other toes)?"

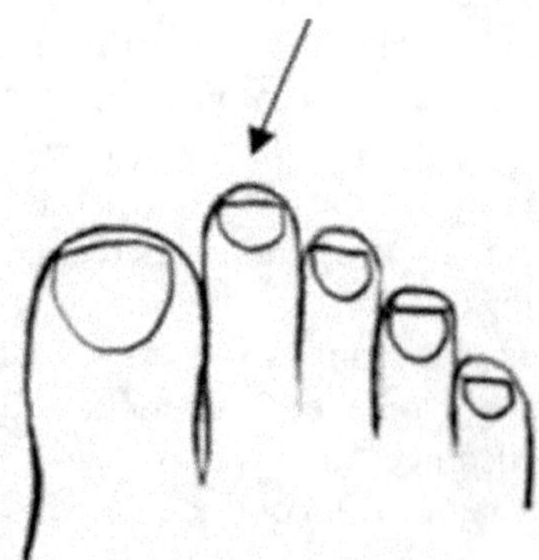

In Harrison (2010), we noted participants "yes" or "no" answers with respect to having a longer second toe. We aimed to compare differences between those with a longer second toe and those without a longer second toe with respect to responses on various established psychological inventories that tap into behaviors and traits typically associated with androgens and with lower 2D:4D finger ratios. We studied left-handedness (Geschwind & Galaburda, 1985; Manning, 2002); competitiveness (Dabbs, 2000; Manning & Taylor, 2001); aggression (Archer, 1991); exercise (Manning, 2002; Voracek, Reimer, Ertl, & Dressler, 2006); sociosexuality (proclivity towards uncommitted sex; Hönekopp, Voracek, & Manning, 2006; Simon et al., 2004); and sexual orientation (Rahman & Wilson, 2003; Robinson & Manning, 2000).

About 42% of participants reported having a longer second toe. Surprisingly, there were no sex differences. One might have expected a greater frequency of men with longer second toes if second toe length is an index of androgen and men typically have higher levels of androgens than do women. Nonetheless, because previous literature consistently has documented male-female differences in testosterone, androgen-linked behaviors, and 2D:4D, we conducted our analyses for men and women separately (Harrison, 2010).

Sure enough, as reported in Harrison (2010) we found that for both men and women, a longer second toe was related to left-handedness as measured by the Edinburgh Handedness Inventory (EHI; Oldfield, 1971). There was a positive relation between having a longer second toe and Competitiveness Orientation Inventory (COI) scores (Gill, 1986) for women, but not for men. There was only one significant finding relating second toe length with aggression; women with a longer second toe has higher physical aggression scores, as measured by the Buss-Perry Aggression Questionnaire-Short Form (BPAQ-SF; Buss & Perry, 1992) physical subscale. For men, a longer second toe predicted exercise frequency, as measured by the Godin Exercise Questionnaire (Godin & Shephard, 1985). This was not true for women. Finally, for both men and women, a second toe configuration did not predict sexual orientation as measured by the Kinsey Scale (Kinsey et al., 1948), and it did not predict sociosexuality (i.e., the propensity toward uncommitted sex) as measured by the SOI inventory (Simpson & Gangestad, 1991).

The association between a longer second toe and left handedness is strong evidence for androgenization. However, the value of a longer second toe as a predictor of behavior, at least in this study (Harrison, 2010), was largely limited to assessments of women. Women with a longer second toe have a higher likelihood of being competitive and physically aggressive. Why would there be a demonstrable effect in women, but not in men? As Fink (2004) explained, men are generally more competitive. With a wider variation in competitiveness in women, androgenization effects would be more pronounced. Also, women typically have less testosterone, and therefore are more sensitive to its effects (Bancroft, 2002).

Some evidence from other researchers suggests that those with a longer second toe have more skilled athleticism. Professional athletes tend to have a longer heel-to-second-toe length compared to heel-to-first-toe length; non-athletes exhibit a reversed pattern (Kulthanan et al., 2004).

Examples of Morton's toe, or Greek foot—a longer second toe configuration. Bottom right: Male subject's second toe is so pronounced that it protrudes from his cast, having severely broken his foot cliff diving. Read: adventurous = more testosterone?

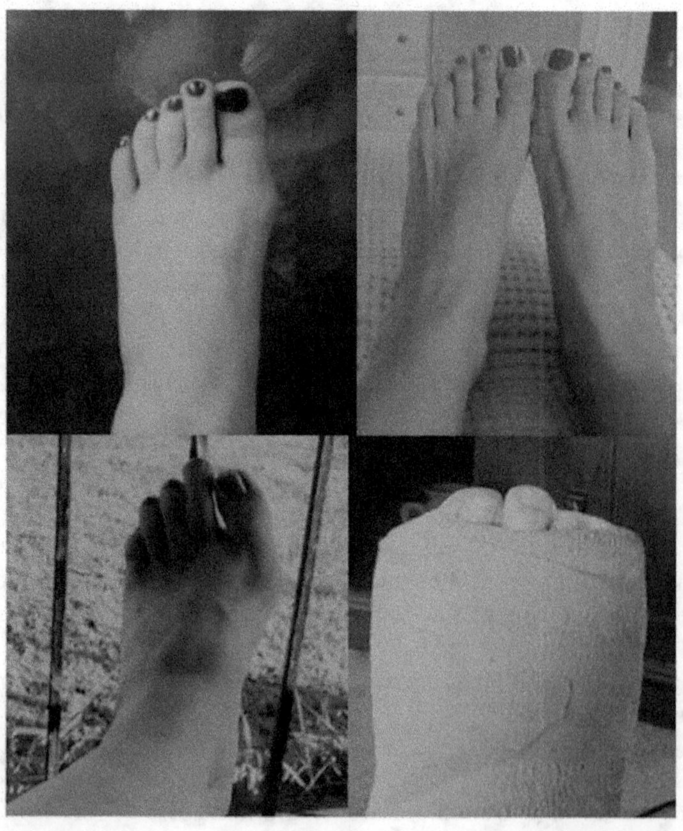

It appears that a longer second toe has long been associated with power, formidability, and the ideal, as ancient Greek art tends to feature a longer second toe (in fact, as stated earlier, a foot with a longer second toe is sometimes called "Greek foot,"), as do other masterpieces like Botticelli's

Venus in *The Birth of Venus* (1486), Bouguereau's cupid in *L'Amour et Psych* (1899), and many of Leonardo da Vinci's works. Even the Statue of Liberty in the United States, a powerful symbol of freedom, has a longer second toe.

Unsurprisingly, evidence suggest that not a lot of people want to work with feet and toes. Noting the obvious avenue of research ripe for the taking (no pun intended) vis-à-vis toe 2D:4D, we wondered why people were just not engaging in this scholarly pursuit. We are confident that our bright, fellow psychological scientists can come up with an accurate measurement of toe lengths, so what is the issue? Maybe they just don't want to study toes. We (Harrison & McFalls, 2012) asked psychology students about their perceptions of feet and toes, with items such as, "Do you think toes/feet are gross?", "Do you mind touching someone else's toes/feet?" and "Would you ever want to conduct research with feet?" Consolidated responses indicate a pervasive aversion towards feet.

Our review of the literature reveals strong evidence why an aversion to feet is likely adaptive. Even in healthy people, bacteria found on feet include those that cause acne and loss of vision; endocarditis and sarcoidosis; Staph infections, meningitis, and sepsis; gangrene, respiratory tract and urinary tract infections; diarrhea (*E. coli* can be found on healthy feet); and purification (see Harrison & McFalls, 2012). Further, an element contributing to foot odor, isovaleric acid, can cause neurological, metabolic, and digestive abnormalities (Kanda, Yagi, Fukuda, Nakajimi, Ohta, & Nakata, 1990). In our paper we asserted that "human feet can offer a veritable smorgasbord of illness causing bacteria" (p. 9). It is no wonder that three-quarters of our college student sample said they would avoid having a romance with someone who had noisome feet.

We (Harrison & McFalls, 2012) stated that "Repulsion to feet may confer an advantage to the repulsed" (p. 10). When something smells foul, our body is signaling to us that we should avoid that stimulus. Nonetheless, perhaps our feet were not always as repulsive throughout human evolution. We contemporary humans are "habitually shod," even though the human foot is biologically adapted to walking barefoot on natural surfaces (D'Aout, Pataky, De Clercq, & Aerts, 2009). Our constant wearing of shoes may contribute to the bacteria growth we observe on modern human feet (Ramsey, 1996).

That being said, our "smelly feet" may have been adaptive in our ancestral past. According to Leakey's *Unpalatability Hypothesis* (1967), potent human body odors served as an advertisement to our predators of the unpalatability of our species' flesh. Having malodorous feet that left a scent trail may have dissuaded our predators with keen olfactory senses from following our paths and pursuing us as prey. Foot odor may seem repulsive to us, but more importantly, it would also be repulsive to our predators.

Stepping Forward

There are obvious next steps in this research. It would be informative to examine continuous, versus categorical, data on the relation between second toe length and behaviors and mental processes linked to testosterone. For example, we might ask questions like, "Are women with even longer second toes that much more competitive?" We contend this would be an intriguing line of inquiry. Further, since the foundation for this research was an interest in 2D:4D finger ratios, it would be prudent to find a viable way to measure toe ratios precisely for comparison with finger ratios; researchers have had a difficult time doing this. Moreover, we suggest exploring the connection between having a longer second toe and performance in challenge situations (in situ testing). Crewther and colleagues (2015) showed that those with lower finger 2D:4D ratios respond more intensely, with a corresponding rise in testosterone and cortisol levels, in a physically competitive challenge scenario. We predict this effect will be found in those with a longer second toe. It would make for a very interesting study.

Even as a gross diagnostic tool (gross in both the omnibus and the disgust sense), it is worth pursuing the connection between longer second toe and conditions linked to androgenization and to finger 2D:4D, such as those named in the previous chapter. In our estimation, it is likely that a longer second toe is related to conditions like congenital adrenal hyperplasia (CAH), polycystic ovary syndrome (PCOS), autism, and substance abuse. Further, although we did not find associations between a longer second toe and the measures of sexuality we administered, and we did not find many effects for men, evidence from finger 2D:4D studies lead us to conjecture potential relationships between toe length and various aspects of sexuality. Researchers may want to explore whether longer second toe (again, as viewed downward from your cranium), and more sophisticated measurements thereof, predict male fertility (testicle volume, sperm count, and decreased time to partner pregnancy) and penis size, gender identity, and sexual orientation.

Top: Detail of Botticelli's The Birth of Venus (1486);
Bottom left, The Statue of Liberty's toes (New York, USA)
Bottom right, the toes of a competitive woman, Marissa's fierce niece.

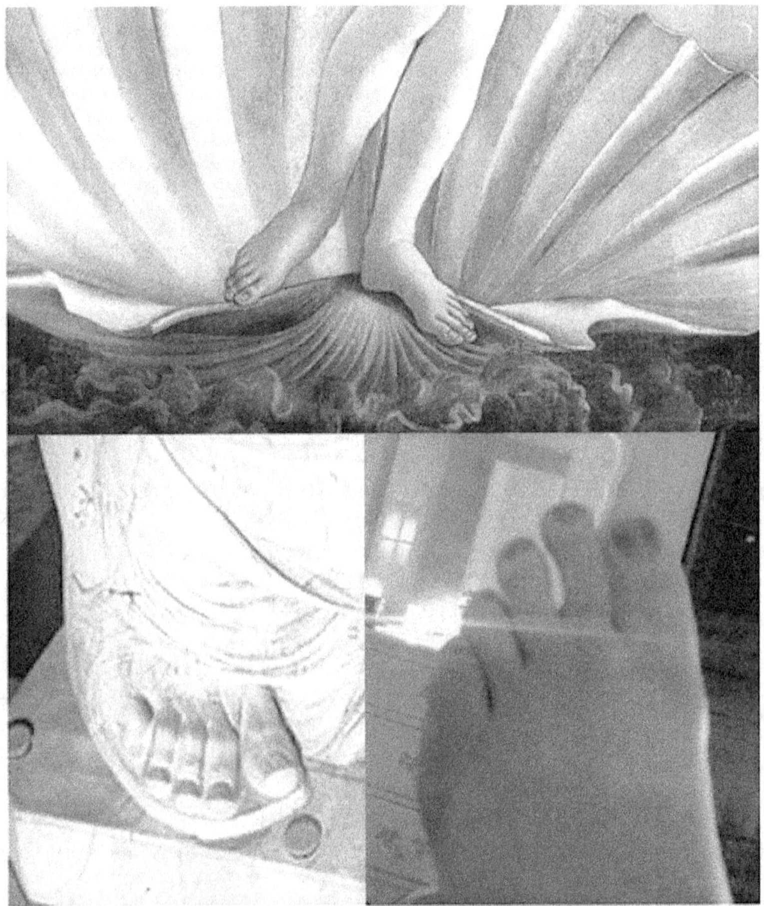

Art images in public domain

Conclusion

Further research can provide more evidence to corroborate empirically the connections between second toe lengths, or toe lengths in general, and behavior and mental processes to allow for a more complete understanding. Until then, note that if she has a longer second toe, don't be surprised that she is a fierce competitor.

References

Archer, J. (1991). The influence of testosterone on human aggression. *British Journal of Psychology, 82*(1), 1-28. https://doi.org/10.1111/j.2044-8295.1991.tb02379.x

Bancroft, J. (2002). Sexual effects of androgens in women: Some theoretical considerations. *Fertility and Sterility, 77* (Suppl 4:S55-9), 55-59.

Bareither, D. (1995). Prenatal development of the foot and ankle. *Journal of the American Podiatric Medical Association, 85*(12), 753-764. https://doi.org/10.7547/87507315-85-12-753

Brison, N., Debeer, P., & Tylzanowski, P. (2013). Joining the fingers: A *HOXD13* story. *Developmental Dynamics, 243*(1), 37-48. https://doi.org/10.1002/dvdy.24037

Buss, A., & Perry, M. (1992). The aggression questionnaire. *Journal of Personality and Social Psychology, 63*(3), 452-459. http://dx.doi.org/10.1037/0022-3514.63.3.452

Crewther, B. T., Cook, C. C., Kilduff, L. P., & Manning, J. T. (2015). Digit ratio (2D:4D) and salivary testosterone, oestradiol and cortisol levels under challenge: Evidence for prenatal effects on adult endocrine responses. *Early Human Development, 91*(8), 451-456. doi: 10.1016/j.earlhumdev.2015.04.011

Dabbs, J. (2000). *Heroes, rogues, and lovers: Testosterone and behavior.* New York, NY: McGraw-Hill.

D'Aout, K., Pataky, T., De Clercq, D., & Aerts, P. (2009). The effects of habitual footwear use: Foot shape and function in native barefoot walkers. *Footwear Science, 1*(2), 81-94. https://doi.org/10.1080/19424280903386411

Decherchi, P. (2005). Dudley Joy Morton's foot syndrome. *La Presse Médicale, 34*(22), 1737-1740. https://doi.org/10.1016/S0755-4982(05)84262-9

Fernández, P. J., Mongle, C. S., Leakey, L., Proctor, D. J., Orr, C. M., Patel, B.A....Jungers, W. L. (2018). Evolution and function of the hominin forefoot. *Proceedings of the National Academy of Sciences (PNAS) of the United States of America, 115*(35), 8746-8751. https://doi.org/10.1073/pnas.1800818115

Fink, B., Manning, J., & Neave, N. (2004). Second to fourth digit ratio and the big five personality traits. *Personality and Individual Differences, 37*(3), 495-503. https://doi.org/10.1016/j.paid.2003.09.018

Geschwind, N., & Galaburda, A. (1985). Cerebral lateralization: Biological mechanisms, associations, and pathology: I. A hypothesis and a program for research. *Archives of Neurology, 42*, 428-459. doi: 10.1001/archneur.1985.04060050026008

Gill, D. (1986). Competitiveness among females and males in physical activity classes. *Sex Roles, 15*(5-6), 233-257.

Godin, G., & Shephard, R. (1985). A simple method to assess exercise behavior in the community. *Canadian Journal of Sport Sciences, 10*(3), 141-146.

Harrison, M. A. (2010). An exploratory study of the relationship between second toe length and androgen-linked behaviors. *Journal of Social, Evolutionary, and*

Cultural Psychology, 4(4), 241-253. http://dx.doi.org/10.1037/h0099286

Harrison, M. A., & McFalls, A. J. (2012). A primal reaction to fetid feet? A brief report. *Human Ethology Bulletin*, 27(3), 8-13.

Hönekopp, J., Voracek, M., & Manning, J. (2006). 2nd to 4th digit ratio (2D:4D) and number of sex partners: Evidence for effects of prenatal testosterone in men. *Psychoneuroendocrinology, 31*(1), 30-37. doi: 10.1016/j.psyneuen.2005.05.009

Kanda, F., Yagi, E., Fukuda, M., Nakajima, K., Ohta, T., & Nakata, O. (1990). Elucidation of chemical compounds responsible for foot malodour. *British Journal of Dermatology, 122*(6), 771-776.

Kinsey, A., Pomeroy, W., & Martin, C. (1948). *Sexual behavior in the human male.* Philadelphia, PA, and London, UK: W. B. Saunders.

Kulthanan, T., Techkampuch, S., & Donphongam, N.D. (2004). A study of footprints in athletes and non-athletic people. *Journal of the Medical Association of Thailand, 87*(7), 788-793.

Larsen, W. J. (2002). *Human embryology, 3rd ed.* Philadelphia, PA: Elsevier.

Leakey L.S. B. (1967). Development of aggression as a factor in early human and pre-human evolution. In C. Clemente & D. Lindsley (Eds). *Brain function, vol. V. Aggression and defense.* Berkeley: University of California Press, 1–33.

Manning, J. T. (2002). *Digit ratio: A pointer to fertility, behavior, and health.* New Brunswick, NJ: Rutgers University Press.

Manning, J. T., Barley, L., Walton, J., Lewis-Jones, D. I., Trivers, R. L., Singh, D., Thornhill, R.….Szwed, A. (2000). The 2nd:4th digit ratio, sexual dimorphism, population differences, reproductive success: Evidence for sexually antagonistic genes? *Evolution and Human Behavior, 21*(3), 163-183. http://dx.doi.org/10.1016/S1090-5138(00)00029-5

Manning, J., & Taylor, R. (2001). Second to fourth digit ratio and male ability in sport: Implications for sexual selection in humans. *Evolution and Human Behavior, 22*(1), 61-69. https://doi.org/10.1016/S1090-5138(00)00063-5

McFadden., D., & Shubel, E. (2002). Relative lengths of fingers and toes in human males and females. *Hormones and Behavior, 42*, 495-500. doi:10.1006/hbeh.2002.1833

Minami, K. (1952). The digit formula in Japanese fetus. II. Study on the relative length between the 1st toe and 2nd toe. *Okajimas Folia Anatomica Japonica 24*, 295. https://www.jstage.jst.go.jp/article/ofaj1936/24/5-6/24_295/_article/-char/ja/

Mortlock, D. P., & Innis, J. W. (1997). Mutation of HOXA13 in hand-foot-genital syndrome. *Nature Genetics, 15*(2), 179-180. doi: 10.1038/ng0297-179

Ogilvie-Harris, D. J., Carr, M. M., & Fleming, P. J. (1995). The foot in ballet dancers: The importance of second toe length. *Foot & Ankle International, 16*(3), 144-147. https://doi.org/10.1177/107110079501600307

Oldfield, R. (1971). The assessment and analysis of handedness: The Edinburgh inventory. *Neuropsychologia, 9*(1), 97-113. https://doi.org/10.1016/0028-3932(71)90067-4

Oztekin, H. H., Boya, H., Nalcakan, M., & Ozcan, O. (2007). Second-toe length and forefoot disorders in ballet and folk dancers. *Journal of the American Podiatric Medical Association, 97*(5), 385-388.

https://doi.org/10.7547/0970385

Rahman, Q., & Wilson, G. (2003). Sexual orientation and the 2nd to 4th finger length ratio: Evidence for organizing effects of sex hormones or developmental instability? *Psychoneuroendocrinology, 28*(3), 288–303.

Ramsey, M. (1996). Foot odor: How to clear the air. *The Physician and Sportsmedicine, 24*(8), 91-92.

Robinson, S., & Manning, J. (2000). The ratio of 2nd to 4th digit length and male homosexuality. *Evolution and Human Behavior, 21*(5), 333–345. doi: 10.1016/S1090-5138(00)00052-0

Simon, J., et al. (2005). Testosterone patch increases sexual activity and desire in surgically menopausal women with hypoactive sexual desire disorder. *Clinical Endocrinology & Metabolism, 90*(9), 5226-5233. doi: 10.1210/jc.2004-1747

Simpson, J., & Gangestad, S. (1991). Individual differences in sociosexuality: Evidence for convergent and discriminant validity. Journal of Personality and Social Psychology, 60(6), 870-883. http://dx.doi.org/10.1037/0022-3514.60.6.870

Tas, E., et al. (2017). Familial deletion of the HOXA gene cluster associated with Hand-Foot-Genital syndrome and phenotypic variability. *American Journal of Medical Genetics Part A, 173*(1), 221-224. doi: 10.1002/ajmg.a.37981

Voracek, M., Reimer, B., Ertl, C., & Dressler, S. (2006). Digit ratio (2D:4D), lateral preferences, and performance in fencing. *Perceptual and Motor Skills, 103*(2), 427-446. doi: 10.2466/pms.103.2.427-446.

Chapter 7

BODY RATIOS

Cultivate your curves - they may be dangerous but they won't be avoided.

-Mae West

As a society, we are often concerned about our body weight, making the abundance of available diet and weight loss programs a lucrative industry. However, in addition to paying attention to the overall size of our bodies, it is actually the shape of our bodies that provide important information about weight and muscle distribution. Certain body ratios such as waist-to-hip ratio (WHR), shoulder-to-hip ratio (SHR), and waist-to-chest ratio (WCR) act as a proxy for measures of central adiposity and muscle mass. In this chapter, we review how these body ratios can serve as markers of health, attractiveness, and even reproductive status.

Following the advent of puberty, body configuration begins to show significant sexual dimorphism, with females developing an hourglass shape and males an inverted triangle or "V-shape" (i.e., broad shoulders and narrow waist). Activational sex hormone exposure that occurs during puberty has been implicated in the development of these different body configurations between the sexes (Mondragón-Ceballos, Granados, Cerda-Molina, Chavira-Ramírez, & Leonor Estela Hernández-López, 2015; Singh, 1993). Throughout early adulthood, the sexes differ greatly in body shape, but these differences eventually tend to decline with age (Wells, Treleaven, & Cole, 2007).

Body ratios appear to be important sex-specific mate-selection features, and they influence judgments of attractiveness, age, and desirability (Dijkstra & Buunk, 2001; Horvath, 1981; Hughes & Gallup, 2003; Singh, 1995). As such, there are differential preferences in opposite-sex body morphology for men and women, as it has been well documented that women tend to have a preference for males with a tapering "V" physique (Lavrakas, 1975), whereas males tend to prefer females with an hourglass figure (Gitter, Lomranz, Saxe, & Bar-Tal, 1983).

We have evolved to be attracted to sex-specific body types that signal mate quality. When we desire someone with a particular body shape, proximately, it is because we think that person is "sexy" or "hot." Ultimately, millions of years of human evolution have shaped our unconscious abilities to determine a good mate and therefore, good genes. Therefore "sexy" signals good genes. Here we present well-researched topics on body shapes and ratios, and we consider some of the interesting research and theories that have emerged about these concepts over the past several decades. Whereas this is not a systematic literature review, we highlight research we believe has help shaped our understanding of the links between certain body ratios with certain behaviors and traits.

Waist-to-hip Ratio (WHR)

Waist-to-hip ratio (WHR) is measure of the circumference of the narrowest point of the waist divided by the widest point of the hips. A small WHR would be indicative of a more hourglass shaped figure. WHR is thought to reflect a critical feature of the female body shape and is a good representation of the distribution of body fat (Wells, 2007).

Prior to puberty, the body shapes of boys and girls are relatively similar (Swami, 2006; Wells, 2007). Noticeable sex differences in typical body shape emerge after puberty because of activational sex hormone exposure that occurs during this time (Singh, 1993; Wells, 2007). Estrogen inhibits fat deposit in the abdominal region while increasing fat deposit in the gluteofemoral region (the buttocks and thighs; Swami, 2006) whereas testosterone promotes fat deposit in the abdominal region and inhibits deposits in the gluteofemoral region (Björntorp, 1997).

Hence, women develop greater amounts of body fat in the lower part of the body (referred to as *gynoid* fat distribution) and men have greater amounts of fat in the upper body (*android* fat distribution; Swami, 2006). These sex differences in body distribution remain throughout most adulthood with women typically having a lower WHR than men. Then, during menopause, due to the reduction of estrogen, women's WHR tends to increase and becomes more similar to the masculine figure (Arechiga, Prado, Canto, & Carmenati, 2001).

Hourglass figure

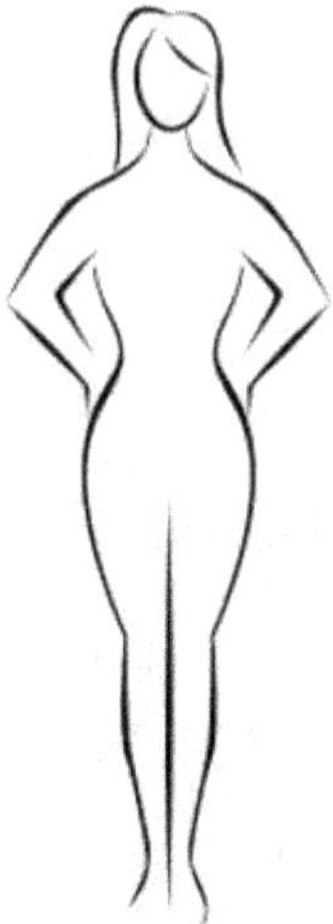

Image by Succubus MacAstaroth (2008)

WHR, therefore, is a prominent body feature that is indicative of one's hormonal profile and is purported to be a reliable signal of a woman's age, fertility, and health (Singh & Randall, 2007). Lower levels of WHR indicate greater levels of circulating estrogen, responsible for fat deposits in the thighs and buttocks, while higher WHR is associated with greater levels of testosterone which contributes to fat deposits in the abdomen (DeRidder et al., 1990; Elbers, Asscheman, Seidell, Megens, & Gooren, 1997; Furnham, Tan, & McManus, 1997). Attraction to women with a lower WHR allows selection of a more viable mate.

The range of WHR for healthy, pre-menopausal Caucasian women is between 0.67 and 0.80 (Lanska, Lanska, Hartz, & Rimm, 1985) and for healthy Caucasian men is between 0.85 to 0.95 (Jones, Hunt, Brown, & Norgan, 1986). These sex differences in body shape stay pronounced throughout most of early to mid-adulthood and are defining sexually dimorphic features (Wells, Treleaven, & Cole, 2007). As a matter of fact, WHR can be used to infer the sex of ambiguous figures when other cues to sex are not provided and regardless of the individual's actual sex (Pazhoohi & Liddle, 2012).

Interestingly, subtle changes in WHR have been observed in accordance to daylight and temperature, with the highest values occurring during the summer and the lowest during the winter (Svartberg, Jorde, Sundsfjord, Bønaa, & Barrett-Connor, 2003). These seasonal changes in WHR can be accounted for by the seasonal variation in total and free testosterone whereby the lowest testosterone levels occurred in months with the highest temperatures and longest hours of daylight. This finding further demonstrates how WHR and testosterone are inversely related.

WHR and Attractiveness

Singh (1993; 1994a; 1994b; 1995; 2002) was one of the first researchers in evolutionary psychology to investigate the role of WHR in mate value. He conducted a series of studies that demonstrated the importance of WHR in women's attractiveness. Most importantly, he found that, instead of highly slender women being deemed the most attractive, it was normal weight female figures with a low (0.7) WHR that were evaluated as being the most attractive as well as possessing more desirable qualities such as youthfulness (Singh, 1994). Many others have been able to replicate his findings that low WHRs in women are consistently judged to be the most attractive, healthy, and youthful regardless of body weight (Crossley, Cornelissen, & Tovée, 2012; Furnham, Tan, & McManus, 1996; Henss, 2000; Rempala & Garvey, 2007).

Despite the wealth of studies that support Singh's findings, there are a few studies that fail to replicate men's preference for a low WHR. For example, Henss (1995) found that a 0.8 WHR, and not a 0.7 WHR, was rated as the most attractive figure. Underweight figures were rated as more attractive than normal weights, while overweight figures and the figures with the largest WHR were still rated as the least attractive. Puhl and Boland (2001) also found that a model with a higher WHR (0.86) was rated as more attractive than a model with a 0.7 WHR. DeSoto and Kopp (2003) challenged the findings that men preferred higher WHR by critiquing the type of stimuli used. They claimed that the use of two-dimensional photographs did not accurately display the true WHR of a woman, because the pictures may not fully capture the bulk of curviness if it comes from the derriere. This is an important point because others would naturally be viewed in three-dimensional form and not two-dimensional form throughout the course of human evolution.

Considering the above, it was quite amazing that Singh first demonstrated that a WHR of 0.7 represented the ideal female body measure by presenting rather rudimentary line drawn figures to raters (Singh 1993; Singh & Luis,

1995). Subsequent studies have presented more realistic color photographs as stimuli that were digitally manipulated to depict a lower and higher WHR, and these studies have also shown that lower WHR related to attractiveness (Henss, 2000). Even more sophisticated 3-D images have since been presented to raters to evaluate ideal WHR measures. Among Caucasian observers examining 3-D images where both the size and shape of their ideal partner could be manipulated, it was found that women thought the ideal female body should have a body mass index (BMI) = 18.9 and WHR = 0.70, and this was very similar to the ideal partner set by men which was a BMI = 18.8 and WHR= 0.73 (Crossley, Cornelissen, & Tovée, 2012). The authors of this study noted how these ideals represented a lower BMI than the actual BMI of 39 out of the 40 women examined. The ideal male body set by the men was BMI = 25.9 and WHR= 0.87, which was also very similar to the ideal partner determined by the women of a BMI = 24.5 and WHR= 0.86. While there tends to be agreement between male and female observers, WHR seems to have differing importance to the sexes. Male observers seemed to favor low WHR because they found the images to be desirable, sexy, and attractive, whereas women favored low WHR because of perceived health differences (Rempala & Garvey, 2007).

The perception of a WHR of 0.7 as ideal (Henss, 2000; Singh, 1993a, 1993b, 1994a; Singh & Suwardi, 1995) does not seem to be significantly affected by the raters' ethnicity, gender, or age (Markey et al., 2002; Singh & Suwardi, 1995). In fact, preferences for both WHR and body mass index (BMI) do not vary with observer age (George, Swami, Cornelissen, & Tovée, 2008). Even blind men who have no previous visual experience exhibit a preference for low female WHR when assessing female body shapes through touch alone (Karremans, Frankenhuis, & Arons, 2010). The fact that the assessment of WHR extends beyond our visual sense highlights its importance as a significant, evolved marker of mate value.

Attractiveness judgements showing a preference for a 0.7 WHR tend to happen quickly and spontaneously even when images are presented for brief exposure times or in rapid succession (Schützwohl, 2006). Even small, incremental changes in WHR affected perceptions of attractiveness in a similar direction as when examining differences using larger increments of WHR (Rempala & Garvey, 2007). This is an indication of the sensitivity of our detection system for evaluating WHR.

Not only does WHR influence men's perceptions of attractiveness, but it also influences their memory of that woman. Men had a superior memory for the appearance and biographical information of women with attractive WHRs (range 0.6-0.8; Fitzgerald, Horgan, & Himes, 2016). This finding embodies what the authors referred to as men having an "adaptive memory," a tendency to remember information that has greater adaptive value to them to make better fitness-related, mate selection decisions.

WHR and Desirability

WHR plays a large role in the mate selection by men. WHR was shown to be a strong predictor of male ratings of the female target's desirability to date, to have as a one-time sexual encounter, and to have as a longer-term relationship partner (Braun & Bryan, 2006). In our study (Hughes & Gallup, 2003), we found that women with low WHR reported sexual intercourse at an earlier age, more sexual partners, more extrapair copulations (EPC), and having engaged in more instances of intercourse with people who were involved in another relationship (i.e., having themselves been EPC partners). Perhaps because men find women with low WHR so attractive, these women are frequently sought after as sexual partners. Women also tend to get jealous of other women if that potential rival has a relatively low WHR (Dijkstra & Buunk, 2001; & Buunk & Dijkstra, 2005), as low WHR women pose more of a competitive threat. Buss, Shackelford, Choe, Buunk, and Dijkstra (2005) documented that women from the United States, Korea, and the Netherlands reported more distress over same-sex rivals who had a more attractive body than they have.

The influence of WHR on overall mating patterns has also been observed at the population level. Across 68 countries examined worldwide, the proportion of divorced individuals in a population correlated positively with sexual dimorphism in WHR, negatively with female WHR and had no correlation with male WHR (Chiappa & Singh, 2017). This finding further demonstrates the role WHR plays in men's mating strategies. It also may be the case that females with lower WHR will divorce more frequently than women with high WHR because they have more opportunity to find another mate.

One study examined the potential role of WHR preference in the assortative mating hypothesis of autistic spectrum disorder (ASD). Increased levels of prenatal androgens (testosterone) have been implicated in the etiology of ASD (Baron-Cohen, Knickmeyer, & Belmonte, 2005; Manning, Baron-Cohen, Wheelwright, & Sanders, 2001). Fathers of children with autistic spectrum disorder had not showed a preference for women with a lower WHR approximating the 0.7 range that is associated with lower circulating testosterone in women (Brosnan & Walker, 2009). Thus, a father's preferences for mates would have placed their offspring in position of having a higher prenatal testosterone environment which would put offspring at a higher risk for ASD.

Advertising WHR

Given the appeal of an image of exaggerated hips relative to waist, women find ways to highlight these features. Women seem to advertise their WHR when they walk and tend to sway their hips more in a lateral motion (Mather & Murdoch, 1994). Consider the Hollywood movie star Marilyn Monroe, thought to be the epitome of beauty and femininity. Her "walking" scene in the movie *Niagara*, where her hips markedly swayed side to side, is considered one of the most iconic scenes of all time. It has been reported that Marilyn would cut one of her heels shorter than the other to allow for her hips to sway even more as she walked (Summers, 1985).

Marilyn Monroe, known to be very intelligent in addition to beautiful, was onto something. Experimentally, it was demonstrated that when a woman had a wider range of hips motion while walking, it created a perception of an exaggerated WHR, and she was therefore seen as being even more attractive by men (Doyle, 2009). Bodies in motion can provide a dynamic source of information important in the assessment of a woman's WHR and should be incorporated in future research versus just examining still photos of figures.

The human voice also can advertise WHR. In our research, we found that women with attractive voices tend to have lower WHR (Hughes, Dispenza, & Gallup, 2004). In fact, people can accurately estimate the WHR of women simply from hearing their voice sample (Hughes, Harrison, & Gallup, 2009). We had independent raters listen to a speaker recite numbers from one to 10 and choose that speaker's WHR from an array of line drawings. Participants were able to select the correct WHR for the speaker at a rate greater than chance (Hughes et al., 2009). Thus, it appears that a woman's WHR is advertised through both her walk and talk.

Perceptions of WHR

Observer Traits. Men's own physical quality and desirability affect their evaluation of women's figures based upon WHR. Lower mate value men, as determined by their self-rating of being less desirable and who had below-typical WHR, were less discriminating in their assessment of women's WHR, whereas men with higher mate values gave higher ratings to female models who had a WHR of 0.72 or lower (Brase & Walker, 2004). These individual differences in ratings probably do not reflect actual alterations in attractiveness preferences per se; rather, it is the result of the observer taking into account his own mate value and therefore targeting the most attractive individual that he could be successful in courting.

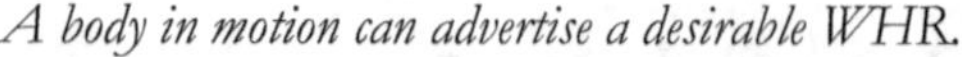

A body in motion can advertise a desirable WHR.

Symmetry and WHR. Perception of WHR also seems to be influenced by body symmetry when evaluating women. When women were assessed using rear nude photos, the effect of WHR on attractiveness ratings were more negatively associated as body asymmetry decreased (Perilloux, Webster, & Gaulin, 2010). Nevertheless, female figures with low WHRs were judged to be more attractive than figures with high WHRs, regardless of their degree of breast asymmetry (Singh, 1995). Needless to say, figures with low WHR and symmetrical breasts were deemed the most attractive and healthiest of all figures examined. Again, receiver psychology shows that what is attractive informs the unconscious motivation to choose the best potential reproductive partner.

Beyond Subjective Ratings

Evidence for men's preferences for WHR extends beyond just subjective ratings of attractiveness. For instance, men show activation in the reward centers of the brain (e.g., nucleus accumbens, anterior cingulate cortex) when viewing nude female bodies surgically altered to express the ideal 0.7 WHR (Platek & Singh, 2010). Stated another way, viewing a woman with an ideal body proportion affects men's brains like taking an addictive drug does. Alternatively, men's neural reward centers were unaffected when viewing changes in women's BMI. There is also electrophysiological evidence that perceived sexual attraction of female bodies varies according to WHR. Male viewers showed increases in event-related potential (ERPs) (i.e., increases in cognitive and sensory processing in the brain) when viewing female figures that had a WHR of 0.7, particularly if those figures were displayed as nude rather than clothed and shown as front view versus back view (Zotto & Pegna, 2017).

Men also spend a greater amount of time visually fixating on women's WHR and breasts relative to other body regions. These data are derived from studies that utilize eye-tracking equipment to record visual fixations, dwell times, and initial fixations when examining pictures of women (Dixson, Grimshaw, Linklater, & Dixson, 2011). Interestingly, men looked more often and for longer periods of time at women's breasts regardless of the their WHR, but they rated women with a WHR of 0.7 as the most attractive regardless of their breast size.

Despite this evidence for visual fixation of a woman's WHR, another study found that patterns of eye movements when recording where observers look to assess women's WHR did not correspond to where they looked when assessing attractiveness. Rather, it appeared that the same regions that male and female observers fixated upon when assessing body fat were the same places they looked when judging attractiveness. In contrast, WHR fixations showed a different pattern from the attractiveness fixations and covered different body features (Cornelissen, Hancock, Kiviniemi, George, & Tovée, 2009). These findings question whether an assessment of WHR is actually being made directly during attractiveness judgments.

Cultural Influences

Some researchers claim that preferences for WHR vary with the ecology/environment as demonstrated in some cross-cultural examinations. For instance, Hadza men who live as hunter-gatherers in Tanzania showed a preference for heavier women regardless of WHR (Wetsman & Marlowe, 1999), and subsequent analyses of this group showed that they actually preferred high WHRs (Marlowe & Wetsman, 2001). In this subsistence-oriented society, thinness probably indicates poorer health and the inability to sustain the energetically expensive work required of the women to forage. Thus, men tend to prefer women with more fat to spare and realize that a woman who is too thin may have less capacity to support pregnancy and lactation.

Similarly, the Shiwiar men who live in the Ecuadorian Amazonia and come from another forager-horticulturist society seem to use both WHR and body weight in their assessments of female sexual attractiveness (Sugiyama, 2004). The Shiwiar tend to prefer not only higher-body-fat women, but also women with higher WHR figures because they appeared to weigh the most. Nevertheless, when differences in body weight were minimized, Shiwiar men exhibited a preference for WHR lower than the mean of local woman.

Another study examining the Hazda of Tanzania showed that the men preferred a lower profile WHR that had greater protruding buttocks than did American men, but preferred higher frontal WHR than American men (Marlowe, Apicella, & Reed, 2005). This disparity in overall WHR may not be that different between these two cultures. Rather, they differ in terms of desiring a woman either with wider hips or with more protruding buttocks. It may be the case that people living in a harsher environment prefer signals of formidability compared to signals of fertility (see Batres & Perrett, 2014).

When examining preferences for women's weight and body shape between samples from Britain and Greece, BMI was found to be the primary determinant of women's physical attractiveness in both cultures, whereas WHR emerged as a significant predictor for only the Greek sample but not the British sample (Swami, Antonakopoulos, Tovée, & Furnham, 2006). Swami and colleagues concluded that certain cultural ideals and gender roles accounted for these variations of perception of the female body.

There are known cultural variations for average measures for WHR of both men and women which may contribute to any differences seen in WHR preferences across cultures. For instance, when examining 19 different populations, women in Czech Republic had the highest WHR, whereas women in Perth had the lowest WHR, and the range of the mean values across populations varied substantially for waist and hip circumference (Molarius, Seidell, Sans, Toumilehto, & Kuulasmaa, 1999). As an example of one such population where measures may influence perception, Polish participants showed a preference for underweight women (BMI = 17.3) with a small WHR, with men preferring a 0.7 WHR and women preferring even lower WHR at 0.66 (Kościński, 2013).

Still, Singh (2002) asserted that WHR is not a byproduct of modern cultural influence, and he claims cross-cultural data reliably indicates male preferences for low WHR in women. Other investigations have also emphasized how various cultural groups use similar criteria for judging the ideal woman's body shape, and only body weight was variable. For example, Indonesian men, African-American men, and Caucasian men all rated women's figures similarly whereby they found the most normal weight figures with a feminine WHR to be the most attractive and youthful and did not judge overweight figures as attractive or healthy regardless of their WHR (Singh & Luis, 1995).

Another study had shown that African-American men were more likely to choose heavier figures as ideal than Caucasian American men did, but both ethnic groups chose figures with a low WHR as ideal, with African American men more likely to choose those with an even lower WHR (Freedman, Carter, Sbrocco, & Gray, 2004).

Furnham, McClelland, and Omer (2003) also found little cross-cultural difference in the preference for a WHR of 0.7 when rating women's figures, rather, the cross-cultural difference lied with respect to weight preferences. In another investigation, both British and Kenyan participants favored lighter figures over heavier figures, but the British participants thought the heavier figures had greater fecundity while the Kenyans gave higher fecundity ratings to the lighter figures. Similarly, participants recruited from Greece, Uganda, and the United Kingdom rated figures with a 0.7 WHR in the light weight category as attractive, healthy, fertile, youthful and willingness to engage in short- and long-term relationships (Furnham, Moutafi, & Baguma, 2002). The only cultural difference was that Ugandans also showed a preference for 0.5 WHR in the heavy weight category. What we can glean from these cross-cultural examinations is that preferences for low WHR seem consistent, but preferences for body weight tends to vary across cultures.

WHR and Health

WHR is a predictor of several diseases and is used to determine health risks such as for cardiovascular disorders, Type 2 diabetes, hypertension, gall bladder disease, and endometrial, ovarian and breast cancer (Folsom, et al., 1993; Huang, Willet, and Colditz, 1999; Misra, and Vikram, 2003; Sayeed et al., 2003; Singh, 1993; Tseng, 2008; Wang & Hoy, 2004).

WHR is such a strong predictor of cardiovascular disease for both men and women that precise predictions can be made in terms of risk based on slight changes in WHR. Every 0.01 increase in WHR is associated with a 5% increase risk of future cardiovascular events when adjusting for age and cohort characteristics (de Koning., Merchant, Pogue, & Anand, 2007). When examining adult Tehranian men, WHR was shown to be a better screening measure for cardiovascular risk factors than other anthropometric indicators such as BMI, waist circumference, and waist-to-height ratio in (Esmaillzadeh, Mirmiran, & Azizi, 2004). Likewise, WHR was one of the strongest obesity indicators related to cardiovascular risks in a sample of middle-aged Finnish men and women (Hu, Tuomilehto, Silventoinen, Barengo, & Jousilahti, 2004). Because WHR has also been shown to be the best single indicator of cardiovascular risk factors, researchers have recommended that health professionals should include waist measurements in their routine clinical examination of adult patients.

WHR is also an integral part of one's cardiovascular profile as relates to cholesterol levels which can influence cardiovascular risk. Changes in middle-aged women's WHR over a three-year period correlated with both decreases in HDL and with activity (Wing, Matthews, Kuller, Meilahn, & Plantinga, 1991). When considering all ages combined, the optimal cut-off points for cardiovascular risk was having a 0.9 WHR for men and 0.8 WHR for women (Dobbelsteyn, Joffres, MacLean, Flowerdew & The Canadian Heart Health Surveys Research Group, 2001).

Just as with the assessment of cardiovascular risks, it is recommended that the assessment of chronic kidney disease should also utilize WHR rather than BMI as an anthropomorphic measure of obesity. WHR has a strong association with increased risk of reduced kidney function/disease and mortality, as opposed to BMI (Elsayed et al., 2008).

Waist-to-height ratio has also shown to be a better obesity index than body mass index and waist-to-hip ratio for predicting diabetes, hypertension, and lipidemia (lipids in the blood) (Sayeed et al., 2003). Moreover, WHR was directly related to breast cancer mortality in postmenopausal women (but not in premenopausal women) after adjusting for age, BMI, family history, estrogen receptor status, tumor stage diagnosis and treatment (Borugian et al., 2003).

It is important to consider ethnic differences in WHR and how they related to ascertaining cutoff values for certain health risks. For instance, there is some evidence to suggest that people of Asian descent should have a lower waist circumference cutoff than Europeans, whereas it may be appropriate for African American, Hispanic, and Middle Eastern populations to use the same current cutoffs for Europeans. However, the evidence is far from conclusive (see Lear, James, Ko, & Kumanyika, 2010). Further, unlike in other populations, some Asian cultures examined showed no evidence that WHR predicts type 2 diabetes better than BMI (Qiao & Nyamdorj, 2010). Evidently, there are cultural and genetic differences that contribute to incidence rates across different populations.

Because lower WHR is associated with a number of health and fertility benefits, it seems that men use this as an important cue when selecting a mate, especially for men who exhibit high levels of disgust to pathogens (i.e., pathogen avoidance). Men's pathogen disgust was positively associated with their preferences for lower WHR female partners (Lee, Brooks, Potter, Brendan, & Zietsch, 2015). Similarly, attractiveness judgements and judgement reaction times based on WHR had related more closely to health than to fecundity or pregnancy judgements (Schützwoh, 2006). Men want to select mates who are healthy, and WHR connotes health in women. In the eye of the beholder, those judging someone with a lower WHR as more attractive are, ultimately, being drawn to a healthier partner.

WHR and Psychological Functioning

In addition to its relation to physical health, evidence suggests WHR is associated with psychological and cognitive functioning. As an example, Hintsanen et al. (2010) found that WHR was positively associated with a higher fearful attachment style that is characterized by the tendency to fear rejection and avoid desired close relationships.

A large-scale, cross-sectional study showed that among older women aged 65-79 who had a low WHR, the higher their BMI, the poorer cognitive function (Kerwin et al., 2010). This relationship was not the case for similar aged women who had a high WHR. Typically having more central fat mass (a high WHR), was associated with higher cognitive function. Interestingly, another study found that female figures with higher WHRs (0.9 and 1.0) were in fact perceived as more intelligent than those with lower WHR (Furnham, Petrides, & Constantinides, 2005).

In contrast, Lassek and Gaulin (2008) showed that women with lower WHRs and their offspring have significantly higher scores on tests of cognitive ability. In addition, offspring of low-WHR teen mothers had children with fewer information processing issues than what is typically seen of children of teen moms. As underscored by Lassek and Gaulin, these findings show that WHR may be indicative of assets during neurodevelopment, providing further insight into men's evolved preferences for low WHR women.

Waist-to-hip ratio (WHR) is an index of many health, fertility, and psychological traits.

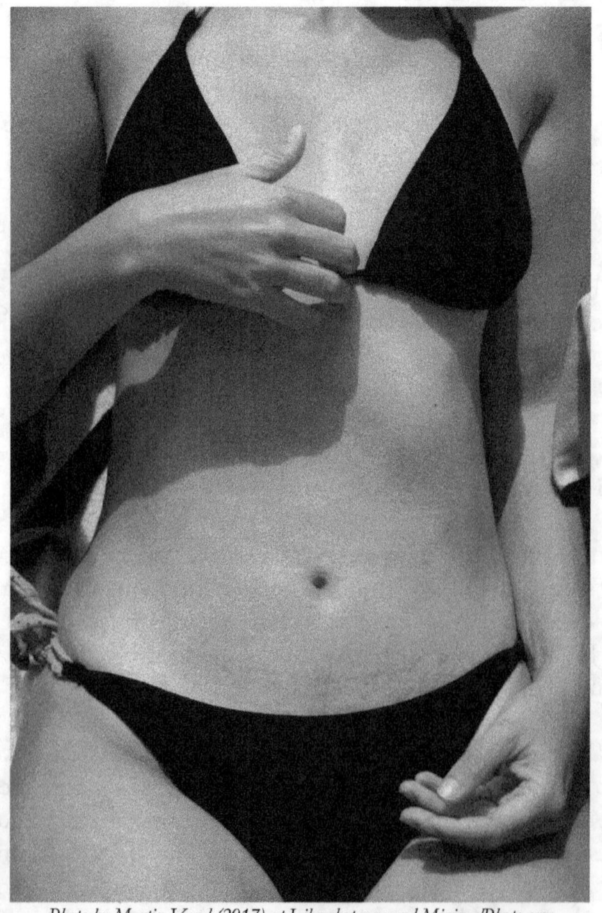

Photo by Martin Vorel (2017) at Libreshot.com and MinimalPhoto.com

WHR and Reproductive Status

WHR provides many cues to a women's reproductive status and can be used to index a female's reproductive potential. For instance, WHR was found to significantly associate with history of infertility, number of live births, age at first live birth, and replacement estrogen use (Kaye, Folsom, Prineas, Potter, & Gapstur, 1990). Because circulating levels of estrogen and testosterone in females affect WHR, it is measure that is directly linked to fertility, reproductive age, and reproductive capability and measures of WHR can provide information regarding one's hormonal profile.

A narrow waist signals that a female is not currently pregnant and WHR had a significant effect on participants' judgements of the pregnancy of the stimuli figures (Furnham & Reeves, 2006). Broad hips relative to a waist can also feature the ability for a woman to bear children (Hughes & Gallup, 2003), as often referenced as having "birthing hips."

There is evidence that higher WHR women may have difficulty conceiving. Women with higher WHRs have more irregular menstrual cycles (van Hooff et al., 2000) which could present some difficulty for timing conception. Further, married women with a higher WHR had more difficulty becoming pregnant and had their first live birth at a later age than married women with lower WHR (Kaye, Folsom, Prineas, & Gapstur, 1990). The probability of successful pregnancy induction is also affected by WHR; women with higher WHR (> 0.8) had lower pregnancy rates than women with lower WHR for in-vitro fertilization procedures (Waas et al., 1997). Women who participated in donor insemination programs also had a lower probability of conception if their WHR was greater than 0.8, after controlling for age, BMI, and parity (Zaadstra et al., 1993). It was speculated that the increased testosterone production of women with high WHR had impacted the viability and development of the embryo.

WHR may also be indicative of a woman's ovulatory status. For instance, naturally cycling women tend to gain a small amount of weight as ovulation nears which allows for their WHR to decrease during this time (Kirchengast & Gartner, 2002). The fact that a woman's WHR is lower during ovulation as compared to other phases of the menstrual cycle (Singh, Davis, & Randall, 2000), makes her appear more attractive during a time when she is likely to conceive. These patterns do not occur in women on hormonal contraceptives since they are no longer ovulating mid-cycle. However, cyclical variations in WHR is up for some debate. Other studies were unable to confirm that women's WHR were lower near ovulation and that it is a reliable cue for ovulatory status (Bleske-Rechek et al., 2011).

Because WHR is related to a number of reproductive outcomes for women, it makes sense that perception of female fecundity maps onto measures of WHR. This is indeed the case. Lower WHR female figures were judged to have greater fecundity across several weight categories (Tassinary & Hansen, 1998). Just as with ratings of attractiveness, the female figures judged to be the most fecund were those in the moderate weight category with a 0.7 WHR.

WHR and Age

WHR is also good indicator of age. In both sexes, the most prominent trend for increasing WHR was observed in those who were over the age of 45 (Lahti-Koski, Pietinen, Männistö, & Vartianien , 2000). Especially for women who undergo menopause, the tendency for more central body shape to develop with age is well-established and older women tend to accumulate more central fat distribution and increased WHR (Taylor, Keil, Gold, Williams, Goudling, 1998). Compared with premenopausal women, postmenopausal women have a wider waist circumference, a higher WHR, and had five times the chance of having central adiposity than premenopausal women, even after controlling for BMI and other confounding factors (Donato, Fuchs, Oppermann, Bastos, & Spritzer, 2006). Because women are not fertile after menopause which takes place around age 50 (Gold, 2011), determining age from WHR allows a partner to discern a viable mate.

WHR and Body Weight

WHR tends to increase not only with age but also with body mass index (BMI) in both men and women (Laws, Terry, & Barrett-Connor, 2011). BMI tends to correlate with the size of the chest and waist in men and with the hips and bust in women (Wells, Treleaven, & Cole, 2007).

Singh (1994a) demonstrated that heavier female figures with low WHR were judged as more attractive and healthier than thinner figures with higher WHR. Based on this data, Singh concluded that female attractiveness and perceptions of ideal female shape are more influenced by WHR than overall body size. Furnham, Swami, and Shah (2006) also found that the effects of WHR on attractiveness were greater than body weight. Another unique way that examined how WHR influences attractiveness judgements independent of BMI was to evaluate the before and after photos of women who had undergone micro-fat grafting surgery (Singh & Randall, 2007). Participants judged post-operative women with lower WHRs as more attractive than their pre-operative photos and this was independent of the women's BMI and whether the woman gained or lost weight after the surgery.

It should be noted that some researchers have stressed that BMI is a much more critical factor than WHR for attractiveness assessments (Kościński, 2013; Tassinary & Hansen, 1998; Swami, 2006), and some researchers have found that the effects of BMI were stronger than WHR for both attractiveness and youthfulness ratings (Furnham, Petrides, & Constantinides, 2005). Swami and colleagues (2006) showed that regardless of cultural setting, BMI was the primary determinant of women's attractiveness. In addition to judging attractiveness, the effects of women's body weight were also considerably stronger than the effects of body shape for perceptions of a woman's emotional stability, family-orientedness, agreeableness, and conscientiousness (Henss, 1995). Given the mixed evidence in the literature, it would be prudent to assume that the effects of BMI and WHR are interdependent and need to be studied jointly rather than in isolation.

WHR and Breasts

Women with both large breasts and narrow waists were rated as youthful, attractive, and were desired as mates for both short- and long-term relationships (Singh & Young, 1995). Large breasts enhance attractiveness ratings when evaluating both slender and heavy female figures so long as those figures have a low WHR (Furnham, Dias, & McClekkand, 1998). In other words, if a figure had high WHR, large breasts actually decreased attractiveness ratings with the one exception of men rating heavier women. In this instance, it was possible that a large bustline made the female figure appear to have a lower WHR than she actually did, thus allowing the female figure to be perceived as more attractive.

Another study found no direct effects of preferences for breast size unless considering its interaction with a female figure's WHR (Furnham, Swami, & Shah, 2006). The fact that men rate a 0.7 WHR figure as most attractive independently of breast size, even though they spent more time looking at the breasts (as examined using eye-tracking equipment), further confirms the notion that the WHR is a key feature in the appraisal of physical attractiveness of female bodies by male observers (Dixson., Grimshaw, Linklater, & Dixson, 2011).

Perception of breast and WHR attractiveness also tends to be influenced by the observer's culture as well as the target female's ethno-cultural affiliation. For instance, South African men rated high-WHR black figures with large breasts and the high-WHR white figures with small breasts as most attractive whereas British Caucasians and British Africans showed a preference for high-WHR black figures with small breasts and high-WHR white figures with large breasts (Swami, Jones, Einon, & Furnham , 2009).

Male WHR

What about the WHR of men? The WHR of men does not appear to be as important in women's preferences of male body shape as it is for men's preferences of female body shape. Nonetheless, women typically prefer male figures that are of normal weight and have a WHR in the typical male range (with a WHR of either 0.9 or 1.0) and judged them to be not only the most attractive, but the healthiest (Asthana, 2000; Singh, 1995). Despite men who have WHR in the typical male range, women cared more about the weight of a man, and all underweight and overweight male figures were not judged to be highly attractive or healthy.

Nonetheless, male WHR factors into female mate choice and there are a few reasons why this may be the case. Just as with women, WHR can reflect a man's hormonal profile. It has been shown that central obesity (as defined as waist circumference > 100 cm or WHR > 0.95) was related to longitudinal change in sex steroid hormones in men (specifically dehydroepiandrosterone sulphate, or DHEAS) whereas elevated BMI was not (Derby, Zilber, Brambilla, Morales, & McKinlay, 2006). As such, WHR can be indicative of a man's age, because with age men's central adiposity increases and there is also a decline in testosterone. WHR in men also predicts social dominance and leadership behavior. For instance, when placed in a group setting, men with higher WHR were rated by other group members as behaving more like a leader, was rated by independent observers as being more dominant, and they even rated their own behavior as being more assertive (Campbell, Simpson, Steward, & Manning, 2002). Women are likely to find these dominant men as attractive mates.

Behavioral Determinants of WHR

Despite the strong influence of hormones on WHR, several behavioral indices can also influence measures of WHR. For instance, an increase in WHR is associated with heavy alcoholic drinking and smoking presumably since those behaviors increase levels of adrenal cortisol production which is linked to central weight gain (Laws, Terry, & Barrett-Connor, 2011). The association between drinking and WHR tends to be stronger in women than men, regardless of the specific type of alcoholic beverage consumed (i.e., wine or beer). Likewise, a study conducted in France also showed that alcohol consumption is positively associated with WHR and waist girth and was independent of BMI for both men and women (Dallongeville et al., 1998). Further investigations of the connection between alcohol use and WHR revealed that the two have a J-shaped relationship such that those who drink small amounts of alcohol per day actually show a lower WHR than non-drinkers, but drinking larger amounts per day (with exact amounts dependent upon the type of alcoholic drinks consumed) had increased WHR in an exponential manner (Lukasiewics, Mennen, Bertrais, Arnault, Preziosi, Galan, & Hercberg, 2005).

Exercise also seems to influence measures of WHR. The WHR of men and women who reported regular exercise was lower than those who did not (Laws et al., 2011) and WHR was significantly and negatively associated with physical activity (Kaye, Folsom, Prineas, Potter, & Gapstur, 1990). Unlike exercise, however, when it comes to diet, there is little association between dietary factors and WHR with the exception of alcohol consumption (Laws et al., 2011). WHR is also negatively associated with education (Kaye et al., 1990). Nonetheless, it appears that only a marginal amount of WHR variation can be explained by such factors as education level or lifestyle and age and BMI account for the most variation in WHR (Lahti-Koski, Pietinen, Männistö, & Vartianien, 2000). Needless to say, even the marginal associations between certain lifestyle factors with WHR suggest that the deposition of fat in the abdominal region as compared to the gluteal region is influenced by factors other than just hormones and/or genetics. Thus, when selecting a mate based upon the WHR, you may not only be selecting someone with a good hormonal profile, but also one with a healthy lifestyle.

Shoulder-to-hip Ratio (SHR)

A body ratio that plays particular importance in men's attractiveness is shoulder-to-hip ratio (SHR), or the relative width of the shoulders to the hips. This is a measure of upper body size and mass. A high SHR would signify broad shoulders with narrower hips, indicative of a "V" shape. For men, measures of SHR are of importance because they correlate positively to testosterone levels (Kasperk et al., 1997) and are related to both muscle development (Evans, 1972) and to skeletal morphology (Kasperk et al., 1997). Accordingly, there were likely selective pressures for men to evolve upper body mass and strength, in part, to have better fighting ability for male-male competition, better locomotion for sport/hunting, and a greater ability to provide protection of their mates (Frederick & Haselton, 2007; Hughes & Gallup, 2003; Pazhoohi, Hosseinchari, & Doyle, 2012). Whereas measures of the waist are primarily influenced by abdominal fatness, the breadth of the shoulders is more closely related to physique and lean mass (Wells, 2009). Thus, unlike women's shape that tends to shift across the lifespan due to WHR, male upper body shape tends to remain relatively more stable (Wells, Treleaven, & Cole, 2007).

Dominance. Shoulder-to-hip ratio (SHR) is a physical feature that has been linked to dominance. Men perceive other men with high SHR as more dominant and men tend to pay more attention to the shoulders of potential rivals (Buunk & Dijkstra, 2005). Men are also more jealous of other men with high SHR and are more likely to view them as potential rivals (Dijkstra & Buunk, 2001). Even women with high SHR evoked more jealousy by other female competitors and were perceived as physically and socially dominant than women with low SHR (Dijkstra & Buunk, 2001). Further, men who have broader shoulders tend to have higher hand-grip strength (shown to be a reliable sign of physical health and muscle function) who, in turn, tend to be more aggressive than men with low hand grip strength values (Gallup, White, & Gallup, Jr. 2007).

Females in the ancestral environment would have been far more gracile (smaller, fragile) compared to robust males, and compared to modern women. It would have been beneficial for an ancestral female to choose a dominant male as a partner for protection of her and her offspring. We are certainly not saying that a modern woman "needs a man" to survive. We are saying that in the environment of evolutionary adaptedness (EEA), a female who had male protection would be more likely to survive than a female who did not have male protection. Therefore, what endures in women today is a preference for a higher male SHR, a phenotypic indicator of dominance.

Attractiveness. SHR is a critical factor that influences male body attractiveness (Dijkstra & Buunk, 2001; Mautz Wong, Peters & Jennions, 2013; Wells, 2009). Both sexes tend to judge male attractiveness by their shoulder width and upper body taper (Lavrakas, 1975; Horvath 1979). In fact, men's SHR accounted for a much larger proportion of variance (79.6%) in female attractiveness ratings of men's bodies than did men's height and penis size (Mautz et al., 2013).

Ideal ranges of SHR have been gleaned from measures of fashion models featured in style magazines who were wearing bathing suits (Dijkstra & Buunk, 2001). From these measures, male fashion models had an average SHR measure of 1.39 ($SD = 0.09$) as opposed members of the general population with an average SHR of 1.21. Likewise, female fashion models also had higher SHR ($M = 1.23$, $SD = 0.05$) than other women (SHR =

1.08). Whereas these data suggest that larger SHR is attractive for women as it is for men, there is little empirical evidence to demonstrate that female SHR is important for mate selection. If having a higher SHR makes a woman slightly more attractive, it may just be that broader shoulders give the appearance of having a relatively smaller waist. Women with broader SHR are viewed as more dominant (Dijkstra & Buunk, 2001), which may or not be seen as an attractive trait by men. If women with broader shoulders appear more dominant, then it makes sense why woman started to wear shoulder pads as a fashion trend in the 1980s when they began to enter the male-dominated work force.

Women are attracted to men with a higher SHR, or a tapering "V" shape

Image courtesy of www.powerathletehq.com
Providers of strength and conditioning programming

Several studies have examined women's preferences for men with broader shoulders in different ways. For instance, Dixson, Halliwell, East, Wignarajah, and Anderson (2003) conducted a study where participants were presented with figures of men's backs and found that women were more attracted to the figure with a greater muscular, mesomorphic physique. Individuals with mesomorphic somatotypes are those that have large bones and broad shoulders (Sills, 1950). Likewise, when observing line drawings of men's physiques, both men and women thought men with broader shoulders and more muscular chests were more attractive

(Horvath, 1981). Shoup and Gallup (2008) took pictures of their male participants' faces, measured their SHR, and presented their photos to female participants to rate for attractiveness. They found that women rated the faces of men with high SHRs as attractive, despite the fact that they only viewed the men from the neck up.

Women with greater resource scarcity (i.e., low socioeconomic status) and who score high on ratings of pathogen disgust prefer men with even higher SHR (Lee, Brooks, Potter, Brendan, & Zietsch, 2015). The argument is that if environmental factors influence women's SHR preferences, then SHR must be an important cue of evolutionarily beneficial traits such as health, high pathogen avoidance, and the ability to acquire or compete for resources which could beneficial for women with resource scarcity.

In one of our own investigations, we (Hughes & Gallup, Jr., 2003) showed that men with high SHRs had more sexual opportunity; high SHR men tend to engage in sexual intercourse at an early age, have more sexual partners in their lifetime, have more affair partners, and were more likely to be selected by women involved in another relationship to serve as her affair partner (Hughes & Gallup, Jr., 2003; Gallup, White, & Gallup, Jr., 2007).

Interestingly, a study found that women used a similar measure of waist-to-shoulder ratio (WSR) as a standard for assessing the desirability male targets as potential one-time sexual partners, but not as longer-term partners (Braun & Bryan, 2006). In other words, women especially find men with a more "manly" tapering "V" body shape (i.e., larger shoulders and a smaller waist) to be more desirable for a one-time sexual encounter than those of shoulders and waist of nearly equal size.

So, why are women selecting men with broader shoulders as attractive mates? First, broad shoulders and narrow hips signal physical dominance (Dijkstra & Buunk, 2001) and masculinity in males (Evans, 1972; Lippa, 1983). Second, women could benefit by choosing a higher SHR partner because of their health and the thought that they are less likely to succumb to disease, can avoid pathogen transmission, and consequently, their offspring could inherit these health benefits (Frederick & Haselton, 2007). Third, body shape can signal both immunocompetence and hormonal quality because it is dependent upon testosterone (Kasperk et al., 1997). Fourth, it is possible that men with larger SHR are displaying other traits that women find attractive. For example, in a sample of Iranian men, as men's SHR increased, so did their body esteem and self-efficacy (Pazhoohi, Hosseinchari, & Doyle, 2012). If men with greater SHR experience earlier sex and greater access to sex partners because women find their masculine physique attractive, then it would make sense that they develop a higher self-reported body esteem and self-efficacy. This, in turn, may make them even more attractive to women in a cyclical fashion.

Advertising SHR. Men seem to realize that their broad shoulders are of importance in female assessment, and they tend to exaggerate these features when they walk. When men walk, they tend to show greater motion of their shoulders and a larger extent of lateral sway of the upper body, "a swagger," than women do (Murray, Kory, & Sepic, 1970; Johnson et al., 2007). In fact, differences in lateral body sway are important in gender identification such that others expect that men will tend to swing their shoulders more side to side whereas women will tend to swing their hips more than shoulders when they walk (Mather & Murdoch, 1994).

What makes a male body "hot?"

Image courtesy of www.powerathletehq.com
Providers of strength and conditioning programming

SHR and Voice. Because men's SHR is influenced by testosterone (Kasperk et al., 1997), it seems to be linked to other features that are influenced by testosterone. Male voice is one such feature that is affected by sex hormones and testosterone produces lower pitched voices (Dabbs & Mallinger, 1999). The pitch (i.e., fundamental frequency) of a man's voice is negatively associated with SHR, such that men with larger upper body musculature tend to have lower-pitched voices (Evans, Neave, & Wakelin, 2006). Women prefer lower male voices (Feinberg, Jones, Little, Burt, & Perrett, 2005). As such, in our research, we found that ratings of voice attractiveness made by women positively correlates with SHR in men (Hughes, Dispenza, & Gallup, 2004). Interestingly, people can accurately estimate the SHR of men simply from hearing their voice sample (Hughes, Harrison, & Gallup, 2009). We found that when presented with a recorded male voice, listeners could select that person's body type from an array at a rate better than chance. Further, SHR is related to measures of formant dispersion in male voices and formant dispersion is often indicative of a man's body size (Evans et al., 2006).

Waist-to-chest Ratio (WCR)

Another proportional body measure that seems to influence the perception of attractiveness is waist-to-chest ratio (WCR), particularly for men. Men who have a narrower waist and broader chest (i.e., a low WCR) and show signs of muscularity are viewed by women as more attractive (e.g., Dixson et al., 2003; Franzoi & Herzog, 1987; Maisey, Vale, Cornelissen, & Tovée, 1999; Swami & Tovée, 2008). Simply put, greater chest muscularity is linked to higher attractiveness ratings (Hovath, 1981). In fact, WCR is more of a predictor of male attractiveness as rated by women (accounting for 56% variance) than is male BMI (accounting for only 12.7% variance) and male WHR (not a significant predictor; Maisey, Vale, Cornelissen, & Tovée, 1999). Likewise, among men from urban settings, WCR was the primary component of male attractiveness ratings, with BMI playing a smaller role and WHR not reaching significance (Swami & Tovée , 2005). Thus, it appears that it is the shape of the male body rather than the size of the male body is of importance for women's assessment of the physical features of men.

This male shape that women prefer is one that is consistent with physical strength and muscularity in the upper body. However, there seems to be a happy medium in terms of the levels of desired male masculinity (as defined by traits such as SHR, WCR, and facial masculinity) that women prefer. Women tend to think men with very high levels of masculinity (very low WCR) are unattractive because these men may be volatile, threatening, dangerous, and less likely to show commitment, whereas men with very low levels of masculinity (very high WCR) are unattractive because they are viewed as weak or submissive (Frederick & Haselton, 2007). When examining 3-D images made by Caucasian observers, the ideal female body determined by women was a WCR= 0.67, similar to the ideal partner set by men which was a WCR = 0.69 (Crossley, Cornelissen, & Tovée, 2012). The ideal male body set by the men was much higher at a WCR= 0.74, and the ideal partner set by the women which was a WCR = 0.77.

Similarly to women's assessments, when men evaluate other men, WCR is also a more important component in their assessment of male attractiveness than is body mass index (BMI; Swami & Tovée, 2008), demonstrating the importance that men place on upper body build when comparing to other men. Interestingly, gay men showed an even stronger preference for lower WCRs than heterosexual men when assessing the attractiveness of other men. This indicates a greater idealization of upper-body muscularity for potential same-sex mates. In addition to evaluations made by others, larger chest-to-waist ratios (CWR) positively correlate with self-ratings of men's own attractiveness levels (Weeden & Sabini, 2007).

Body Perceptions. Men with lower WCR are perceived as being more physically dominant, physically fit, and are more able to serve as protectors of their loved ones (Coy, Green, & Price, 2014). Alternatively, men who have greater WCR are victims of negative biases when evaluated by both sexes and are thought to be lazier, lonelier, and more likely to get teased than men with lower WCRs (Swami et al., 2008). This finding further demonstrates how those who are perceived as being unattractive can be stigmatized and falls in line with the well-known "what-is-beautiful-is-good" stereotype (Dion, Berscheid, & Walster, 1972). Further, when men's body parts are sexualized by the media, the focus of the objectification tends to be placed on how muscular and v-shaped the male bodies are and highlight the broad chests, narrow waists, and muscular arms (Frith & Gleeson, 2004; Gervais, Vescio, & Allen, 2012). Like women, when men see these muscular ideals in the media, they can become dissatisfied with their own body image which can lead to depression, eating disorders, steroid use, or excessive exercise (Harvey & Robinson, 2003; Morry & Staska, 2001; Tiggemann, Martins, & Kirkbride, 2007).

Individual Differences. Women's own mate value influences their preferences for male WCR. Women with a more attractive, lower volume-height index showed stronger preferences for attractive, lower WCR men, but no other female rater characteristics such as their WHR, self-perceived attractiveness, or sociosexuality (propensity toward casual sex) predicted the strength of preference for attractive male WCR (Price, Pound, Dunn, Hopkins, & Kang, 2013).

Self-Mate Value. Men's own mate value, as determined by their WCR, impacts their belief system. Men who have lower WCR and are more masculine tend to be less egalitarian in terms of believing that resources should be distributed equally in social groups (Price, Kang, Dunn, & Hopkins, 2011). This finding makes sense in that those who are more dominant and therefore have greater social status would benefit more from an environment of social inequality where they could reap the afforded benefits over others.

Women's Waist and Chest. For women, WCR does not appear to be of much importance when it comes to mate assessment as it is for men. WCR was not found to be a significant predictor of female attractiveness, especially when compared to BMI which accounted for more than 74% of variance in attractiveness ratings (Maisey, Vale, Cornelissen, & Tovée, 1999). Instead of considering measures of WCR for women (which is indicative of a sign of chest muscularity), an equivalent measure may be the examination of breast-to-underbreast ratio in relation to WHR. Women who have larger breasts (high breast-to-underbreast ratio) and narrower waists (low WHR) have higher fecundity rates as assessed by daily estrogen and progesterone levels, and this is the case especially during mid-cycle, which could increase the chances of conception (Jasieńska, Ziomkiewicz, Ellison, Lipson, & Thune, 2004). Hence, men tend to pay attention to the chest and waists of women because they serve as prominent cues to fecundity and health, rather than serve as an index of muscularity as it is for men.

Conclusion

The body shape of men and women as measured in ratios of the waist, hips, and chest are prominent morphological features related to attractiveness, desirability, health reproduction, age, sex, and hormonal profiles. Science has shown that a target's body morphology plays a prominent role in our perceptions of what we find is sexually attractive. These body measures are important for our capacity to select viable mates who possess adaptive traits. In other words, we are attracted to those whose bodies signal to us high mate value and thus, a greater likelihood of passing on our genes.

References

Asthana, S. (2000). Female judgement of male attractiveness and desirability for relationships: Role of waist-to-hip ratio (WHR). *Psycho-Lingua, 30*(1), 61-64.

Arechiga, J., Prado, C., Canto, M., and Carmenati, H. (2001). Women in transition-menopause and body composition in different populations. *Collective Anthropology, 25*, 443-448.

Baron-Cohen, S., Knickmeyer, R. C., & Belmonte, M. K. (2005). Sex differences in the brain: Implications for explaining autism. *Science, 310*, 819-823. doi:10.1126/science.1115455.

Batres, C., & Perrett, D. I. (2014). The influence of the digital divide on face preferences in El Salvador: People without internet access prefer more feminine men, more masculine women, and women with higher adiposity. *PLOS One, 9*(7), e100966. https://doi.org/10.1371/journal.pone.0100966

Bleske-Rechek, A., Harris, H. D., Denkinge, K., Webb, R. M., Erickson, L., & Nelson, L. A. (2011). Physical cues of ovulatory status: A failure to replicate enhanced facial attractiveness and reduced waist-to-hip ratio at high fertility. *Evolutionary Psychology, 9*(3), 336–353. https://doi.org/10.1177/147470491100900306

Borugian, M. J., Sheps, S. B., Kim-, C., Olivotto, I. A., Van Patten, C., Dunn, B. P., Coldman, A. J., Potter, J. D., Gallagher, R. P., & Hislop, T. G. (2003). Waist-to-hip ratio and breast cancer mortality. *American Journal of Epidemiology, 158*(10), 963-968. https://doi.org/10.1093/aje/kwg236

Björntorp, P. (1997). Body fat distribution, insulin resistance, and metabolic diseases. *Nutrition, 12*(9), 795-803. https://doi.org/10.1016/S0899-9007(97)00191-3

Brase, G. L., & Walker, G. (2004). Male sexual strategies modify ratings of female models with specific waist-to-hip ratios. *Human Nature, 15*(2), 209–224. https://doi.org/10.1007/s12110-004-1020-x

Braun, M. F., & Bryan, A. (2006). Female waist-to-hip and male waist-to-shoulder ratios as determinants of romantic partner desirability. *Journal of Social and Personal Relationships, 23*(5) 805-819. doi: 10.1177/0265407506068264

Brosnan, M., & Walker, I. (2009). A preliminary investigation into the potential role of waist hip ratio (WHR) preference within the assortative mating hypothesis of autistic spectrum disorders. *Journal of Autism and Developmental Disorders, 39*(1), 164-171. doi: 10.1007/s10803-008-0615-1

Buunk, B. P., & Dijkstra, P. (2005). A narrow waist versus broad shoulders: Sex and age differences in the jealousy-evoking characteristics of a rival's body build. *Personality and Individual Differences, 39*(2), 379-389. https://doi.org/10.1016/j.paid.2005.01.020

Buss, D. M., Shackelford, T. K., Choe, J., Buunk, B. P., Dijkstra, P. (2005). Distress about mating rivals. *Personal Relationships, 7*(3), 235-243. https://doi.org/10.1111/j.1475-6811.2000.tb00014.x

Campbell, L., Simpson, J. A., Stewart, M., & Manning, J. G. (2002). The formation of status hierarchies in leaderless groups: The role of male waist-to-hip ratio. *Human Nature, 13*(3), 345–362. https://doi.org/10.1007/s12110-

002-1019-0

Chiappa, P., & Singh, S. (2017). Sexual dimorphism in waist-to-hip ratio and divorce frequency in human populations. Evolutionary Behavioral Sciences, 11(3), 221-241. https://doi.org/10.1037/ebs0000100

Cornelissen, P. L., Hancock, P. J. B., Kiviniemi, V., George, H. R., & Tovée, M. J. (2009). Patterns of eye movements when male and female observers judge female attractiveness, body fat and waist-to-hip ratio. *Evolution and Human Behavior, 30*(6), 417–428. https://doi.org/10.1016/j.evolhumbehav.2009.04.003

Coy, A. E., Green, J. D., & Price, M. E. (2014). Why is low waist-to-chest ratio attractive in males? The mediating roles of perceived dominance, fitness, and protection ability. *Body Image, 11*(3), 282-289. doi:10.1016/j.bodyim.2014.04.003

Crossley, K. L., Cornelissen, P. L., & Tovée, M. J. (2012). What is an attractive body? Using an interactive 3D program to create the ideal body for you and your partner. *PLOS ONE, 7*(11), 1-11. https://doi.org/10.1371/journal.pone.0050601

Dabbs, J. J., & Mallinger, A. (1999). High testosterone levels predict low voice pitch among men. *Personality and Individual Differences,27*, 801–804.

Dallongeville, J., Marécaux, N., Ducimetière, P., Ferrières, J., Arveiler, D., Bingham, A., Ruidavets, J. B., Simon, C., & Amouyel, P. (1998). Influence of alcohol consumption and various beverages on waist girth and waist-to-hip ratio in a sample of French men and women. *International Journal of Obesity, 22*, 1178-1183. https://doi.org/10.1038/sj.ijo.0800744

de Koning, L., Merchant, A. T., Pogue, J., & Anand, S. S. (2007). Waist circumference and waist-to-hip ratio as predictors of cardiovascular events: meta-regression analysis of prospective studies. *European Heart Journal, 28*(7), 850-856. https://doi.org/10.1093/eurheartj/ehm026

Derby, C. A., Zilber, S., Brambilla, D., Morales, K. H., McKinlay, J. B., (2006) Body mass index, waist circumference and waist to hip ratio and change in sex steroid hormones: The Massachusetts Male Ageing Study. *Clinical Endocrinology, 63*(1) https://doi.org/10.1111/j.1365-2265.2006.02560.x

DeRidder, C. M., Bruning, P. F., Zonderland, M. L., Thijssen, J. H. H., Bonfrer, J. M. G., Blankenstein, M. A., et al. (1990). Body fat mass, body fat distribution, and plasma hormones in early puberty in females. *The Journal of Clinical Endocrinology and Metabolism, 70*(4), 888–893.

DeSoto, M. C., & Kopp, K. J. (2003). Predicting female attractiveness: A second look at thinness and waist-to-hip ratio. *Sexualities, Evolution & Gender, 5*(2), 83–88. https://doi.org/10.1080/14616660310001632572

Dijkstra, P., & Buunk, B. P. (2001). Sex differences in the jealousy-evoking nature of a rival's body build. *Evolution and Human Behavior, 22*, 335-341. https://doi.org/10.1016/S1090-5138(01)00070-8

Dion, K. K., Berscheid, E., & Walster, E. (1972). What is beautiful is good. *Journal of Personality and Social Psychology, 24*, 285–290.

Dixson, B. J., Grimshaw, G. M., Linklater, W. L., & Dixson, A. F. (2011). Eye-tracking of men's preferences for waist-to-hip ratio and breast size of women. *Archives of Sexual Behavior, 40*(1), 43-50.

https://doi.org/10.1007/s10508-009-9523-5

Dixson, A. F., Halliwell, G., East, R., Wignarajah, P., & Anderson, M. J. (2003). Masculine somatotype and hirsuteness as determinants of sexual attractiveness to women. *Archives of Sexual Behavior, 32*(1), 29-39. doi:10.1023/A:1021889228469

Dobbelsteyn, C. J., Joffres, M. R., MacLean, D. R., & Flowerdew, G. (2001). A comparative evaluation of waist circumference, waist-to-hip ratio and body mass index as indicators of cardiovascular risk factors. The Canadian Heart Health Surveys. *International Journal of Obesity, 25*, 652-661. https://doi.org/10.1038/sj.ijo.0801582

Donato, G. B., Fuchs, S. C., Oppermann, K., Bastos, C., & Spritzer, P. M. (2006). Association between menopause status and central adiposity measured at different cutoffs of waist circumference and waist-to-hip ratio. *The Journal of The North American Menopause Society, 13*(2), 280-285. https://doi.org/10.1097/01.gme.0000177907.32634.ae

Doyle, J. F. (2009). A woman's walk: Attractiveness in motion. *Journal of Social, Evolutionary, and Cultural Psychology, 3*(2), 81-92. http://dx.doi.org/10.1037/h0099329

Elbers, J. M. H., Asscheman, H., Seidell, J. C., Megens, A. J., & Gooren, L. J. G. (1997). Long-term testosterone administration increases visceral fat in female to male transsexuals. *The Journal of Clinical Endocrinology and Metabolism, 82*, 2044–2047.

Elsayed, E. F., Sarnak, M. J., Tighiuoart, H., Griffith, J. L., Kurth, T., Salem, D. N., Levey, A. S., & Weiner, D. E. (2008). Waist to hip ratio, body mass index and subsequent kidney disease and death. *American Journal of Kidney Diseases, 52*(1), 29-38. https://doi.org/10.1053/j.ajkd.2008.02.363

Esmaillzadeh, A., Mirmiran, P., & Azizi, F. (2004). Waist-to-hip ratio is a better screening measure for cardiovascular risk factors than other anthropometric indicators in Tehranian adult men. *International Journal of Obesity, 28*, 1325-1332. https://doi.org/10.1038/sj.ijo.0802757

Evans, R. B. (1972). Physical and biochemical characteristics of homosexual men. *Journal of Consulting and Clinical Psychology, 39*(1), 140-147. http://dx.doi.org/10.1037/h0033203

Evans, S., Neave, N., & Wakelin, D. (2006). Relationships between vocal characteristics and body size and shape in human males: An evolutionary explanation for a deep male voice. *Biological Psychology, 72*(2), 160-163. http://dx.doi.org/10.1016/j.biopsycho.2005.09.003

Evans, S., Neave, N., Wakelin, D., & Hamilton, C. (2008). The relationship between testosterone and vocal frequencies in human males. *Physiology and Behavior, 93*, 783-788. https://doi.org/10.1016/j.physbeh.2007.11.033

Feinberg, D. R., Jones, B. C., Little, A. C., Burt, D. M., & Perrett, D. (2005). Manipulations of fundamental and formant frequencies influence the attractiveness of human male voices. *Animal Behaviour, 69*, 561–568.

Fitzgerald, C. J., Horgan, T. G., & Himes, S. M. (2016). Shaping men's memory: The effects of a female's waist-to-hip ratio on men's memory for her appearance and biographical information. *Evolution and Human Behavior, 37*(6), 510–516.

https://doi.org/10.1016/j.evolhumbehav.2016.05.004

Folsom, A. R., Kaye, S. A., Sellers, T. A., Hong, C., Cerhan, J. R., Potter, J. D., & Prineas, R. (1993). Body fat distribution and 5-year risk of death in older women. *Journal of the American Medical Association, 269*, 483-487.

Franzoi, S. L., & Herzog, M. E. (1987). Judging physical attractiveness: What body aspects do we use? *Personality & Social Psychology Bulletin, 13,* 19-33.

Frederick, D. A., & Haselton, M. G. (2007). Why is muscularity sexy? Tests of the fitness indicator hypothesis. *Personality and Social Psychology Bulletin, 33*(8), 1167-1183.

Freedman, R. E. K., Carter, M. M., Sbrocco, T., & Gray, J. J. (2004). Ethnic differences in preferences for female weight and waist-to-hip ratio: A comparison of African American and White American college and community samples. *Eating Behaviors, 5*(3), 191–198. https://doi.org/10.1016/j.eatbeh.2004.01.002

Frith, H., & Gleeson, K. (2004). Clothing and embodiment: Men managing body image and appearance. *Psychology of Men & Masculinity, 5*, 40–48. doi:10.1037/1524-9220.5.1.40

Furnham, A., Dias, M., & McClelland, A. (1998). The role of body weight, waist-to-hip ratio, and breast size in judgements of female attractiveness. *Sex Roles, 39*(3-4), 331-326. https://doi.org/10.1023/A:1018810723493

Furnham, A., McClelland, A., & Omer, L. (2003). A cross-cultural comparison of ratings of perceived fecundity and sexual attractiveness as a function of body weight and waist-to-hip ratio. *Psychology, Health & Medicine, 8*(2), 219–230. https://doi.org/10.1080/1354850031000087609

Furnham, A., Moutafi, J., & Baguma, P. (2002). A cross-cultural study on the role of weight and waist-to-hip ratio on female attractiveness. *Personality and Individual Differences, 32*(4), 729-745. https://doi.org/10.1016/S0191-8869(01)00073-3

Furnham, A., Petrides, K. V., & Constantinides, A. (2005). The effects of body mass index and waist-to-hip ratio on ratings of female attractiveness, fecundity, and health. *Personality and Individual Differences, 38*(8), 1823–1834. https://doi.org/10.1016/j.paid.2004.11.011

Furnham, A., & Reeves, E. (2006). The relative influence of facial neoteny and waist-to-hip ratio on judgements of female attractiveness and fecundity. *Psychology, Health & Medicine, 11*(2), 129–141. https://doi.org/10.1080/13548500500155982

Furnham, A., Swami, V., & Shah, K. (2006). Body weight, waist-to-hip ratio and breast size correlates of ratings of attractiveness and health. *Personality and Individual Differences, 41*(3), 443-454. https://doi.org/10.1016/j.paid.2006.02.007

Furnham, A., Tan, T., & McManus, C. (1997). Waist-to-hip ratio preferences for body shape: A replication and extension. *Personality and Individual Differences, 22*(4), 539–549. https://doi.org/10.1016/S0191-8869(96)00241-3

Gallup, A. C., White, D. D., & Gallup, G. G. Jr. (2007). Handgrip strength predicts sexual behavior, body morphology, and aggression in male college students. *Evolution and Human Behavior, 28*(6), 423-429.

doi:10.1016/j.evolhumbehav.2007.07.001

George, H. R., Swami, V., Cornelissen, P. L., & Tovée, M. J. (2008). Preferences for body mass index and waist-to-hip ratio do not vary with observer age. *Journal of Evolutionary Psychology, 6*(3), 207–218. https://doi.org/10.1556/JEP.6.2008.3.4

Gervais, S. J., Vescio, T. K., & Allen, J. (2012). When are people interchangeable sexual objects? The effect of gender and body type on sexual fungibility. *British Journal of Social Psychology, 51*(4), 499-513

Gitter, A. G., Lomranz, J., Saxe, L., & Bar-Tal, Y. (1983). Perceptions of female physique characteristics by American and Israeli students. *Journal of Social Psychology, 121*, 7-13.

Gold, E. B. (2011). The timing of the age at which natural menopause occurs. *Obstetrics and Gynecology Clinics of North America, 38*(3), 425-440. doi: 10.1016/j.ogc.2011.05.002

Harvey, J. A., & Robinson, J. D. (2003). Eating disorders in men: Current considerations. *Journal of Clinical Psychology in Medical Settings, 10*, 297–306.

Henss, R. (1995). Waist-to-hip ratio and attractiveness: Replication and extension. *Personality and Individual Differences, 19*(4), 479–488. https://doi.org/10.1016/0191-8869(95)00093-L

Henss, R. (2000). Waist-to-hip ratio and female attractiveness Evidence from photographic stimuli and methodological considerations. *Personality and Individual Differences, 28*(3), 501–513. https://doi.org/10.1016/S0191-8869(99)00115-4

Hintsanen, M., Jokela, M., Pulkki-Råback, L., Viikari, J. S. A., & Keltikangas-Järvinen, L. (2010). Associations of youth and adulthood body-mass index and waist-hip ratio with attachment styles and dimensions. *Current Psychology: A Journal for Diverse Perspectives on Diverse Psychological Issues, 29*(3), 257–271. https://doi.org/10.1007/s12144-010-9084-8

Horvath, T. (1981). Physical attractiveness: The influence of selected torso parameters. *Archives of Sexual Behavior, 10*(1), 21-24. https://doi.org/10.1007/BF01542671

Hu, G., Toumilehto, J., Silventoinen, K., Barengo, N., & Jousilahti, P. (2004). Joint effects of physical activity, body mass index, waist circumference and waist-to-hip ratio with the risk of cardiovascular disease among middle-aged Finnish men and women. *European Heart Journal, 25*(24), 2212-2219. https://doi.org/10.1016/j.ehj.2004.10.020

Huang, Z., Willet, W. C., and Colditz, G. A. (1999). Waist circumference, waist:hip ratio, and risk of breast cancer in the Nurses' Health Study. *American Journal of Epidemiology, 150*, 1316-1324.

Hughes, S. M., Dispenza, F. & Gallup, G. G., Jr. (2004). Ratings of voice attractiveness predict sexual behavior and body configuration. *Evolution and Human Behavior, 25*, 295-304. https://doi.org/10.1016/j.evolhumbehav.2004.06.001

Hughes, S. M., & Gallup, Jr., G. G. (2003). Sex differences in morphological predictors of sexual behavior: Shoulder to hip and waist to hip ratios. *Evolution and Human Behavior, 24*(3), 173-178. https://doi.org/10.1016/S1090-5138(02)00149-6

Hughes, S. M., Harrison, M. A. & Gallup, G. G., Jr. (2009). Sex-specific body configurations can be estimated from voice samples. *Journal of Social, Evolutionary, and Cultural Psychology, 3*(4), 343-355. Mehta, S. K. (2014). Waist Circumference to Height Ratio in Children and Adolescents. *Clinical Pediatrics,* 1-7. https://doi.org/10.1177/0009922814557784

Jasieńska, G., Ziomkiewicz, A., Ellison, P. T., Lipson, S. F., & Thune, I. (2004). Large breasts and narrow waists indicate high reproductive potential in women. *The Royal Society, 271*(1545), 1213-1217.

Johnson, K. L., Gill, S., Reichman, V., & Tassinary, L. G. (2007). Swagger, sway, and sexuality: Judging sexual orientation from body motion and morphology. *Journal of Personality and Social Psychology, 93*(3), 321-334. https://doi.org/10.1037/0022-3514.93.3.321

Jones, P. R., Hunt, M. J., Brown, T. P., & Norgan, N. G. (1986). Waist-hip circumference ratio and its relation to age and overweight in British men. *Human Nutrition. Clinical Nutrition, 40*(3), 239-247.

Karremans, J. C., Frankenhuis, W. E., & Arons, S. (2010). Blind men prefer a low waist-to-hip ratio. *Evolution and Human Behavior, 31*(3), 182-186. https://doi.org/10.1016/j.evolhumbehav.2009.10.001

Kasperk, C., Helmboldt, A., Borcsok, I., Heuthe, S., Cloos, O., Niethard, F., & Ziegler, R. (1997). Skeletal site-dependent expression of the androgen receptor in human osteoblastic cell populations. *Calcified Tissue International, 61*(6), 464-473.

Kaye, S., A., Folsom, A. R., Prineas, R. J., Potter, J. D., & Gapstur, S. M. (1990). The association of body fat distribution with lifestyle and reproductive factors in a population study of postmenopausal women. *International Journal of Obesity, 14*(7), 583-591.

Kerwin, D. R., Zhang, Y., Kotchen, J. M., Espeland, M. A., Van Horn, L., McTigue, K. M., … Hoffmann, R. (2010). The cross-sectional relationship between body mass index, waist hip ratio, and cognitive performance in postmenopausal women enrolled in the Women's Health Initiative. *Journal of the American Geriatrics Society, 58*(8), 1427-1432. https://doi.org/10.1111/j.1532-5415.2010.02969.x

Kirchengast, S., & Gartner, M. (2002). Changes in fat distribution (WHR) and body weight
across the menstrual cycle. *Collegium Antropologicum, 26*, 47-57.

Kościński, K. (2013). Attractiveness of women's body: Body mass index, waist–hip ratio, and their relative importance. *Behavioral Ecology, 24*(4), 914-925. https://doi.org/10.1093/beheco/art016

Lahti-Koski, M., Pietinen, Pirjo, Männistö, S., & Vartianinen, E. (2000). Trends in waist-to-hip ratio and its determinants in adults in Finland from 1987 to 1997. *The American Journal of Clinical Nutrition, 72*(6), 1436-1444. https://doi.org/10.1093/ajcn/72.6.1436

Lanska, D. J., Lanska, M. J. Hartz, A.J., & Rimm, A. A. (1985). Factors influencing anatomic location of fat tissue in 52,953 women. *International Journal of Obesity, 9*(1), 29-38.

Lassek, W. D., & Gaulin, S. J. C. (2008). Waist-hip ratio and cognitive ability: Is gluteofemoral fat a privileged store of neurodevelopmental

resources? *Evolution and Human Behavior, 29*(1), 26–
34. https://doi.org/10.1016/j.evolhumbehav.2007.07.005

Lavrakas, P. J. (1975). Female preferences for male physiques. *Journal of Research in Personality, 9*(4), 324–334. https://doi.org/10.1016/0092-6566(75)90006-9

Laws, A., Terry, R. B., & Brrett-Connor, E. (2011). Behavioral covariates of waist-to-hip ratio in Rancho Bernardo. *American Journal of Public Health, 80*(11), 1358-1362. https://doi.org/10.2105/AJPH.80.11.1358

Lear, S. A., James, P. T., Ko, G. T., & Kumanyika, S. (2010). Appropriateness of waist circumference and waist-to-hip ratio cutoffs for different ethnic groups. *European Journal of Clinical Nutrition, 64*, 42-61. https://doi.org/10.1038/ejcn.2009.70

Lee, A. J., Brooks, R. C., Potter, K. J., & Zietsch, B. P. (2015). Pathogen disgust sensitivity and resource scarcity are associated with mate preference for different waist-to-hip ratios, shoulder-to-hip ratios, and body mass index. *Evolution and Human Behavior, 36*(6), 480-488. https://doi.org/10.1016/j.evolhumbehav.2015.07.002

Lippa, R. (1983). Sex typing and the perception of body outlines. *Journal of Personality, 51*(4), 667–682. https://doi.org/10.1111/j.1467-6494.1983.tb00873.x

Lukasiewics, E., Mennen, L. I., Bertrais, S., Arnault, N., Preziosi, P., Galan, P., & Hercberg, S. (2005). Alcohol intake in relation to body mass index and waist-to-hip ratio: the importance of type of alcoholic beverage. *Public Health Nutrition, 8*(3), 315-320. https://doi.org/10.1079/PHN2004680

Maisey, D. S., Vale, E. L. E., Cornelissen, P. L., & Tovée., M. J. (1999). Characteristics of male attractiveness for women. *The Lancet, 353*, 1500.

Manning, J. T., Baron-Cohen, S., Wheelwright, S., & Sanders, G. (2001). The 2nd to 4th ratio and autism. *Developmental Medicine and Child Neurology, 43*, 160–164. doi:10.1017/S0012162201000317

Markey, C. N., Tinsley, B. J., Ericksen, A. J., Ozer, D. J., & Markey, P. M. (2002). Preadolescent's perceptions of females' body size and shape: Evolutionary and social learning perspectives. *Journal of Youth and Adolescence, 31*(2), 137--146.

Marlowe, F., Apicella, C., & Reed, D. (2005). Men's preferences for women's profile waist-to-hip ratio in two societies. *Evolution and Human Behavior, 26*, 458-468. https://doi.org/10.1016/j.evolhumbehav.2005.07.005

Marlowe, F., & Wetsman, A. (2001). Preferred waist-to-hip ratio and ecology. *Personality and Individual Differences, 30*(3), 481-489. https://doi.org//10.1016/S0191-8869(00)00039-8

Mather, G., & Murdoch, L. (1994). Gender discrimination in biological motion displays based on dynamic cues. *Proceedings: Biological Sciences, 258*(1353), 273-279. http://dx.doi.org/10.1098/rspb.1994.0173

Mautz, B.S., Wong, B. B. M., Peters R. A., & Jennions, M. D. (2013). Penis size interacts with body shape and height to influence male attractiveness. *PNAS, 110*(17) 6925-6930. www.pnas.org/cgi/doi/10.1073/pnas.1219361110

Misra, A., and Vikram, N. (2003). Clinical and pathophysiological consequences of abdominal adiposity and abdominal adipose tissue depots. *Nutrition, 19*,

456-457.

Molarius, A., Seidell, J. C., Sans, S., Tuomilehto, J., & Kuulasmaa, K. (1999). Waist and hip circumferences, and waist-hip ratio in 19 populations of the WHO MONICA Project. *International Journal of Obesity, 23*, 116-125. https://doi.org/10.1038/sj.ijo.0800772

Mondragón-Ceballos, R., Granados, M., Cerda-Molina, A. L., Chavira-Ramírez, R., & Hernández-López, L. E. (2015). Waist-to-hip ratio, but not body mass index, is associated with testosterone and estradiol concentrations in young women. *International Journal of Endocrinology, 6*, 654046. http://dx.doi.org/10.1155/2015/654046

Morry, M., & Staska, S. (2001). Magazine exposure: Internalization, self-objectification, eating attitudes, and body satisfaction in male and female university students. *Canadian Journal of Behavioral Science, 33*, 269-279.

Murray, M. P. Kory, R. C. Sepic, S. P. (1970). Walking patterns of normal women. *Archives of Physical Medicine and Rehabilitation*, 51, 637-650.

Pazhoohi, F., Hosseinchari, M., & Doyle, J. F. (2012). Iranian men's waist-to-hip ratios, shoulder-to-hip ratios, body esteem and self-efficacy. *Journal of Evolutionary Psychology, 10*(2), 61-67. http://dx.doi.org/10.1556/JEP.10.2012.2.2

Pazhoohi, F., & Liddle, J. R. (2012). Identifying feminine and masculine ranges for waist-to-hip ratio. *Journal of Social, Evolutionary, and Cultural Psychology, 6*(2), 227–232. https://doi.org/10.1037/h0099212

Perilloux, H. K., Webster, G. D., & Gaulin, S. J. C. (2010). Signals of genetic quality and maternal investment capacity: The dynamic effects of fluctuating asymmetry and waist-to-hip ratio on men's ratings of women's attractiveness. *Social Psychological and Personality Science, 1*(1), 34–42. https://doi.org/10.1177/1948550609349514

Platek, S. M., & Singh, D. (2010). Optimal waist-to-hip ratios in women activate neural reward centers in men. *PLoS One, 5*(2). https://doi.org/10.1371/journal.pone.0009042

Price, M. E., Kang, J., Dunn, J., & Hopkins, S. (2011). Muscularity and attractiveness as predictors of human egalitarianism. *Personality and Individual Differences, 50*(5), 636-640.

Price, M. E., Pound, N., Dunn, J., Hopkins, S., & Kang, J. (2013). Body shape preferences: Associations with rater body shape and sociosexuality. *PLoS One, 8*(1), 1-10.

Puhl, R. M., & Boland, F. J. (2001) 'Predicting female physical attractiveness: Waist-to-hip ratio versus thinness', *Psychology, Evolution and Gender* 3, 27–46.

Qiao, Q., & Nyamdorj, R. (2010). Is the association of type II diabetes with waist circumference or waist-to-hip ratio stronger than that with body mass index? *European Journal of Clinical Nutrition*, 30-34. https://doi.org/10.1038/ejcn.2009.93

Rempala, D., & Garvey, K. (2007). Sex differences in the effects of incremental changes in waist-to-hip ratio. *Journal of Social, Evolutionary, and Cultural Psychology, 1*(3), 86–97. https://doi.org /10.1037/h0099825

Sayeed, M. A., Mahtab, H., Larif, Z. A., Khanam, P. A., Ahsan, K. A., Banu, A., & Azad Khan, A. K. (2003). Waist-to-height ratio is a better obesity index than body mass index and waist-to-hip ratio for predicting diabetes, hypertension and lipidemia. *Bangledesh Medical Research Council Bulletin, 29*(1), 1-10.

Schützwohl, A. (2006). Judging female figures: A new methodological approach to male attractiveness judgments of female waist-to-hip ratio. *Biological Psychology, 71*(2), 223–229. https://doi.org/10.1016/j.biopsycho.2005.04.005

Shoup, M. L., & Gallup, G. J. (2008). Men's faces convey information about their bodies and their behavior: What you see is what you get. *Evolutionary Psychology, 6*(3), 469-479. doi:10.1177/147470490800600311

Sills, F. D. (1950). A factor analysis of somatotypes and of their relationship to achievement in motor skills. *Research Quarterly. American Association for Health, Physical Education and Recreation, 21*(4), 424-437.

Singh, D. (1993). Adaptive significance of female physical attractiveness: Role of waist-to-hip
ratio. *Journal of Personality and Social Psychology, 65*(2), 293.

Singh, D. (1994a). Is thin really beautiful and good? Relationship between waist-to-hip ratio (WHR) and female attractiveness. *Personality and Individual Differences, 16*(1), 123–132. https://doi.org/10.1016/0191-8869(94)90116-3

Singh, D. (1994b). Ideal female body shape: Role of body weight and waist-to-hip ratio. *International Journal of Eating Disorders, 16*(3), 283 - 288.

Singh, D. (1995). Female health, attractiveness, and desirability for relationships: Role of breast asymmetry and waist-to-hip ratio. *Ethology and Sociobiology, 16*(6), 465-481. https://doi.org/10.1016/0162-3095(95)00073-9

Singh, D. (1995). Female judgment of male attractiveness and desirability for relationships: Role of waist-to-hip ratio and financial status. *Journal of Personality and Social Psychology, 69*(6), 1089–1101. https://doi.org/10.1037/0022-3514.69.6.1089

Singh, D. (2002). Female mate value at a glance: Relationship of waist-to-hip ratio to health, fecundity, and attractiveness. *Neuroendocrinology Letters Special Issue, 23*, 81-91.

Singh, D., & Luis, S. (1995). Ethnic and gender consensus for the effect of waist-to-hip ratio on judgment of women's attractiveness. *Human Nature, 6*(1), 51-65. https://doi.org/10.1007/BF02734135

Singh, D., & Randall, P. K. (2007). Beauty is in the eye of the plastic surgeon: Waist-hip ratio (WHR) and women's attractiveness. *Personality and Individual Differences, 43*(2), 329–340. https://doi.org/10.1016/j.paid.2006.12.003

Singh, D., Davis, M., & Randall, P. (200). Flaunting ovulation: Lower WHR, enhanced self-perceived attractiveness, and increased sexual desire. Paper presented at the 13th Human Behavior and Evolution Society meeting, University College London, London.

Singh, D., & Suwardi, L. (1995). Ethnic and gender consensus for the effect of waist-to-hip ratio on judgment of women's attractiveness. *Human Nature, 6*(1), 51–66.

Singh, D., & Young, R. K. (1995). Body weight, waist-to-hip ratio, breasts, and hips: Role in judgments of female attractiveness and desirability for relationships. *Ethology and Sociobiology, 16*(6), 483-507. https://doi.org/10.1016/0162-3095(95)00074-7

Sugiyama, L. S. (2004). Is beauty in the context-sensitive adaptations of the beholder? Shiwiar use of waist-to-hip ratio in assessments of female mate value. *Evolution and Human Behavior, 25*(1), 51–62. https://doi.org/10.1016/S1090-5138(03)00083-7

Swami, V. (2006). The influence of body weight and shape in determining female and male physical attractiveness. In A. M. Columbus (Ed.), *Advances in psychology research., Vol. 56.* (Vol. 56, pp. 45–70). Hauppauge, NY: Nova Science Publishers.

Swami, V., Antonakopoulos, N., Tovée, M. J., & Furnham, A. (2006). A critical test of the waist-to-hip ratio hypothesis of women's physical attractiveness in Britain and Greece. *Sex Roles, 54*(3–4), 201–211. https://doi.org/10.1007/s11199-006-9338-3

Swami, V., Furnham, A., Amin, R., Chaudhri, J., Joshi, K., Jundi, S., Miller, R., Mirza-Begum, J., Beghum, F. N., Sheth, P., & Tovée, M. J. (2008). Lonelier, lazier, and teased: The stigmatizing effect of body size. *The Journal of Social Psychology, 148*(5), 577-593.

Swami, V., Jones, J., Einon, D., & Furnham, A. (2009). Men's preferences for women's profile waist-to-hip ratio, breast size, and ethnic group in Britain and South Africa. *British Journal of Psychology, 100*(2), 313–325. https://doi.org/10.1348/000712608X329525

Swami, V., & Tovée, M. J. (2005). Male physical attractiveness in Britain and Malaysia: A cross-cultural study. *Body Image, 2*(4), 383-393. https://doi.org/10.1016/j.bodyim.2005.08.001

Swami, V., & Tovée, M. J. (2008). The muscular male: A comparison of the physical attractiveness preferences of gay and heterosexual men. *International Journal of Men's Health, 7*(1), 59-71.

Summers, A. (1985). *Goddess: The secret lives of Marilyn Monroe.* New York, NY: Open Roads Integrated Media.

Svartberg, J., Jorde, R., Sundsfjord, J., Bønaa, K. H., & Barrett-Connor, E. (2003). Seasonal variation of testosterone and waist to hip ratio in men: The Tromsø Study. *The Journal of Clinical Endocrinology & Metabolism, 88*(7), 3099-3104. https://doi.org/10.1210/jc.2002-021878

Tassinary, L. G., & Hansen, K. A. (1998). A critical test of the waist-to-hip-ratio hypothesis of female physical attractiveness. *Psychological Science, 9*(2), 150–155. https://doi.org/10.1111/1467-9280.00029

Taylor, R. W., Keil, D., Gold, E. J., Williams, S. M., & Goulding, A. (1998). Body mass index, waist girth, and waist-to-hip ratio as indexes of total and regional adiposity in women: evaluation using receiver operating characteristic curves. *The American Journal of Clinical Nutrition, 67*(1), 44-49. https://doi.org/10.1093/ajcn/67.1.44

Tiggemann, M., Martins, Y., & Kirkbride, A. (2007). Oh to be lean and muscular: Body image ideals in gay and heterosexual men. *Psychology of Men & Masculinity, 8*, 15–24. doi:10.1037/1524- 9220.8.1.15

Tseng, C. (2008). Waist-to-height ratio and coronary artery disease in Taiwanese

Type 2 diabetic patients. *Nature Publishing Group, 16*(12), 2754-2759. https://doi.org/10.1038/oby.2008.430

Van Hooff, M. H., Voorhorst, F. J., Kaptein M.B., Hirasing, R.A., Koppenaal, C, & Schoemaker, J. (2000). Insulin, androgen, and gonadotropin concentration, body mass index, and waist to hip ratio in the first years after menarche in girls with regular menstrual cycle, irregular menstrual cycles, or Oligomenorrhea. *Journal of Clinical Endocrinology and Metabolism, 85*, 1394–1400.

Wang, Z., & Hoy, W. E. (2004). Waist circumference, body mass index, hip circumference and waist-to-hip ratio as predictors of cardiovascular disease in Aboriginal people. *European Journal of Clinical Nutrition, 58*, 888-893. https://doi.org/10.1038/sj.ejcn.1601891

Waas, P., Waldenström, U., Rössner, S., & Hellberg, D. (1997). An android body fat Distribution in female impairs the pregnancy rate of *in-vitro* fertilization-embryo transfer. *Human Reproduction, 12*, 2057–2060. https://doi.org/10.1093/humrep/12.9.2057

Weeden, J., & Sabini, J. (2007). Subjective and objective measures of attractiveness and their relation to sexual behavior and sexual attitudes in university students. *Archives of Sexual Behavior, 36*, 79-88.

Wells, J. C. K., Treleaven, P. & Cole, T. J. (2007). BMI compared with 3-dimensional body shape: The Sizing Survey. *American Journal of Clinical Nutrition, 85*, 419-425.

Wells, J. C. K. (2007). Sexual dimorphism of body composition. *Best Practice & Research Clinical Endocrinology & Metabolism, 21*(3), 415-430. https://doi.org/10.1016/j.beem.2007.04.007

Wells, J. C. K. (2009). Sexual dimorphism of body composition. *Best Practice and Research Clinical Endocrinology and Metabolism, 21*(3), 415-430. http://10.1016/j.beem.2007.04.007

Wetsman, A., & Marlowe, F. (1999). How universal are preferences for female waist-to-hip ratios? Evidence from the Hadza of Tanzania. *Evolution and Human Behavior, 20*(4), 219–228. https://doi.org/10.1016/S1090-5138(99)00007-0

Wing, R. R., Matthews, K. A., Kuller, L. H., Meilahn, E. N., & Plantinga, P. (1991). Waist to hip ratio in middle-aged women: Associations with behavioral and psychosocial factors and with changes in cardiovascular risk factors. *Arteriosclerosis, Thrombosis, and Vascular Biology, 11*(5), 1250-1257. https://doi.org/10.1161/01.ATV.11.5.1250

Zaadstra, B. M., Seidell, J. C., Van Noord, P.A., te Velde, E. R., Habbema, J. D., Vrieswijk, B. & Karbaat, J. (1993). Fat and female fecundity: Prospective study of effect of body fat distribution on conception rates. *British Medical Journal, 306*, 484-487. https://doi.org/10.1136/bmj.306.6876.484

Zotto, M., & Pegna, A. J. (2017). Electrophysiological evidence of perceived sexual attractiveness for human female bodies varying in waist-to-hip ratio. *Cognitive, Affective & Behavioral Neuroscience, 17*(3), 577–591. https://doi.org/10.3758/s13415-017-0498-8

Chapter 8

BODY SCENT

Follow your nose! It always knows!

-Toucan Sam, Kellogg's Cereal

Human body scent plays a role in interpersonal attraction and can signal certain qualities about an individual. There is a long-held belief that humans do not have a pronounced olfactory sense and, therefore, smell is less influential in our assessments of others. However, this idea has been argued to be untrue (see Shephard, 2004). Many researchers have stressed the importance of the human sense of smell and how it has been underestimated in the past (Grammer, Fink, & Neave, 2004).

The idea that we either do not value or place little emphasis on our sense of smell is reflected in our language. We often have difficulty finding the words to describe a smell, and it seems that our vocabulary is lacking for adjectives that allow us to properly verbalize our olfactory experiences (Barkat-Defradas, 2016). We frequently find ourselves describing scents by using linguistics with additional cross-sensory descriptors (e.g., "a sweet smell," "a rosy smell" "smells like linens") rather than using descriptors that solely identify a scent alone (e.g., "musky") (see Gallup & Cameron, 1992). These biases away from scent-oriented language may be of particular concern for those in industries who need to exploit their sense of olfaction such as professional wine tasters, perfume testers, or food critics.

Nevertheless, several research studies have demonstrated the importance of the human sense of smell, particularly how human body odor impacts attraction, mate selection, and the recognition of others and their traits. In this chapter, we review some of the literature that demonstrates how body scent can provide information about a person's mate quality, age, gender, kin, fertility, diet, physical and mental health, sexual orientation, and personality.

The Production and Detection of Body Odors and Pheromones

Human body odors are secreted from various areas of the body such as the scalp, the mouth, the anal-genital region, the feet, the armpits (i.e., referred to as the axillae or axillary glands), and other skin surfaces, especially when sweating (Yamazaki et al., 2010). Axillary odor in adults appears to be the most distinguishing because of the relatively high concentration of both eccrine and apocrine glands in this area (Havlicek et al., 2017).

As for the detection of scent, odor molecules can reach olfactory receptor cells in two ways: 1) the orthonasal route carried in by inhaled air, and 2) the retronasal route which is carried from the back of the oral cavity through the nasopharynx into the back of the nasal cavity (Shephard, 2004). The first route is usually used to test smell perception, and the latter is usually used for smelling foods and liquids and can combine with taste to give the complex sensation of flavor.

Pheromones. Aside from conspicuous body odors that can be knowingly detected, humans have a separate, albeit more underdeveloped, accessory olfactory system that is thought to be dedicated solely for the detection of pheromones. Pheromones are defined as "airborne chemical signals that are released by an individual into the environment and which affect the physiology or behavior of other members of the same species" (Stern & McClintock, 1998). In other words, pheromones are released by an organism so as to communicate information to members of their species (conspecifics).

There is evidence to suggest that human pheromones (chemosignals that some consider external hormones) are released through axillary sweat glands (Beier, Ginez, & Schaller, 2005), and these chemical signals can subtly affect attraction in humans. The understanding of pheromonal communication may be clearer if we think of dogs that will often sniff one another for identification, sniff territorial claims (e.g., smell another dog's urine on a fire hydrant), or sniff a female to determine if she is "in heat."

Human pheromones are purportedly found in underarm axillary secretions.

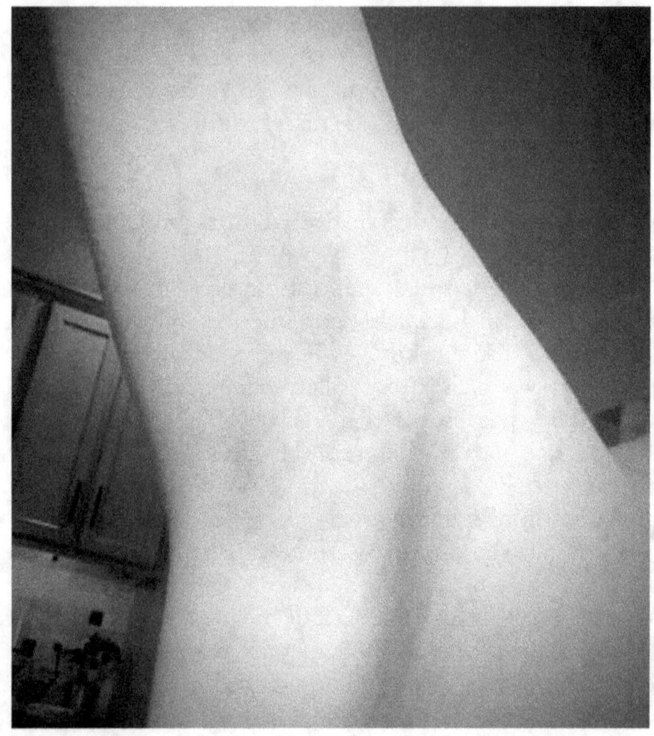

In humans, the vomeronasal organ (VNO), purported to be a set of receptors located near but separate from the olfactory receptors, is thought to be responsible for the subtle detection of pheromones and it sends the information to the accessory olfactory bulb in the brain (Keller, Baum, Brock, Brennan, Bakker, 2009). Monti-Bloch and colleagues (1998) described the human VNO as a tubular organ bilaterally located underneath the mucosal lining of the anterior nasal septum, lined with pseudostratified epithelium which grows during fetal development until birth. Some researchers claim the foundation for a VNO is visible in human fetuses up to 19 weeks.

Other researchers have claimed that some adult humans have a vestigial VNO, or at least a VNO "pit," (see Meredith, 2001). Although the topic of its existence and location is debated, the VNO in humans is said to be a functional organ responding to species-specific substances secreted in human skin (Monti-Bloch, Diaz-Sanchez, Jennings-White, Berliner, 1998).

In many other species such as in canines and rodents, this accessory olfactory system is closely connected to the hypothalamus in the brain whose functions tie to reproduction. As such, this systems' detection of odors appear to influence reproductive behaviors and can trigger neuroendocrine changes that can lead to accelerating puberty, inducing estrus, blocking pregnancy, and increasing testosterone in males exposed to the urine of females in estrus (Keller et al., 2009). Whereas the impact of pheromones on the behavioral and reproductive biology of humans may not be exactly akin to other animals, several studies indicate that humans indeed use olfactory communication and are able to produce and perceive certain pheromones (Grammer, Fink, & Neave, 2004).

In humans, there is some evidence to support the function of pheromones in mate choice. Again, a pheromone is not perceived consciously. Saxton, Little, and Roberts (2008) conducted a well-designed experiment where they primed participants with a control substance or a putative human pheromone found in higher concentrations in men, 4,16-androstadien-3-one (androstadienone). Participants then attended a speed-dating event. Subsequently, women primed with androstadienone ascribed overall higher attractiveness ratings to their male speed-dating targets.

Androstadienone, derived from testosterone, is found in men's axillary sweat.

Along these lines, Cerda-Molina and colleagues (2013) conducted interesting research evincing that axillar and vulvar secretions from women influence heterosexual men's ratings of women's attractiveness. Women's odors collected around the women's ovulation (high fertility) phase of the menstrual cycle increased testosterone in men who smelled the secretions. Also, after smelling the periovulatory compounds, men reported an increased interest in sex. Odors from women's luteal phase (low fertility prior to menstruation) decreased testosterone. Cerda-Molina et al. provided valuable evidence that psychoneuroendocrinological changes occur with exposure to body odors, although particular pheromones triggering these experimental changes were not identified. The authors noted that increased testosterone not only increases sexual readiness, but also facilitates responses to intra-male competition.

It is important to emphasize that studies presented in the chapter sometimes reference detectible body odors, whereas others allude to the unconscious influences of indiscernible pheromones. It may not be possible to delineate between the two since our understanding of human pheromones is incomplete. Vaglio underscored this idea nicely, stating "the search for these semiochemicals [pheromones] is still an elusive goal," and "the race is still on to capture and define human scents" (p. 279).

The Scent of Kin

Like other mammals, humans are capable of discriminating between kin and non-kin by solely using olfactory cues (Porter, 1999). The capacity to recognize kin happens early in life. Neonates as young as 2 weeks of age who breast feed can recognize their mother's axillary odors in comparison to non-parturient women or unfamiliar women (Cernoch & Porter, 1985; Vaglio, 2009). Apparently, breast feeding allows infants the exposure needed to become familiarized with their mother's unique olfactory signature because infants who are bottle-fed were unable to discriminate between their mother's odor and that of other women, nor could recognize their own father's odor.

Just as infants can recognize their mothers postpartum, mothers can recognize their infants. Within days after birth, mothers are able to reliably identify garments worn by their own infants from those worn by other infants (Porter, Cernoch & McLaughlin, 1983) and could identify their own babies when sniffing the heads of different infants while blindfolded (Russell, Mendelson & Peeke, 1983). Further, one does not have to be related to an individual to assess kin relations. Unacquainted individuals can also match offspring to their parents based solely on body odor (Porter,

Cemoch, & Balogh, 1985). Because infants are so highly dependent and care is essential for their survival, the recognition of kin through odor could facilitate both the elicitation and provisioning of such care from those who have a vested interest in their survival.

A mother appreciating the smell of her child.

The fact that the scent of relatives can be identified suggests that close biological relatives share somewhat similar odor signatures (Porter, 1999). The best example of this comes from evidence that body odor of identical (i.e., monozygotic) twins show high resemblance (Roberts et al., 2005), which makes sense as they share 100% or their genes which should code for their body odor signature. It is presumed that what facilitates this kin recognition is the result of genetically mediated similarities in bodily biochemistry and metabolism (Porter, 1999).

In the same vein, there is evidence for the ability to self-recognize from odors as adults (McBurney, Levine, & Cavanaugh, 1977), but this is not so in children (pre-pubertal and pubertal) who were unable to recognize their own odor or the odors of other family members (Ferdenzi, Schaal, & Roberts, 2010). However, children seem to improve with age in their kin recognition abilities (Ferdenzi et al., 2010). Further, women appear to be better at recognizing their own odors than are men, despite the fact that women rated their own axillary secretions as smelling less pleasant than men rating their own body odors (Platek, Burch, & Gallup, Jr., 2001). The opposite was found previously, whereby women judged their own odors as smelling pleasant whereas men judged their odors more often as unpleasant. Despite these sex differences, just as people rate their own voices as sounding more attractive than others do (Hughes & Harrison, 2013), typically, people rate their own odors as smelling more pleasant than other raters do (McBurney, Levine, & Cavanaugh, 1977).

The Scent of Dissimilar Mates

In terms of kin recognition, it is also important to identify those with whom we should avoid mating due to genetic relatedness and the sharing of a high proportion of genes in common. For instance, women did not find the scents of men who they perceived resembled a close relative's scent as sexy or attractive, although they did not assess these scents negatively (Sorokowska, Butovskaya, Veselovskaya, 2015). These results show that women would probably not consider men whose body odor indicates high genetic similarity as a mate perhaps as a mechanism for incest avoidance. From an evolutionary perspective, mating with a relative would be disadvantageous because there is a greater likelihood that relatives share similar deleterious alleles in common, and if combined in a homozygous manner, could potentially cause many negative outcomes, including sterility and reduced survival, a result termed as inbreeding depression (Charlesworth & Willis, 2009). Perhaps scent helped promote the origin of culturally universal incest taboos that are seen throughout most of the world.

Along these lines of assessing genetic relatedness through scent, several studies have documented that individuals prefer the body scent of opposite-sex individuals with major histocompatibility complex (MHC) genes that are dissimilar to their own (Jacob, McClintock, Zelano, & Ober, 2002; Thornhill, Gangestad, Miller, Scheyd, McCollough, & Franklin, 2003; Wedekind, & Füri, 1997; Wedekind Seebeck, Bettens, & Paepke, 1995). MHC is a highly polymorphic group of genes that encodes for proteins essential for pathogen defense vis-à-vis T (thymus) cells, and thus plays a central role in immune system functioning (Baker & Evavold, 2017; Penn & Potts, 1999). These products contribute to an individual's body odor and body odor can therefore be used as a guide to identify possible mates with similar/dissimilar genotypes (Santos, Schinemann, Gabardo, & Bicalho, 2005). It is believed that the MHC-dissimilarity of parents increases the immune competence of offspring (i.e., heterozygote advantage). Thus, any observed mate preferences based on MHC dissimilarity could have been a means to react to pathogen pressures. In addition to enhancing immunocompetence of offspring, selecting MHC dissimilar mates could also be a mechanism to avoid inbreeding (Huchard, Baniel, Schliehe, Diecks, & Kappeler, 2013; Penn & Potts, 1999) and therefore result in more viable offspring.

When testing for MHC complementarity, naturally ovulating women rated the scents of MHC-dissimilar men wearing T-shirts they slept in as smelling more pleasant than MHC-similar men (Wedekind et al., 1995). The odors of MHC-dissimilar men also reminded women of their current or former romantic partners than had the odors of MHC-similar men (Wedekind et al., 1995). Other researchers found that women preferred the scent of men with only an intermediate MHC-match based on HLA alleles inherited from their fathers (Jacob, McClintock, Zelano, & Ober, 2002).

Some studies have demonstrated this odor preference for MHC dissimilarity in only one sex and not the other. For instance, Thornhill and colleagues (2003) found that men preferred scents of women with common MHC alleles different from their own scent whereas women did not show such preferences. On the other hand, Santos et al. (2005) only found a significant correlation between MHC-dissimilarity and odor preferences when female smellers evaluated male sweat odors, but not when men evaluated women's odors. Moreover, in another study, Roberts and colleagues (2008) found that only women who were in a relationship preferred the scents of MHC-dissimilar men, whereas women who were single preferred the scents of MHC-similar men suggesting that partnered women may seek to improve offspring quality through extra-pair pairings (Roberts, Gosling, Carter, & Petrie, 2008). Overall, these studies provide interesting data with respect to how people may display odor preferences associated with particular genes that code for immunological functioning.

The processing of body scent to make certain judgments about others can operate at the unconscious level. The argument is that through human evolution we are endowed with mechanisms that help us identify someone who is or is not an appropriate mating target. This is likely not a conscious reaction, but our nervous system has evolved to send olfactory warnings that someone may have genes that are too similar to our own to facilitate an ideal matching scenario.

The Scent of Attractive Mates

There is additional evidence to support the idea that human body odor influences mate choice, particularly for women. Women tend to show preferences for the body odor of men that signal good mate quality, especially during the fertile part of their cycle when the possibility of conception occurring is most pertinent. Women seem to rate high mate value men as more attractive during ovulation when their sensitivity to the scent of androstenone is enhanced (Gangestad & Thornhill, 1998; Thornhill & Gangestad, 1999). Androsenone is one of the first putative human pheromones to be identified, but it is still a topic of debate in the literature (see Havlicek, Murray, Saxton, & Roberts, 2010). Nonetheless, there are several pieces of evidence that attractiveness of body odor correlates with good gene indicators.

For example, women in the fertile phase of their cycle demonstrated preferences for the scents of men with higher testosterone levels (Thornhill, Chapman, & Gangestad, 2013). Likewise, women in the fertile phase preferred axillary odor of men who scored high on a dominance scale (Havlicek, Roberts, & Flegr, 2005). These findings corroborate with several studies showing women's preferences for more masculine faces when in the fertile phase of their cycle (Penton-Voak et al. 1999; Penton-Voak & Perrett 2000). Dominance is associated with higher testosterone (Mazur & Booth, 1998), and therefore could indicate a man's health and viability.

Men with more attractive body odor as rated by women were also more likely to have lower, 2D:4D digit ratios, which, as reviewed in Chapter 5, low 2D:4D ratio is thought to be an indicator of higher levels of prenatal testosterone and is associated with dominance, health, and male vigor (Roberts et al., 2011). Further, men who displayed relatively more attractive nonverbal behavior were also rated to have more attractive body odor (Roberts et al., 2011). It was assumed that attractive male movement also relates to dominance and perhaps self-confidence, just as axillary odor and dominance are associated (Havlicek et al., 2005).

Interestingly, the preference for dominant male odors was stronger for fertile women in stable relationships than fertile single women (Havlicek et al., 2005). It is believed women often display a mating strategy that entails seeking genetically superior men as extra-pair partners while concurrently having another in-pair partner willing to invest in the long-term (Thornhill & Gangestad, 2003). This idea may explain why women in committed relationships found dominant male odors so attractive during the time when they could conceive, perhaps to cuckold their in-pair mate.

As discussed elsewhere in this book, several studies have documented that women in the fertile phase of their menstrual cycle also prefer the scent of symmetrical men (Gangestad & Thornhill, 1998; Rikowski & Grammer,

1999; Thornhill et al., 2003). The relationship between fertility risk and female preferences for symmetrical men became even stronger when men's showering and fragrance use were controlled for in the analysis (Thornhill & Gangestad, 1999). Again, one of the proximate mediators thought to be responsible for this mid-cycle preference shift is the level of certain female sex hormones; women's progesterone levels were found to be negatively correlated with the preference for the scent of symmetrical men while estrogen levels were positively related (Garver-Apgar, Gangestad, & Thornhill, 2008).

Just like female raters, men also assess the odors of other symmetrical men as more intense, pleasant, and attractive in comparison to the odors of asymmetrical men (Borráz-León, Cerda-Molina, & Mayagoitia-Novales, 2017). In fact, the testosterone levels of symmetrical men decreased when they smelt the odor of asymmetrical men suggesting that men may be able to "sniff out" their potential rivals, and because asymmetrical men pose less threat, the observed decrease in testosterone is thought to inhibit competitive behaviors. In addition to symmetry, there was a positive relationship between male body odor and male facial attractiveness as rated by women in the most fertile phase of their menstrual cycle (Rikowski & Grammer, 1999). Likewise, the more attractive men rated women's faces, the sexier they perceived their body odor. Thus, body odor and facial attractiveness seem to be conveying similar mate quality information.

Women Stress Scent. There are sex differences in the importance that men and women place on body scent when selecting mates. Women seem to be more reliant on olfactory cues whereas men use visual cues for both partner choice and during sexual arousal (Havlicek et al., 2008). A survey that examined the importance that men and women place on various sensory-physical traits during mate selection confirmed this sex difference. Women rated man's smell to be more important than his looks, voice, or how his skin feels when selecting a lover (Herz & Inzlicht, 2002). With the exception of pleasantness, the influence of smell also outranked all other social factors measured and was even more valued than money or ambition/resource potential. In contrast, men rated a woman's physical looks as the most desirable trait and as more important than any other factor except for pleasantness. Not only did women evaluate body odor as more important in their mate choice responses than did men, but women had a more intense response to odor cues overall.

The Scent of Romantic Partners

Odors perceived as similar to a romantic partner's odor were assessed as more pleasant, and female raters assessed the odor donors that smelled similar to their partners as sexy, tender, physically attractive, reliable, and as having a greater potential to be a good father to their children (Sorokowska, Butovskaya, Veselovskaya, 2015). Further, partnered women who reported to be satisfied with their current relationship evaluated smells which they found similar to their partner's smell in a highly positive way. This finding suggests that either women are using certain odor cues they find appealing when first selecting their partners or they have been conditioned to like the smell of their partner and have associated that scent with hedonic value.

The more in love a woman reported being with her romantic partner, the worse she performed in identifying the body odor of an opposite-sex friend (who could be a potential mate) but not her boyfriend's or same-sex friend's body odors (Lundström & Jones-Gotman, 2009). The rationale provided to explain this finding was that romantic love deflects attention away from potential new partners rather than towards the present partner. They stipulated that changes are likely mediated by circulating neuropeptides.

The Scent of Sexual Orientation

There have been a few studies that have tested whether sexual orientation has any bearing on preferences for body odor. One study showed that the perception of axillary odors was associated with both gender and sexual orientation (Martins et al., 2005). A complex interaction emerged from their results. Gay men preferred the odors of other gay men and heterosexual women. Heterosexual men showed no differential preference between heterosexuals of either sex or for lesbians, but preferred lesbians' scent over gay male donors. Both heterosexual women and lesbian women preferred odors from heterosexuals of either gender over gay men and lesbian women, but preferred odors from lesbian women over gay men. Interestingly, all groups except for homosexual men showed a lower preference for the scent of homosexual men. However, this last finding could not be replicated. In fact, a later study showed that heterosexual women rated the body odor of homosexual men as more, not less, pleasant, sexier, and preferable than that of heterosexual men (Sergeant, Dickins, Davies, & Griffiths, 2007). Clearly sexual orientation impacts olfactory function, but it is less clear how exactly this is the case due to inconsistent findings.

Other studies have examined the influence of sexual orientation on the perception of body odor using physiological measures. For instance, a study examining event-related potentials of homosexual and heterosexual individuals showed that the body odors of desirable partners were processed at an earlier level than non-desired partners (Lübke, Hoenen & Pause, 2012.). In other words, gay men, heterosexual men, and lesbian women had responded with shorter latencies to the odors of donors who were of their preferred gender. Men's sexual orientation also significantly impacts their perception of androstenone, a chemosignal that humans have specific receptors for and is one of the major contributing substances to human body odor. Homosexual men displayed significantly higher olfactory sensitivity to the odor of androstenone than heterosexual men, but they did not differ from heterosexual men in their subjective judgements of or emotional response to androstenone (Lübke, Schablitsk, & Pause, 2009). These findings further the idea that we may be more in tune with the odors of potential mates we desire.

The Scent of Fertility

There is a long-standing assumption that unlike many other mammals, human females have concealed ovulation whereby men do not know when a woman is fertile during her menstrual cycle. However, empirical evidence from human odor studies suggests that ovulation may not be entirely masked, and female odors/pheromones provide some clues that unveil the timing of a woman's fertility.

One of the first studies to test this idea had women wear tampons across their menstrual cycle so that they could extract the vaginal secretion odors and present them in vitro to independent male raters blind to what they were smelling (Doty, Ford, Preti, & Huggins, 1975). They found that men rated the vaginal odors of women sampled during the ovulatory phase as slightly more pleasant, albeit in neutral range, than samples extracted from other phases of the cycle.

More recent studies have corroborated such findings. For instance, Singh and Bronstad (2001) discovered that men evaluated the scent of shirts worn by women while they were fertile as more pleasant and sexy than the scent of shirts worn by women during the non-fertile phase of their menstrual cycle. Similarly, Havlicek, Dvořáková Bartoš, and Flegr, (2006) found that the scents of women in the follicular or fertile phase were rated as smelling the least intense and the most attractive as compared to other phases of the menstrual cycle. In addition, the attractiveness of body odor varied during all phases of the cycle, as well (i.e., follicular, luteal, and menstrual). Although the magnitude of these cyclic changes was considerably less than differences seen between women, they were nonetheless perceivable and may play a role in directing sexual activity (Havlicek et al., 2006). Men may be able to use smell as a mechanism for monitoring menstrual cycle phase in current or prospective sexual partners.

One criticism regarding the design of these studies is the verification of whether odors were truly being collected while a woman was ovulating. Gildersleeve, Haselton, Larson, Pillsworth (2012) sought to correct for this issue. They collected samples of woman's natural body scent across the menstrual cycle after wearing cotton gauze pads under both underarms for a period of 24 hours. One collection was done during the woman's high-fertility period which was verified by ovulation urine test kits, and the other collection occurred during the low-fertility time verified by the date of the women's menstruation. They found that not only could men accurately discriminate between the low- and high-fertility odor samples, but men thought the high-fertility scents were more attractive. The authors suggest that high-fertility body scents may increase men's testosterone levels which, in turn, could direct a man's mating effort toward those women.

Men's preference for the odors of women during mid-cycle was more pronounced than it was for women rating the odors of other women (Kuukasjarvi et al., 2004). This finding makes sense as it would be more important for men than women to detect the reproductive status of women in order to reproduce. Nonetheless, female raters showed a trend similar to men, although not significant, suggesting that women may also have some ability to detect the reproductive status of other women, perhaps for reasons related to intrasexual competition.

How long can these scents last? Men were still able to decipher and prefer the shirts worn by fertile women even after the shirts were kept at room temperature for a week, emphasizing how intense the scent is (Singh & Bronstad, 2001). It is also important to note that no changes of the smell of women's worn T-shirts were observed across the menstrual cycle in women using hormonal oral contraception (Kuukasjarvi et al., 2004). Women on the pill serve as a good control group because they do not ovulate, and consequently, should not display these body odor changes. This finding also implies that women's body odors may have a hormonal basis; this effect is sex hormone dependent presumably as a result of changing amounts or ratios of estrogen and progesterone.

Fertility Tips. Another study examined the tip earning rates of exotic dancers across their menstrual cycles. Dancers who were naturally cycling earned more tips when they were ovulating whereas dancers on birth control experienced no earning peak prior to menstruation (Miller, Tybur, & Jordan, 2007). Either the women could have been acting differently to secure greater tips during ovulation or it could be possible that the pheromones released during ovulation made male clients more attracted to the women which led to their greater financial endowments. In other words, women's cycling hormones may influence men's attraction and sexual approach behavior (Gildersleeve et al., 2012).

Given the evidence of detection of body odor changes across the menstrual cycle, Havlicek and colleagues (2006) suggested that the fertile period in human females should be not be considered as concealed, rather just non-advertised.

Pregnancy Scent. In addition to detecting the fertile time in a woman's menstrual cycle through body scent, it also seems possible to determine whether a woman is pregnant from her body odor. Specific chemicals were detected in axillae and areola of pregnant women that showed systematic fluctuations during pregnancy and in women lactating after delivery (Vaglio et al., 2009). As such, men rate samples of axillary odor of women in their second trimester as most pleasant (Lenochová & Havlicek 2011). Pregnant women not only smell more attractive to men, but also to insects. Pregnant women get bitten more by mosquitos (Ansell et al., 2002) presumably because levels of short-chain fatty acids made their body odor more appealing to the insects (Smallegange et al., 2009).

The Scent of Gender

Several studies have documented that the assessment of gender via body odor occurs at a level greater than chance (Doty Orndorff, Leyden, & Klingman, 1978; Hold & Schleidt 1977; Russell, 1976; Schleidt 1980) and judgments are more accurate when rating the opposite sex (Sorokowska, Sorokowski, & Szmajke, 2012). However, this effect is not necessarily very robust. Doty et al. (1978) found only a small proportion of their observers predicted the sex of the odor donor above chance levels. Likewise, Hold and Schleidt (1977) found that only one third of their participants were capable of distinguishing male from female odors, but their sample was very small (10 subjects). Interestingly, another study showed both male and female axillary odors were rated as more masculine than feminine, regardless of the sex of the donor (Mutic et al., 2015). Further, hygienic procedures can diminish personal odors and suppress the ease at which distinctions between male and female odors can occur (Schleidt, 1980). It may be the case that we attribute male dominance and physical activity to sweat, thereby perceiving any body odor as masculine. In contrast, women will often use fragrances and perfumes to mask their natural body odors so we may not associate the smell of sweat with femininity.

DoD photo by Marine Lance Cpl. G. Kindred, public domain.

Evidence has long suggested that women tend to be more accurate than men in recognizing the sex of a donor on the basis of body odor (Hold & Schleidt, 1977). This accuracy of women detecting gender from odors occurs regardless of oral contraception use (Wedekind & Füri, 1997). Given that women tend to be overall slightly more sensitive to various odors than men (Doty and Cameron, 2009), it makes sense that they may be more perceptive in appraising gender from body scent. Furthermore, women value olfactory cues more than men in both sexual and non-sexual contexts (Havlicek et al., 2008). Nevertheless, contrary to these studies, Sorokowska et al. (2012) did not find that women were any more accurate than men in assessing donor odor sex, so there is some debate as to whether such a sex difference in this ability exists.

Assigning gender to a donor's odor sample may be accomplished by the perceived intensity and pleasantness of the axillary odor. Female body odor is typically rated as more pleasant and less intense than male body odor (McBurney et al., 1976; Hold and Schleidt, 1977). Alternatively, stronger and less pleasant odors are more frequently assigned to a male gender category (Doty, Orndorff, Leyden, & Kligman, 1978). Wedekind and Füri (1997) also found that smellers tended to ascribe more pleasant body odors as female and more unpleasant ones as male regardless of whether actual gender of the donor. Likewise, more intense odors are stereotypically attributed as male than female, independent of the actual sex of the odor donor (Doty et al., 1978). To our knowledge, there was only one study that showed male body odors were actually rated as more pleasant than were female body odors, but the odors were only evaluated by female raters (Sorokowska, Sorokowski, & Havlícek, 2016).

The Scent of Old Age

Does your grandmother's house smell different or is that in your head? Apparently, humans are able to discriminate age based on body odor alone, but this effect is mediated by those who are older age. When body odors were sampled from three age groups categorized as young (20-30 years old), middle-age (45-55), and old-age (75-95), participants were only able of accurately assign body odors for the elderly group but not from the two younger groups (Mitro, Gordon, Olsson, & Lundstrom, 2012). Further, young raters judged body odors from the old age group as smelling less intense and less unpleasant than odors emitted from the other age groups. This contradicts popular anecdotal reports that so-called "old-age odors" are unpleasant. Perhaps if participants were made aware of the true origin of these odors, these odors may have been rated more negatively due to a bias toward old age.

What is driving this effect? When investigating the changes in body odor associated with aging, analysis of skin surface lipids indicated that 2-nonenal, an unsaturated aldehyde that has been linked with a greasy and grassy odor, was detected only in subjects over the age of 40 and there was also an increase in unsaturated fatty acids and lipid peroxides in skin surface lipids (Haze et al., 2001). Yamazaki, Hoshino, and Kusuhara (2010) pointed out that changes in body odor due to aging may be directly related to sweat gland activity and sebum composition or indirectly related to food intake and amounts of physical activity. For these reasons, body odor may function as a barometer for one's physical condition at a given age. From an evolutionary perspective, being able to detect body odor changes across age may be adaptive in eliminating older individuals as possible mates when younger.

The Scent of Diet

Body odor can also provide information about one's diet. For instance, women rated the sweat of men who had a greater intake of fruits and vegetables (as recorded through skin spectrophotometry measures) as more pleasant smelling, and this was independent of their perception of sweat intensity (Zuniga, Stevenson, Mahmut, & Stephen, 2017). Moreover, the odors of men who had self-reported diets that included an intake of fats, meats, eggs, and tofu were rated as smelling more pleasant, whereas men who had greater carbohydrate intake had less pleasant, stronger smelling sweat. Because diet and health often go hand and hand, being able to assess the diet of a potential mate through body odor would be advantageous during mate selection.

Along these lines, garlic has been shown to have many beneficial health effects due to its antioxidant properties and antimicrobial activity, and ingested garlic has been known to create a certain breath and body odor (Tattelman, 2005). While we may think that the body odor garlic produces is aversive, research actually shows that prolonged periods of garlic consumption has positive effects on perceived body odor and an increased dosage of garlic had increased the assessment of odor to be more attractive, pleasant, and less intense (Fialová, Roberts, & Havlicek, 2016). Again, this speaks to the idea of how pleasant-smelling body odor can be revealing of a person's healthy diet.

Another study tested the effects of food deprivation on the quality of body odor (Fialová et al., 2019). They found that body odors were rated as more pleasant, more attractive, and less intense after the restoration of food intake following a 48-hour period of food deprivation as compared to the baseline (i.e., habitual, regular food regimen) and the calorie restriction periods. If body odor is an index of both food quantity and quality of one's diet, then based on these grounds alone, body odor can be important for making wise mate assessments. The fact that the hedonic properties of body odor increased following the reinstitution of food intake after food restriction means that body odor could also provide cues about metabolic efficiency. Moreover, if we consider the numerous health benefits of periodic fasting regimes (e.g., lowered body weight, body fat, total cholesterol, LDL cholesterol, blood pressure; see Seimon et al., 2015), a diet that is popularized today and known as an "intermittent fasting" diet, then these health effects could be consequently reflected in body odor. Intermittent fasting probably was similar to the diet of our ancestors, who likely ate in feast and famine patterns given their foraging and hunting lifestyle (Knight, 2011).

The Scent of Sickness

Some diseases and infections can create a distinct odor that can be detected (Olsson et al., 2014). Volatile compounds found in human body odor resulting from poor health or disease could be the result of either altered metabolism or direct effects from the infectious agents (Havlicek, Fialová, & Roberts, 2017). From an evolutionary perspective, it would be advantageous to detect various pathogens in others as a first defense to optimize avoidance of contagion (Olsson et al., 2014) The idea that odor can trigger a behavioral immune response so as to avoid interpersonal contact with an infected individual was even demonstrated experimentally. Olsson and colleagues (2014) had injected participants with endotoxins in order to activate their immune system and found that, compared to controls who received a placebo, those infected had a more aversive body odor that could be detected by others and observable just within a few hours. This is good evidence that humans seem to detect social cues of sickness through body odor alone.

There are several examples of diseases that produce distinct body odors (for reviews, see Havlicek, Fialová, & Roberts, 2017; Kippenberger et al., 2012). For instance, those suffering from pneumonia and who have tuberculosis tend to have a foul breath odor (Liddell, 1976; Syhre & Chambers, 2008) while those suffering from typhoid fever are said to smell like baked bread (Liddell, 1976). Patients with isovaleric acidemia produce high levels of isovaleric acid in body fluids and urine which causes a distinctive odor of sweaty feet (Tanaka et al., 1968); this acid is shown to cause neurological conditions, so it is no wonder we avoid this fetid scent, as research shows that the bacteria in feet can cause meningitis, sepsis, gangrene, and many other deleterious conditions (see Harrison & McFalls, 2010, for review).

There are specific scents associated with some health conditions, and some evidence suggests these scents can be used as diagnostic tools. Phenylketonuria is a gene mutation disorder that causes a deficiency in the enzyme phenylalanine hydroxylase needed to break down the amino acid, phenylalanine. If phenylalanine is consumed in one's diet, it will convert to phenylpyruvic acid and phenylacetate which are excreted in sweat and urine that gives off a musty smell resembling sweaty locker rooms (Cone, 1968).

Diabetics produce a breath that has a sweet smell because of their elevated levels of ketones producing acetone from their breath (Laffel, 1999). Bacterial vaginosis can cause a cheesy or fishy vaginal odor which is the result production of highly odorous trimethylamine (Wolrath et al., 2005). In fact, changes in vaginal odor can be used by gynecologists as a diagnostic (Anderson, Klink, & Cohrssen, 2004).

Several carcinomas can be identified through a marked odor profile as evidenced by studies showing that dogs can be trained to differentiate between breath or urine odor samples taken from people suffering from lung, bladder, and prostate cancer (Moser & McCulloch, 2010). Apparently, dogs can be used for their keen sense of smell as "cancer detectors." Thus, body odor provides many clues to one's health, and apparently one can "smell sickness."

The Scent of Mental Health

There are claims that psychiatric hospital personnel report that certain psychiatric conditions are associated with peculiar odors (Havlicek, Fialová, & Roberts, 2017). Schizophrenia is one such mental health condition that has long been associated with a certain body odor (Smith & Sines, 1960). Those inflicted with schizophrenia have been shown to have elevated levels of a compound, trans-3-methyl-2-hexenoic acid that has been linked to having a distinct odor (DiNatale et al., 2005; Smith et al., 1969), and this odor might be linked with metabolic enzyme deficiencies (Liddell, 1976). Additionally, other volatile compounds contributing to a breath odor has been associated with schizophrenia (Phillips et al., 1995). Of note, it has been shown that none of these compounds associated with schizophrenia can be attributed to side effects of the neuroleptic medication that is taken as treatment.

There are also some affective states such as anxiety that can influence axillary body odor (Fialová & Havlicek, 2012) and smelling axillary odors associated with a stress response negatively influenced social evaluations in terms of confidence, trustworthiness, and competence (Dalton, Mauté, Jaén, & Wilson, 2013). It would be interesting to see if these findings could be extended to examine those who possess certain anxiety disorders.

The Scent of Personality Traits

Information about an individual's personality may also be conveyed through olfactory cues. Correlations were found between scent ratings and self-assessed personality dimensions of odor donors, particularly for extraversion, neuroticism, and dominance (Sorokowska, Sorokowski, & Szmajke, 2012). These personality traits, in particular, might have stronger connection with substances influencing body odor than other personality traits; evidence suggests that certain hormones, enzymes, and neurotransmitters might directly or indirectly link extraversion, neuroticism, and dominance to the composition of human body odor (for review, see Sorokowska et al., 2012). Furthermore, judgments of dominance were most accurate when participants rated the odor of the opposite sex, suggesting that odor cues are especially important for mating. Ratings of odor attractiveness also predicted targets' personalities (Sorokowska, 2013a). The precise mechanism underlying the association between body odor and personality traits is not well understood. It is presumed that in the case of dominance, both traits may be underpinned by levels of testosterone (Havlicek, Roberts, & Flegr, 2005).

There are some age differences in the accuracy of personality assessment via body odor. It appears that both children and adults could accurately assess neuroticism, whereas only adults could correctly identify dominance (Sorokowska, 2013b). From these findings, the author concluded that the ability to assess personality traits using body odor goes beyond mating contexts and people seem to acquire this competence in childhood. People might learn to assess dominance using body odor only after mate choice becomes relevant, as dominance can indicate that a mate is healthy and fertile because it correlates positively with testosterone (Mazur & Booth, 1998).

The ability to accurately determine both the sex and personality via body odor samples is even evident in those who are blind. Sorokowska and Oleszkiewicz (2019) showed that early blind and later blind people had not differed from sighted individuals in accurately determining the sex and personality from body odor samples, nor did the groups differ in their assessment of perceived intensity, pleasantness, or attractiveness of the odors. These findings are a testament to the fact that visual information does not seem to modulate sensitivity to socially relevant cues transmitted by body odors. Body odors seem to be just as important as visual and auditory cues for assessing some personal attributes about another, including certain personality traits.

Obscuring Body Scents

Given the amount of information that body scent offers, it is a wonder why we often will mask our body odors through the use of certain cosmetic perfumes, colognes, scented deodorants, scented soaps, and other fragrances. The use of these cosmetics can affect body odor perception, and fragrances can interact with body odor creating an individually specific odor mixture (Lenochová et al., 2012). In fact, fragrance use extends beyond the simple masking of unpleasant body odor and it has been shown that people tend to select perfumes that interact well with their own body odor to create positive body odor perceptions (Lenochová et al., 2012). .

The use of fragrances is particularly impactful when assessing attractiveness and when making accurate personality assessments via body odor. For instance, ratings of body odor attractiveness and pleasantness were significantly lower for natural body odors than those who wore fragranced cosmetics, but notwithstanding, the intensity of the odors was rated similarly (Sorokowska, Sorokowski, Havlícek, Koster, & Freiherr, 2016). As for personality assessment, self-assessed neuroticism showed stronger correlations with odor ratings for natural body odors than odors masked with cosmetics use, while odor ratings for dominance significantly predicted self-rated dominance regardless of cosmetic use of the odor donors. The use of perfumes and colognes has also been shown to affect the perception of job applicants. Male interviewers viewed both male and female job applicants less favorably if they wore cologne/perfume, whereas female interviewers viewed them more positively (Baron, 1983). The authors attributed this sex difference to the fact that men had greater difficulty than women ignoring extraneous aspects of the applicant's appearance and grooming which men found interfered with their ability to be an effective interviewer.

The act of masking body odor with fragrances is likely a more recent vintage in our evolutionary history. As mentioned in Chapter 6, it would not have been adaptive for early humans to obscure their body odors when living in the EEA. Leakey's Unpalatability Hypothesis (1967) posits that human's potent body odor advertised the unpalatability of our flesh and served as a defense against predation. So, our survival depended upon our body scent. Today, most of us do not have to contend with and worry about attacks from predators, so we are left with what we may find is a repugnant body odor that we feel compelled to disguise with fragrances and cleansers.

Conclusion

Body odor appears to be another vital tool for assessment that can reveal several attributes including mate quality, age, gender, kin, fertility, diet, physical and mental health, sexual orientation, and personality. Being able to use the sense of smell in addition to our other senses to decipher information about potential mates (whether this occurred consciously or not) probably served us well throughout our ancestral past in selecting more viable mates. Along with the theme of "judging a book by its cover," what we can take from this chapter is that perhaps we should not take things only at *face* value but at *nose* value, as well.

References

Anderson, M. R., Klink K., & Cohrssen, A. (2004). Evaluation of vaginal complaints. *Journal of the American Medical Association (JAMA), 291*(11), 1368-1379. doi:10.1001/jama.291.11.1368

Ansell, J., Hamilton , K. A., Pinder, M., Walraven, G. E. L., & Lindsay, S.W. (2002). Short-range attractiveness of pregnant women to Anopheles gambiae mosquitoes. *Transactions of The Royal Society of Tropical Medicine and Hygiene, 96* (2):113-116. https://doi.org/10.1016/S0035-9203(02)90271-3

Barkat-Defradas, M. (2016). *Words for odours : Language skills and cultural insights.* Newcastle upon Tyne: Cambridge Scholars Publishing

Baker, B. M., & Evavold, B. D. (2017). MHC bias bt T cell receptors: Genetic evidence for MHC and TCR coevolution. *Trends in Immunology, 38*(1), 2-4. https://doi.org/10.1016/j.it.2016.11.003

Baron, R. A. (1983). "Sweet smell of success:"? The impact of pleasant artificial scents on evaluations of job applicants. *Journal of Applied Psychology, 68*(4), 709-713.

Beier, K., Ginez, I., & Schaller, H. (2005). Localization of steroid hormone receptors in the apocrine sweat glands of the human axilla. *Histochemistry and Cell Biology, 123*, 161-165.

Borráz-León, J. I., Cerda-Molina, A. L., & Mayagoitia-Novales, L. (2017). Testosterone level changes after perceiving the body odour of a possible rival in human males: The role of facial symmetry. *Behaviour, 154*(6), 677-691. https://doi-org/10.1163/1568539X-00003437

Cerda-Molina, AL. L. et al. (2013). Changes in men's salivary testosterone and cortisol levels, and in sexual desire, after smelling female axillary and vulvar scents. *Frontiers in Endocrinology, 4*(159). doi: 10.3389/fendo.2013.00159

Cernoch, J. M., & Porter, R. H. (1885). Recognition of maternal axillary odors by infants. *Child Development, 56*, 1593-1598.

Charlesworth, D., & Willis, J. H. (2009). The genetics of inbreeding depression. *Nature Reviews Genetics, 10*, 783-796. https://doi.org/10.1038/nrg2664

Cone, T. E. (1968). Diagnosis and treatment – some diseases syndromes and conditions associated with an unusual odor. *Pediatrics, 41*(5), 993-995.

Dalton, P., Mauté, C., Jaén, C., & Wilson, T. (2013). Chemosignals of stress influence social judgments. *PLoS ONE, 8*(10), 1.

Di Natale, C., Paullese, R., D'Arcangelo, G., Comandini, P., Pennazza, G., Martinelli, E., Rullo, S., Roscioni, M. C., Roscioni, C., Finazzi-Agrò, A., & D'Amico, A. (2005). Identification of schizophrenic patients by examination of body odor using gas chromatography-mass spectrometry and a cross-selective gas sensor array. *Medical Science Monitor, 11*(8), 366-375.

Doty, R. L., & Cameron, E. L. (2009). Sex differences and reproductive hormone influences on human odor perception. *Physiology and Behavior, 97*(2), 213-228. https://doi.org/10.1016/j.physbeh.2009.02.032

Doty, R. L., Ford, M., Preti, G., & Huggins, G. R. (1975). Changes in the intensity and pleasantness of human vaginal odors during the menstrual cycle. *Science, 190*(4221), 1316-1318. https://doi.org/10.1126/science.1239080

Doty, R. L., Orndorff, M. M., Leyden, J., & Kligman, A. (1978). Communication of gender from human axillary odors: Relationship to perceived intensity and hedonicity. *Behavioral Biology, 23*(2), 373-380.

Ferdenzi, C., Schaal, B., & Roberts, C. (2010). Family scents: Developmental changes in the perception of kin body odor? *Journal of Chemical Ecology, 36*, 847-854.

Fialová, J, & Havlicek , J. (2012). Perception of emotion-related odours in humans. *Anthropologie, 50*(1), 95-110.

Fialová, J., Hoffmann, R., Roberts, S. C., & Havlicek, J. (2019). The effect of complete caloric intake restriction on human body odour quality. *Physiology & Behavior*, 112554. https://doi.org/10.1016/j.physbeh.2019.05.015

Fialová, J., Roberts, S. C., & Havlicek, J. (2016). Consumption of garlic affects hedonic perception of axillary body odour, *Appetite, 97*, 8-15. https://doi.org/10.1016/j.appet.2015.11.001

Gallup, G. G., Jr., & Cameron, P. A. (1992). Modality specific metaphors: Is our mental machinery "colored" by a visual Bias? *Metaphor and Symbolic Activity, 7*(2), 93-98.

Gangestad, S. W., & Thornhill, R. (1998). Menstrual cycle variation in women's preferences for the scent of symmetrical men. *Proceedings of the Royal Society B: Biological Sciences, 265*, 927-933.

Garver-Apgar, C. E., Gangestad, S. W., & Thornhill, R. (2008). Hormonal correlates of women's mid-cycle preference for the scent of symmetry. *Evolution and Human Behavior, 29*(4), 223-232. doi:10.1016/j.evolhumbehav.2007.12.007

Gildersleeve, K. A., Haselton, M. G., Larson, C. M., & Pillsworth, E. G. (2012). Body odor attractiveness as a cue of impending ovulation in women: Evidence from a study using hormone-confirmed ovulation. *Hormones and Behavior, 61*(2), 157-166. https://doi.org/10.1016/j.yhbeh.2011.11.005

Grammer, K., Fink, B., & Neave, N. (2004). Human pheromones and sexual attraction. *European Journal of Obstetrics and Gynecology, 118*(2), 135-142. https://doi-org/10.1016/j.ejogrb.2004.08.010

Harrison, M. A., & McFalls, A. J. (2012). A primal reaction to fetid feet? A brief report. *Human Ethology Bulletin*, 27(3), 8-13.

Havlicek, J., Dvořáková, R., Bartoš, L. & Flegr, J. (2006). Non-advertised does not mean concealed: Body odour changes across the human menstrual cycle, *Ethology, International Journal of Behavioural Biology, 112*(1), 81-90. https://doi.org/10.1111/j.1439-0310.2006.01125.x

Havlicek, J., Fialová, J., & Roberts, S.C. (2017). Individual variation in body odor. *Springer Handbook of Odor, Springer.* https://doi.org/10.1007/978-3-319-26932-0_50Havlicek, J., Murray, A. K., Saxton, T. K., Roberts, S.C. (2010). Current issues in the study of androstenes in human chemosignaling. *Vitamins and Hormones, 83*, 47-81. doi: 10.1016/S0083-6729(10)83003-1Havlicek, J., & Roberts, S. C. (2009). MHC-correlated mate choice in humans: A review. *Psychoneuroendocrino 34* (4), 497-512.

Havlicek, J., Roberts, S. C., & Flegr, J. (2005). Women's preference for dominant male odour: Effects of menstrual cycle and relationship status. *Biological Letters, 1*, 256-259. https://doi.org/10.1098/rsbl.2005.0332Havlicek, J., Saxton, T. K., Roberts, S. C., Jozifkova, E., Lhota, S., Valentova, J., & Flegr, J. (2008). He sees, she smells? Male and female reports of sensory reliance in mate choice and non-mate choice contexts. *Personality and Individual Differences, 45*(6), 565-570. https://doi-org.10.1016/j.paid.2008.06.019

Haze, S., Gozu, Y., Nakamura, S., Kohno, Y., Sawano, K., Ohta, H., & Yamazaki, K. (2001). 2-nonenal newly found in human body odor tends to increase with aging. *Journal of Investigative Dermatology, 116*(4), 520-524. https://doi-org.felix.albright.edu/10.1046/j.0022-202X.2001.01287.x

Herz, R. S., & Inzlicht, M. (2002). Sex differences in response to physical and social factors involved in human mate selection: The importance of smell for women. *Evolution and Human Behavior, 23*(5), 359-364. https://doi-org./10.1016/S1090-5138(02)00095-8

Hold, B., & Schleidt, M. (1977). The importance of human odour in non-verbal communication. *Zeitschrift für Tierpsychologie, 43*,225-238. https://doi.org/10.1111/j.1439-0310.1977.tb00072.x

Huchard, E., Baniel, A., Schliehe, Diecks, S., Kappeler, P. M. (2013). MHCdisassortative mate choice and inbreeding avoidance in a solitary primate. *Molecular Ecology, 22*(15), 4071-4086. https://doi.org/10.1111/mec.12349.

Hughes, S. M. & Harrison, M. A. (2013). I like my voice better: Self-enhancement bias in perceptions of voice attractiveness. *Perception, 42,* 941-949. doi:10.1068/p7526

Jacob, S., McClintock, M.K., Zelano, B., & Ober, C. (2002). Paternally inherited HLA alleles are associated with male choice of male odor. *Nature Genetics, 30*, 175-179.

Keller, M., Baum, M. J., Brock, O., Brennan, P. A., & Bakker, J. (2009). The main and the accessory olfactory systems interact in the control of mate recognition and sexual behavior. *Behavioural Brain Research, 200*(2), 268-276.

Kippenberger, S., Havlicek, J., Bernd, A., Thaçi, D., Kaufmann, R., & Meissner, M. (2012). "Nosing Around" the human skin: what information is concealed in skin odour? *Experimental Dermatology, 21*(9), 655-659. https://doi.org/10.1111/j.1600-0625.2012.01545.x

Knight, C. (2011). '"Most people are simply not designed to eat pasta": Evolutionary explanations for obesity in the low-carbohydrate diet movement', *Public Understanding of Science, 20*(5), 706-719. https://doi.org/10.1177/0963662510391733

Kuukasjarvi, S., Eriksson, C. J. P., Koskela, E., Mappes, T., Nissinen, K., & Rantala, M. J. (2004). Attractiveness of women's body odors over the menstrual cycle: The role of oral contraceptives and receiver sex. *Behavioral Ecology, 15*(4), 579-584. https://doi.org/10.1093/beheco/arh050

Laffel, L. (1999). Ketone bodies: a review of physiology, pathophysiology and application of monitoring to diabetes. *Diabetes/Metabolism Research and Reviews, 15*(6), 412-426.

Leakey L.S. B. (1967). Development of aggression as a factor in early human and pre-human evolution. In C. Clemente & D. Lindsley (Eds). *Brain function, vol. V. Aggression and defense.* Berkeley: University of California Press, 1–33.

Lenochová, P., & Havlicek, J. (2011). *Fragrant expectations – Changes of female body odour quality during pregnancy and after delivery.* Paper presented at the VIth European Human Behaviour and Evolution Association Conference, Giessen, Germany

Lenochová, P., Vohnoutová, P., Roberts, P., Oberzaucher, E., Grammer, K., & Havlíče, J. (2012). Psychology of fragrance use: Perception of individual perfume blends reveals a mechanism for idiosyncratic effects on fragrance choice. *PLoS One.* https://doi.org/10.1371/journal.pone.0033810

Liddell, K. (1976). Smell as a diagnostic marker. *Postgraduate Medical Journal, 52* (605), 136-138. http://dx.doi.org/10.1136/pgmj.52.605.136

Lübke, K. T., Hoenen, M., & .Pause, B, M. (2012). Differential processing of social chemosignals obtained from potential partners in regards to gender and sexual orientation. *Behavioral Brain Research, 228*(2), 375-387. https://doi.org/10.1016/j.bbr.2011.12.018

Lübke, K., Schablitsk, S., & Pause, B. M. (2009). Male sexual orientation affects sensitivity to androstenone. *Chemosensory Perception, 2*(3), 154-160.

Lundström, J. N., & Jones-Gotman, M. (2009). Romantic love modulates women's identification of men's body odors. *Hormones and Behavior, 55*(2), 280–284. https://doi-org /10.1016/j.yhbeh.2008.11.009

Martins, Y., Preti, G., Crabtree, C. R., Runyan, T., Vainius, A. A., & Wysocki. C. J. (2005). Preference for human body odors is influenced by gender and sexual orientation. *Psychological Science, 16*(9), 694-701.

Mazur, A., & Booth, A. (1998). Testosterone and dominance in men. *Behavioral Brain Sciences, 21*(3), 353-363. https://doi.org/10.1017/S0140525X98001228

McBurney, D. H., Levine, J. M., & Cavanaugh, P. H. (1977). Psychophysical and social ratings of human body odor. *Personality and Social Psychology Bulletin, 3*(1), 135–138. https://doi-org/10.1177/014616727600300126

Meredith, M. (2001). Human vomeronasal organ function: A critical review of the best and worst cases. *Chemical Senses, 26*(4), 433-445. https://doi.org/10.1093/chemse/26.4.433

Miller, G., Tybur, J. M., & Jordan, B. D. (2007). Ovulatory cycle effects on tip earnings by lap dancers: Economic evidence for human estrus? *Evolution and Human Behavior, 28*(6), 375-381. https://doi.org/10.1016/j.evolhumbehav.2007.06.002

Miller, S. L., & Maner, J. K. (2010). Scent of a woman: Men's testosterone responses to olfactory ovulation cues. *Psychological Science, 21*(2), 276-283. https://doi.org/10.1177/0956797609357733

Mitro, S., Gordon, A. R., Olsson, M. J., & Lundstrom, J. N. (2012). The smell of age: Perception and discrimination of body odors of different ages. *PLoS One, 7*(5). doi: 10.1371/journal.pone.0038110

Monti-Bloch, L., Diaz-Sanchez, V., Jennings-White, C., & Berliner, D. L. (1998). Modulation of serum, testosterone and autonomic function through stimulation of the male human vomeronasal organ (VNO) with pregna-4, 20-diene-3, 6dione. *The Journal of Steroid Biochemistry and Molecular Biology, 65*(1-6), 237-242. https://doi.org/10.1016/S0960-0760(98)00025-9

Moser, E., & McCulloch, M. (2010). Canine scent detection of human cancers: A review of methods and accuracy. *Journal of Veterinary, 5*(3), 145-152. https://doi.org/10.1016/j.jveb.2010.01.002

Mutic, S., Moellers, E. M., Wiesmann, M., & Freiherr, J. (2016). Chemosensory communication of gender information: Masculinity bias in body odor perception and femininity bias introduced by chemosignals during social perception. *Frontiers in Psychology, 20*, 1980. https://doi.org/10.3389/fpsyg.2015.01980

Olsson, M. J., Lundström, J. N., Kimball, B. A., Gordon, A. R., Karshikoff, B., Hosseini, N., ... Lekander, M. (2014). The scent of disease: Human body odor contains an early chemosensory cue of sickness. *Psychological Science, 25*(3), 817-823. https://doi-org/10.1177/0956797613515681

Penn, D. J., & Potts, W. K. (1999). The evolution of mating preferences and major histocompatibility complex genes. *The American Naturalist, 153*(2), 145-164.

Penton-Voak, I. S., & Perrett, D. I. (2000). Female preference for male faces changes cyclically: Further evidence. *Evolution and Human Behavior, 21*(1), 39-48. https://doi.org/10.1016/S1090-5138(99)00033-1

Penton-Voak, I. S., Perrett, D. I., Castles, D. L., Kobayashi, T., Burt, D. M., Murray, L. K. & Minamisawa, R. (1999). Menstrual cycle alters face preference. *Nature, 399*, 741-742. https://doi.org/10.1038/21557

Phillips, M., Erickson, G. A., Sabas, M., Smith, J.P., & Greenberg, J. (1995). Volatile organic compounds in the breath of patients with schizophrenia. *Journal Clinical Pathology, 48*(5), 466-469. https://doi.org/10.1136/jcp.48.5.466

Platek, S. M., Burch, R. L., & Gallup, Jr., G. G. (2001). Sex differences in olfactory self-recognition. *Physiology and Behavior, 73*(4), 635-640. https://doi.org/10.1016/S0031-9384(01)00539-X

Porter, R. H. (1999). Olfaction and human kin recognition. *Genetica, 104*(3), 259-263.

Porter, R. H., Cernoch, J. M., & Balogh, R. D. (1985). Odor signatures and kin recognition. *Physiology and Behavior, 34*(3), 445-448. https://doi-org/10.1016/0031-9384(85)90210-0

Porter, R. H., Cernoch, J. M., & McLaughlin, F. J. (1983). Maternal recognition of neonates through olfactory cues. *Physiology and Behavior, 30*(1), 151-154. https://doi.org/10.1016/0031-9384(83)90051-3

Rikowski, A., & Grammer, K. (1999). Human body odour, symmetry and attractiveness. *Proceedings of the Royal Society B, 266*, 869-874.

Roberts, S. C., Gosling, L. M., Spector, T. D., Miller, P., Penn, D. J., & Petrie, M. (2005). Body odor similarity in noncohabiting twins. *Chemical Senses, 30*(8), 651-656. https://doi-org/10.1093/chemse/bji058

Roberts, S. C., Kralevich, A., Ferdenzi, C., Saxton, T, Jones, B., DeBruine, L., Little, A. & Havlicek, J. (2011). Body odor quality predicts behavioral attractiveness in humans. *Archives of Sexual Behavior, 40*(6), 1111-1117. ISSN 0004-0002

Russell, M. J. (1976). Human olfactory communication. *Nature, 260*, 520–522.

Russell, M. J., Mendelson, T., & Peeke, H. V. S. (1983). Mother's identification of their infant's odors. *Ethology and Sociobiology, 4*(1), 29-31. https://doi.org/10.1016/0162-3095(83)90005-5

Santos, P. S. C., Schinemann, J.A., Gabardo, J., & Bicalho, M.D. (2005). New evidence that the MHC influences odor perception in humans: A study with 58 southern Brazilian students. *Hormones and Behavior, 47*(4), 384-388. https://doi.org/10.1016/j.yhbeh.2004.11.005

Saxton, T. K., Little, A. C., & Roberts, S. C. (2008) Ecological validity in the study of human pheromones. In: Hurst J.L., Beynon R.J., Roberts S.C., Wyatt T.D. (eds.) *Chemical signals in vertebrates, 11th ed.* Springer, New York, NY

Schleidt, M. (1980). Personal odor and nonverbal communication. *Ethology and Sociobiology, 1*(3), 225-231. https://doi.org/10.1016/0162-3095(80)90009-6

Seimon, R. V., Roekenes, J. A, Zibellini, J., Zhu, B., Gibson, A. A., Hills, A. P., Wood, R. E., King, N. A., Byrne, N. M., & Sainsbury, A. (2015). Do intermittent diets provide physiological benefits over continuous diets for weight loss? A systematic review of clinical trials, *Molecular and Cellular Endocrinology, 418*(2), 153-172.

Sergeant, M. J. T., Dickins, T. E., Davies, M. N. O., & Griffiths, M. D. (2007). Women's hedonic ratings of body odor of heterosexual and homosexual men. *Archives of Sexual Behavior, 36*(3), 395-401.

Shepherd, G. M. (2004). The human sense of smell: Are we better than we think? *PLoS Biology, 2*(5), e146. https://doi.org/10.1371/journal.pbio.0020146

Singh, D., & Bronstad, P. M. (2001). Female body odour is a potential cue to ovulation. *Proceedings of the Royal Society of London B: Biological Sciences, 268*(1469), 797-801. https://doi.org/10.1098/rspb.2001.1589

Smallegange, R., Qiu, Y., Bukovinszkiné-Kiss, G., Loon, J. A., Takken, W. (2009). The effect of aliphatic carboxylic acids on olfaction-based host-seeking of the malaria mosquito Anopheles gambiae sensu stricto. *Journal of Chemical Ecology, 35*(8), 933-943. https://doi.org/10.1007/s10886-009-9668-7

Smith, K., & Sines, J. O. (1960). Demonstration of a peculiar odor in the sweat of schizophrenia patients. *AMA Arch Gen Psychiatry*, 2(2), 184-188. doi:10.1001/archpsyc.1960.03590080060010

Smith, K., Thompson, G. F., & Koster, H. D. (1969). Sweat in schizophrenic patients: Identification of the odorous substance. *Science, 166* (3903), 398-399. https://doi.org/10.1126/science.166.3903.398

Sorokowska, A. (2013a). Seeing or smelling? Assessing personality on the basis of different stimuli. *Personality and Individual Differences, 55*(2), 175-179. https://doi.org/10.1016/j.paid.2013.02.026

Sorokowska, A. (2013b). Assessing personality using body odor: Differences between children and adults. *Journal of Nonverbal Behavior, 37*(3), 153-163.

Sorokowska,A., Butovskaya, M., & Veselovskaya, E. (2015). Partner's body odor vs. relatives' body odor: A comparison of female associations. *Polish Psychological Bulletin, 46*(2), 209-213. https://doi.org/10.1515/ppb-2015-0027

Sorokowska, A., & Oleszkiewicz, A. (2019). Body-odor based assessments of sex and personality – Non-significant differences between blind and sighted odor raters. *Physiology and Behavior*, 112573.

Sorokowska, A., Sorokowski, P., Havlicek, J., Koster, E. P., & Freiherr, J. (2016). Body odor based personality judgments: The effect of fragranced cosmetics. *Frontiers in Psychology*, 1-8. doi:10.3389/fpsyg.2016.00530

Sorokowska, A., Sorokowski, P., & Szmajke, A. (2012). Does personality smell? Accuracy of personality assessments based on body odour. *European Journal of Personality, 26*(5), 496-503. https://doi.org/10.1002/per.848

Stern, K., & McClintock, M. K. (1998). Regulation of ovulation by human pheromones. *Nature, 392*, 177-179. https://doi.org/10.1038/32408

Syhre, M., & Chambers, S. T. (2008). The scent of Mycobacterium tuberculosis. Tuberculosis, 88 (4), 317-323. https://doi.org/10.1016/j.tube.2008.01.002

Tanaka, K., Orr, J., & Isselbacher, K. (1968). Identification of β-hydroxyisovaleric acid in the urine of a patient with isovaleric acidemia. *Biochimica et Biophysica Acta (BBA) - Lipids and Lipid Metabolism , 152*(3), 638-641.

Tattelman, E. (2005). Health effects of garlic. *American Family Physician, 72*(1), 103-106.

Thornhill, R., Chapman, J. F., & Gangestad, S. W. (2013). Women's preferences for men's scents associated with testosterone and cortisol levels: Patterns across the ovulatory cycle. *Evolution and Human Behavior, 34*(3), 216-221. https://doi.org/10.1016/j.evolhumbehav.2013.01.003

Thornhill R., & Gangestad S.W. (2003). Do women have evolved adaptation for extra-pair copulation? In Voland E., & Grammer, K. (Eds.) *Evolutionary aesthetics*. Heidelberg, Germany: Springer.

Thornhill, R., & Gangestad, S. W. (1999). The scent of symmetry: A human sex pheromone that signals fitness? *Evolution and Human Behavior, 20*(3), 175-201. https://doi.org/10.1016/S1090-5138(99)00005-7

Thornhill, R., Gangestad, S. W., Miller, R., Scheyd, G., McCollough, J. K., & Franklin, M. (2003). Major histocompatibility complex genes, symmetry, and body scent attractiveness in men and women. *Behavioral Ecology, 14*(5), 668-678. https://doi.org/10.1093/beheco/arg043

Vaglio, S. (2009). Chemical communication and mother-infant recognition. *Communicative and Integrative Biology, 2*(3), 279-281.

Vaglio, S., Minicozzi, P., Bonometti E., Mello, G., & Chiarelli, B. (2009). Volatile signals during pregnancy: A possible chemical basis for mother-infant recognition. *Journal of Chemical Ecology, 35*(1), 131-139. https://doi.org 10.1007/s10886-008-9573-5

Wolrath ,H., Ståhlbom, B. Hallén, A. & Forsum, U. (2005).Trimethylamine and trimethylamine oxide levels in normal women and women with bacterial vaginosis reflect a local metabolism in vaginal secretion as compared to urine. *APMIS, 113* (7-8), 513-516. https://doi.org/10.1111/j.1600-0463.2005.apm_175.x

Wedekind, C., & Füri, S. (1997). Body odor preference in men and women: Do they aim for specific MHC combinations or simply heterozygosity? *Proceedings of the Royal Society B, 264*, 1471-1479. https://doi.org/10.1098/rspb.1997.0204

Wedekind, C., Seebeck, T., Bettens, F., & Paepke, A. J. (1995). MHC-dependent mate preferences in humans. *Proceedings of the Royal Society B: Biological Sciences, 260*(1359), 245-249. https://doi.org/10.1098/rspb.1995.0087

Yamazaki, S., Hoshino, K., & Kusuhara, M. (2010). Odor associated with aging. *Anti-Aging Medicine, 6*, 60-65. https://doi.org/10.3793/jaam.7.60

Zuniga, A., Stevenson, R. J., Mahmut, M. K., & Stephan, I. D. (2017). Diet quality and the attractiveness of male body odor. *Evolution and Human Behavior, 38*(1), 136-143. https://doi.org/10.1016/j.evolhumbehav.2016.08.002

Chapter 9

MINOR PHYSICAL ANOMALIES

Not everything that steps out of line, and thus "abnormal,"
must necessarily be "inferior."

-Hans Asperger

What does schizophrenia *look like?*

Minor physical anomalies (MPAs) are subtle congenital physical abnormalities, with no health or functional relevance, that remain stable after birth. Commonly studied MPAs are those of the head, eyes, ears, mouth, hands, feet, and torso (Compton & Walker, 2009). Documented MPAs include those presented in the accompanying Table, which we compiled from several studies.

A high prevalence of MPAs have been documented in those with mental illness. For example, as many as 60% of patients with schizophrenia have MPAs (Ismail et al., 1998). In comparison, there is a low prevalence in mentally healthy subjects (Sivkov & Akabaliey, 2003). Researchers suggest that MPAs can facilitate an understanding of perturbations of neurodevelopment. That is, the same stressors that cause MPAs to develop might also predispose people to develop mental illness (Compton & Walker, 2009; Schiffman et al., 2002).

Why might this be the case? Ismail and colleagues (1998) stated that "minor physical anomalies are fossilized imprints of early disturbance in embryonic development" (p. 1700). These developmental perturbations are tied to the first trimester of development (Guy, Majorski, Wallace, & Guy, 1983; Steg & Rapoport, 1975) and may occur with central nervous system maldevelopment (Campbell, Geller, Small, Petti, & Ferris, 1978; Hata, Iida, Iwasaka, Negoro, Ueda, & Kishimoto, 2003). Guy and colleagues (1983) emphasized that the emergence of these anomalies is evidence of central nervous system disturbance which may predispose individuals to behavioral and cognitive deficits. Myers et al. (2017) made a critical point that the brain and skin are formed from the same embryonic neuroectodermal tissue, and therefore MPAs may reflect brain development disturbances.

Coloboma of the iris develops before birth.

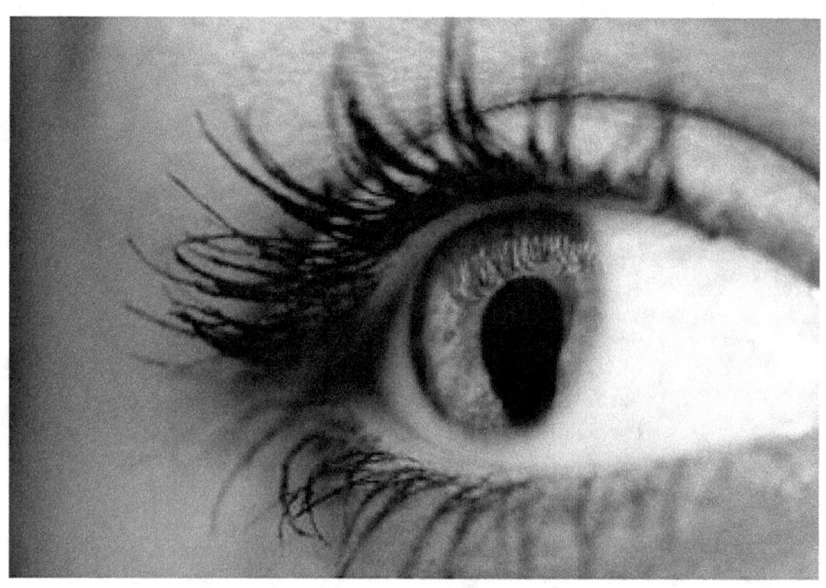

Image from U.S. National Library of Medicine, public domain.

We present here a Table that summarizes different MPAs commonly discussed in the literature. We compiled these findings from the studies noted in this chapter. Whereas MPAs themselves are typically inconsequential, they can be interpreted as signs of underlying conditions and could be used as diagnostic tools (Compton & Walker, 2009; Ozgen, Hop, Hox, Beemer, & van Engeland, 2010).

Commonly Documented Minor Physical Anomalies

Region	Trait
Head	Flat forehead
	Two or more hair whorls
	Frontal bossing (protrusion of skull)
	Flattened occiput (back of skull)
	Brachycephaly (broad, short skull)
	Protruding, malformed, and/or low-set ears
	Adherent ear lobes
	Earlobe crease
Face	Craniofacial asymmetry
	Fused eyebrows
	Hypertelorism (widely spaced eyes)
	Coloboma (missing tissue of the eye)
Mouth	Narrow, broad, or steeped palate
	Tongue asymmetry or furrows
	Rough and smooth spots on tongue
Hands	Curved fifth finger
and	Single palmar (simian) crease
Feet	Arachnodactyly (long digits)
	Digit syndactyly
	Large gap between great (first) toe and second toe
	Overlapping toes
Torso	Flat and pigmented birthmarks
	Polythelia (more than two nipples)
	Wide-set nipples

Note. *From Compton and Walker (2009); Dyshniku, Murray, Fazio, Lykins, & Cantor (2015); Gourion, Goldberger, Bourdel, Bayle, Lôo, and Krebs (2004); Ismail, Cantor-Graae, and McNeil, (1998); Myers et al., 2017; Waldrop, Halverson, and Shetterley (1989); Waldrop, Pedersen, and Bell (1968).*

MPAs are associated with disrupted prenatal development and are prevalent in some psychological conditions. We discuss these below. A higher prevalence of MPAs is related to earlier disease onset and earlier age of first psychiatric hospitalization (Gassab, Aissi, Slama, Gaha, & Mechri, 2013).

Compton and Walker (2009) reported that MPAs are not typically used for clinical diagnoses, but instead may be incidentally observed in patients. They are, however, sometimes documented for investigation purposes, with some researchers having developed and/or refined scales to assess their presence and compare them to unaffected population parameters (Green, Satz, Gaier, Ganzell, & Kharabi, 1989; Ismail et al., 1998; Lane et al., 1997; Waldrop & Halverson, 1972; Waldrop, Halverson, & Shetterley, 1989). Most studies we discuss in this chapter have used these scales to produce MPA scores to examine the relationship between MPAs and various mental health conditions.

Schizophrenia. Schizophrenia is a severe, chronic mental disorder. It is relatively uncommon; in a systematic review of the literature, researchers found a median lifetime morbid risk of 7.2/1000 with a male/female rate ratio of 1.4/1 (McGrath, Saha, Chant, & Welham, 2008). Schizophrenia is a spectrum disorder marked by a variety of symptoms that could include hallucinations, delusions, dysfunctional thought, stereotyped movements, flat affect, and anhedonia. Cognitive symptoms include diminished executive function (making decisions, controlling one's behavior, paying attention), and working memory deficits (National Institute of Mental Health, 2016). The exact causes of schizophrenia are unknown, but scientists believe there is a myriad of genetic, developmental, and stressor events that increase risk of developing the disorder (NIMH, 2016).

Can you determine if someone is at higher risk to develop the condition solely from their appearance? For all intents and purposes, it seems that someone trained for the task could detect morphological signs that signal risk of the disorder. Hands, feet, mouth, and eye MPAs can be used to distinguish patients with schizophrenia from controls (Green et al., 1989; Ismail, Cantor-Graae, & McNeil, 1998). Xu, Chan, and Compton (2011) argued that MPAs are endophenotypes for schizophrenia, meaning that they are manifestations that can be observed by trained persons as signals to disease. Gourion et al. (2004) reported that facial asymmetry, a typically assessed MPA, was a strong discriminator between patients with schizophrenia and controls. Gourion and colleagues stressed the relationship between dysregulated craniofacial and neurodevelopmental processes in schizophrenia.

MPAs have long been associated with dysmorphogenesis in schizophrenia (O'Callaghan, Larkin, Kinsella, & Waddington, 1991). Stated another way, this excess of MPAs in those with schizophrenia substantiates a neurodevelopmental underpinning to the disorder (Compton & Walker, 2009). There must be some developmental perturbation that is contributing to MPA expression and to the illness. In a meta-analysis of 13 relevant empirical articles tying MPAs to schizophrenia, Weinberg and colleagues (2007) found increased presence of MPAs in each of the six anatomical features of focus (eyes, ears, head, mouth, feet, and hands). They reported the largest effect size for the mouth region.

Green and colleagues (1989) also documented that patients with schizophrenia have more MPAs compared to controls, and those with earlier onset had more than those with later onset of the disorder. Whereas both men and women with schizophrenia had a high frequency of mouth MPAs, women with schizophrenia had more head circumference anomalies.

Schiffman et al. (2002) conducted a well-executed, longitudinal study of schizophrenia spectrum disorders. They documented MPAs in children, and 19 years later, found that those with a high number of these physical anomalies developed schizophrenia spectrum disorders at a higher rate than those with fewer MPAs. In addition, those with a high number of MPAs developed schizophrenia spectrum disorders more than they developed other disorders. Schiffman and colleagues asserted that MPAs evince neurodevelopmental stress.

As evidence for a genetic basis, MPAs scores are documented as higher in subjects with first-degree relatives with schizophrenia (Gassab et al., 2013; Gourion et al., 2004; O'Callaghan et al., 1991). Siblings of those with schizophrenia show a higher prevalence of MPAs than controls (Gassab et al., 2013), as do parents of those with schizophrenia (Gourion et al., 2004). Of note, Ismail and colleagues (1998) showed that although siblings of those with schizophrenia had a higher rate of MPAs than controls, there were very few associations between the degree or type of MPA between patient and sibling. One older study linked the presence of multiple anomalies to paternal psychopathology (Steg & Rapoport, 1975). Researchers contend that MPAs are highly heritable. However, like mental illnesses, researchers suggest that mutations and epigenetic forces can mediate MPA development (Compton & Walker, 2009).

Interestingly, Thoma and colleagues (2008) showed that MPAs were not associated with schizotypy, which is a personality type characterized by odd beliefs, paranoia, experiences of unusual sensations, and social anhedonia. Schizotypy is argued by some to fall on the milder end of the spectrum of schizophrenia, and researchers have posited that those expressing schizotypy may possess genetic vulnerability—the "diathesis"—to schizophrenia (Gooding, Tallent, & Matts, 2005; Meehl, 1990; Thoma et al., 2008). Further, those who exhibit increased schizotypal symptoms have an increased risk of psychosis (Gooding et al., 2005). However, Thoma and colleagues found that schizotypy was related to greater fluctuating asymmetry (FA). Whereas both MPAs and FA are indices of developmental instability, Thoma et al. (2008) noted that MPAs develop early on in gestation, whereas FAs can result from developmental perturbations throughout prenatal development, pointing to the importance of studying the timing of stressors in the development of schizophrenia.

Syndactyly of the fingers occurs at about 8 weeks in utero.

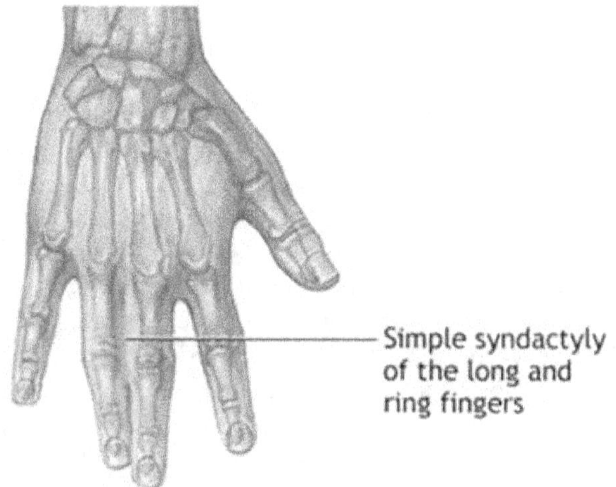

Image from U.S. National Library of Medicine, public domain.

However, a study by Blanchard et al. (2010) found increased MPAs in those with social anhedonia, which is a major characteristic of schizotypy. Further, within the social anhedonia group, Blanchard and colleagues noted that MPAs were positively associated with characteristics of schizoid personality disorder and schizotypal personality disorder. This suggests developmental dysmorphogenesis earlier in utero for these more severe conditions. Similarly, Weinstein et al. (1999) found more MPAs, including dermatoglyphic asymmetry (fingertip ridge symmetry), in those with schizotypal personality disorder compared to those with other personality disorders and those with no disorders. They also stressed the need for further research to focus on perturbations that occur during fetal development. Other researchers have also documented that MPAs are associated with increased dermatoglyphic asymmetry (Green, Bracha, Satz, & Christenson, 1994). Whereas other studies note that MPAs suggest maldevelopment in the first trimester, MPAs related to dermatoglyphic development would occur between weeks 14 and 22 of fetal development, suggesting maldevelopment in the second trimester (Green et al., 1994).

Although an extensive discussion of molecular genetics is beyond the scope of this book, it is worth noting that mouse models of the pathology of schizophrenia can experimentally create analogs to MPAs. To test the dopamine model of schizophrenia (a commonly investigated area), Kato and colleagues (2011) administered neuregulin-1 (NRG1) protein to neonatal mice. NRG1 is implicated in neural connectivity, and NRG1 receptors are highly expressed by dopamine neurons. The introduction of this protein created a hyperdopaminergic state in mice, resulting in dysregulated inhibitory and social behaviors after puberty. These behaviors are similarly seen in humans with schizophrenia. It also caused aberrant midbrain dopamine neuron development. Notably, the mice experienced altered developmental patterns of eyelid opening and teeth compared to controls (Kato et al., 2011). Thus, the experimental manipulation altered both the brain and physical features typically considered in MPA measures. This warrants further investigation.

Psychosis. Would you recognize that someone experiences psychosis by looking at them? That is questionable, but there do appear to be subtle physical differences between those who experience psychosis and those who do not. Psychosis can be a symptom of schizophrenia, but it is also associated with other conditions. Thus, it warrants a separate discussion as it relates to MPAs. McGrath, El-Saadi, and Grim (2002) examined MPAs of the face and head by recruiting individuals with psychosis and controls. They matched 180 pairs for age and sex. Those with wider skull bases, shorter and wider palates, and protruding ears had higher odds of having a psychotic disorder. McGrath et al. noted these features are associated with temporal lobe development, and indeed, reduced temporal lobe volume has been documented in schizophrenia (Turetsky, Cowell, Gur, Grossman, Shtasel, & Gur, 1995). McGrath and colleagues (1995) also documented a connection between MPAs and psychosis, and for male patients, noted an association between MPAs and family history of psychiatric disorder. Akabaliev and colleagues (2014) further documented a connection between MPAs and psychosis, demonstrating that those with schizophrenia had higher MPA scores than did bipolar I patients, with both having higher MPA scores than psychiatrically healthy controls. These findings further substantiate the idea that neurodevelopmental anomalies fall on a continuum for clinical psychosis.

The presentation of MPAs has also been associated with brain gray matter changes in psychosis. (Gray matter in the brain consists mainly of neuron cell bodies and glia). Dean et al. (2006) showed that in people with first-episode psychosis, there was a decrease in grey matter in the prefrontal cortex and precuneus. The precuneus is in the parietal lobe and is related to self-consciousness and sense of agency (Cavanna & Trimble, 2006), and an increase in the thalamus, basal ganglia, and lingual gyrus. The lingual gyrus is in the occipital lobe and is related to visual processing, color perception, and dreaming, and an increased volume has been associated with creative thinking (Zhang et al., 2016). These findings make a lot of sense as psychotic episodes will often involve hallucinations (i.e., visualizations, sensations, and perceptions that have no basis in reality) and a distorted sense of self.

Autism Spectrum Disorder (ASD). Autism spectrum is a group of neurodevelopmental disorders. It is characterized by social and communication impairments and restrictive, repetitive interests (Happé & Ronald, 2008). Autism has a strong genetic component as demonstrated by numerous twin/familial studies, with evidence suggesting disruption of proteins pertaining to increased neuronal connections (Bourgeron, 2015). It is a disorder of multiple impairments and considered one of the most highly heritable disorders (Happé & Ronald, 2008), if not the most heritable of any childhood behavior disorders (Miles & Hilllman, 2000).

Years ago, Campbell and colleagues (1978) observed more physical anomalies in children with autism compared to unaffected siblings and controls. Are there really physical signs of autism? There appear to be. Miles and Hillman (2000) asserted, "The percentage of phenotypically abnormal individuals is higher than generally thought and disagrees with the perception that children with autism are usually normally formed" (p. 245), reporting that 20% of children with autism have an abnormal phenotype. In a carefully designed meta-analysis, Ozgen and colleagues (2010) pointed out that those with autism display an excess of MPAs compared to controls, with a large effect size conveying a robust result.

Manouilenko et al. (2014) documented at least one MPA in each of 50 individuals with ASD in their sample. Those with ASD had more MPAs compared to controls, with most differences emerging in craniofacial areas and hands. Ear shape was also related to autistic traits in those with ASD. High MPAs related to lower functioning in those with ASD. They, like other researchers, stressed that MPAs develop early in utero, at the same time as structures of the central nervous system that may mediate ASD development.

Myers et al. (2017) also found MPAs more frequently in those with autism spectrum disorder (ASD), with monozygotic twins having a higher concordance rate than dizygotic twins, further implicating the role of genes in MPAs. Myers and colleagues suggested the use of MPAs as a diagnostic tool for ASD.

Miles and Hillman (2000) emphasized a need to examine the skewed sex ratio in autism (i.e., more males than females). They found that those with unaffected morphology (physical appearance) were much more likely to be male, whereas those with MPAs were nearly equally male and female. Since a 4:1 male-to-female ratio of autism is commonly reported (Werling & Geschwind, 2013), they argued that autism featuring MPAs might be exhibiting a subtype of autism as a product, at least in part, of disrupted embryogenesis. Using Miles and Hillman's (2000) criteria, Angkustsiri et al. (2014) studied MPAs in a large group of children. Consistent with previous results, they found that ASD children had more physical anomalies than controls.

Miles and colleagues (2005) stressed the need to address the heterogeneity of ASD and recommended dividing autism into two subgroups. Complex autism, they argued, is present in 20% of the autism population. These individuals show evidence of early morphogenesis with increased minor physical anomalies. All others would fall in the essential autism group. Miles et al. reported that individuals in the complex group had increased seizures, lower intelligence scores, more brain abnormalities, and more abnormal EEG activity. Studying disruptions to morphogenesis may allow for better treatment (Miles et al., 2005) and perhaps prevention in the future.

Some researchers have used MPAs as part of the criteria used to assess ASD. Those who have six or more MPAs (known as dysmorphic) are considered to have experienced early developmental dysmorphogenesis and are more likely to have brain structure abnormalities, low IQ, seizures, and genetic syndromes associated with autism (Miles & Hilllman, 2000). In their study, they used MRI scans to examine MPAs of autistic individuals and they found twice the incidence of brain abnormality in phenotypically abnormal subjects compared to phenotypically normal subjects. Affected areas were the frontal, parietal, and temporal lobes, with the majority of disturbances in the structures of the cerebellum. Miles and Hillman noted that "clinical morphology is a powerful tool that allows us to pick out individuals whose structural development was disrupted during early embryogenesis" (p. 248).

Hyperactivity. There is not a lot of published research addressing the connection between MPAs and hyperactivities. However, we include the mention of this research here, because some older studies by prominent experts in MPA analysis, such as Mary Waldrop, documented increased rates of MPAs in hyperactive children. Waldrop and colleagues (1968) found that the presence of MPAs was related to both hyperactivity and impatience in a sample of 74 typically developing 2.5-year-old children. They stated that the more MPAs a child had, the more the child was to be "aggressive, hyperkinetic, and intractable" (p. 399). Waldrop and associates (1978) also conducted brief examinations of newborns, and from documenting MPAs could predict hyperactivity at age 3.

The American Psychiatric Association did not recognize attention-deficit/hyperactivity (ADHD) disorder until 1987, when it included hyperactivity with inattention and impulsiveness as the main symptoms of the disorder (Lange, Reichl, Lange, Tucha, & Tucha, 2010). Therefore, comparing earlier research on MPAs and hyperactivity and later research on MPAs and ADHD is difficult, and this does seem to be a rare pursuit. In one fairly recent study, Minahim and Rohde (2015) examined a sample of intellectually gifted individuals (i.e., I.Q. score > 98th percentile) and found a high frequency of ADHD, with a strong association between ADHD and MPA scores. Again, there is a paucity of recent research on this matter.

Pedophilia. It is not a stretch to say that people tend to assume pedophiles have a "certain look" (Forrest, 2015). Is there scientific truth to this? James Cantor and colleagues (2007) have shown evidence for pedophilogenic factors—including physical traits developed in utero—that predict predisposition to erotic interest in children. These physical factors include MPAs and height.

Dyshniku, Murray, Fazio, Lykins, and Cantor (2015) studied MPAs in pedophiles and other sex offenders. They found that increased MPA scores are associated with penile arousal to child stimuli, number of child (but not adult) sexual victims, and charges of or admitting to possession of child pornography. These associations were stronger with the frequency of craniofacial MPAs compared to peripheral MPAs. Interestingly, most pedophiles in their sample had asymmetrical ears. They also found more MPAs in their sample of pedophiles than they found in samples of individuals with schizophrenia.

Shortened height is also a physical marker that can indicate a risk of pedophilia. Height, leg, and torso length are not typically considered in common scales of MPAs. Nonetheless, we present this research in this chapter for two reasons: first, because some of the research about both MPAs and height was conducted by the same teams; and second, because the evidence from morphological studies of pedophiles, like research on MPAs, points to disturbances in morphogenesis that have given rise to marked psychological problems. A shorter height was offered on the list of evidence for neural maldevelopment in pedophilia which had also included lower IQ scores, decreased visuospatial memory, more frequent childhood head injuries, and atypical white (brain) matter manifestations (see Dyshniku et al., 2015, for review). Thus, like MPAs, height reflects genetic development that can be dysregulated in utero (Cantor, Kuban, Blak, Klassen, Dickey, & Blanchard, 2007).

Fazio, Dyshniku, Lykins, and Cantor (2017) documented that pedophiles had shorter height and leg length compared to other sex offenders. These results are commensurate with what is seen in other biologically mediated neurodevelopmental disorders. Fazio et al. underscored that in addition to prenatal factors, early childhood environment contributes to the development of height. They stressed that height can "serve as a tertiary marker for factors more germane to pedophilogenesis" (p. 510).

Cantor and colleagues (2007) conducted a well-designed study in which they examined the adult heights of men who were sex offenders. They examined height in a large sample of those who were sexually interested in prepubescent children (pedophilic offenders), pubescent children (hebephilic offenders), and adults (teleiophilic offenders), and they also included a control group of men who had committed no known sex offenses and were sexually interested in only adults. They found that pedophile and hebephile offenders were shorter than controls and that pedophilic sex offenders are about 2 cm shorter than controls, even when accounting for age. They noted that teleiophilic offenders were taller than pedophiles but shorter than teleiophilic non-offenders, although those group differences were not statistically significant.

Cantor et al. (2007) stressed that the connection between height and pedophilia is evidence that those with pedophilia were subjected to developmental perturbations in utero. That is, something happened prenatally or during early childhood development that affected physical height development and affected brain development that mediates forces of sexual attraction to inappropriate targets. Proposed factors included infections, environmental toxins, and/or poor nutrition (Cantor et al., 2007). These authors prompted future researchers to explore this phenomenon and other MPAs among those with various paraphilias.

Levenson and Ackerman (2017) conducted a large-scale analysis that corroborates the above findings. The examined the records of 22,228 sex offenders in the United States. They found that pedophiles (defined as having victims age 12 or younger) were about one-quarter inch shorter than sex offenders whose victims were adults. Pedophiles were also .18 inch shorter than sex offenders whose victims were minor teens. Levenson and Ackerman underscored that an examination of the biological underpinnings of sexual deviation is a complex task, and that a consideration of the etiology of pedophilia should take into account neurophysiology and environment, particularly early childhood experiences.

Additional research needs to be conducted in this area to elucidate neurodevelopmental issues in pedophiles, other paraphilias, and other sex offenders. Moreover, whereas the overwhelming majority of sex offenders are men, it would be prudent to examine neurodevelopment in female offenders as well. We must also recognize that there are pedophile offenders who do not exhibit physical issues, and there are likely several other factors that contribute to its etiology. Further, there are certainly people who are shorter with non-detached ears who do not desire or engage in sexually aberrant behaviors.

Conclusion

MPAs are part of the spectrum of congenital abnormalities, less severe than major congenital anomalies such as cleft palate and microcephaly (Compton & Walker, 2009). Both major and minor anomalies may predict predisposition to mental illness. Waddington et al. (2008) demonstrated that the presence of any craniofacial or midline anomaly at birth or in infancy was associated with a doubled risk of developing a schizophrenia spectrum disorder. As researchers have noted (cf. Trixler et al., 2001), examining MPAs that arise in embryonic organogenesis (gestation to day 56) separately from those occurring after organogenesis, (i.e., morphological disturbances), may shed light on the developmental sequences that predispose an individual to schizophrenia (Compton & Walker, 2009).

The evidence presented in this chapter strongly suggests that MPAs co-occur with, and ostensibly have been subjected to, the same dysmorphogenesis that spur maldevelopment in the structures that mediate normal psychological functioning. To treat and ultimately prevent the development of psychological illness, it would be prudent for researchers to consider MPAs as an ontogenetic window of neurodevelopment. So, can you look at someone's physical traits and infer a risk of mental illness? It seems a trained expert might evaluate MPAs and associated conditions. We stress such judgments are best reserved for physicians and mental health professionals.

References

Angkustsiri, K., et al. (2014). Minor physical anomalies in children with autism spectrum disorders. *Autism, 15*(6), 746-760. doi: 10.1177/1362361310397620

Akabaliev, V. H., Sivkov, S. T., & Mantarkov, M. Y. (2014). Minor physical anomalies in schizophrenia and bipolar I disorder and the neurodevelopmental continuum of psychosis. *Bipolar Disorders: An International Journal of Psychiatry and Neurosciences, 16*(6), 633-641. https://doi.org/10.1111/bdi.12211

Blanchard, J. J., Aghevli, M., Wilson, A., Sargeant, M. (2010). Developmental instability in social anhedonia: An examination of minor physical anomalies and clinical characteristics. *Schizophrenia Research, 118*(1-3), 162-167. https://doi.org/10.1016/j.schres.2009.10.028

Bourgeron, T. (2015). From the genetic architecture to synaptic plasticity in autism spectrum disorder. *Nature Reviews Neuroscience, 16*(9), 551-563. doi:10.1038/nrn3992

Campbell, M., Geller, B., Small, A. M., Petti, T. A., & Ferris, S. H. (1978). Minor physical anomalies in young psychotic children. *The American Journal of Psychiatry, 135*(5), 573-575. http://dx.doi.org/10.1176/ajp.135.5.573

Cantor, J. M., Kuban, M. E., Blak, T., Klassen, P. E., Dickey, R., & Blanchard, R. (2007). Physical height in pedophilic and hebephilic sexual offenders. *Sex Abuse, 19*(4), 395-407. https://doi-org.ezaccess.libraries.psu.edu/10.1177/107906320701900405

Cavanna, A. E., & Trimble, M. R. (2006). The precuneus: a review of its functional anatomy and behavioural correlates. *Brain, 129*(3), 564-583. doi:10.1093/brain/awl004

Compton, M. T., & Walker, E. F. (2009). Physical manifestations of neurodevelopmental disruption: Are minor physical anomalies part of the syndrome of schizophrenia? *Schizophrenia Bulletin, 35*(2), 425-436. https://doi.org/10.1093/schbul/sbn151

Dean, K., et al. (2006). Grey matter correlates of minor physical anomalies in the AeSOP first-episode psychosis study. *British Journal of Psychiatry, 189*, 221-228. doi: 10.1192/bjp.bp.105.016337

Dyshniku, F., Murray, M. E., Fazio, R. L., Lykins, A. D., & Cantor, J. M. (2015). Minor physical anomalies as a window into the prenatal origins of pedophilia. *Archives of Sexual Behavior, 44*(8), 2151-2159. doi: 10.1007/s10508-015-0564-7

Fazio, R. L., Dyshniku, F., Lykins, A. D., & Cantor, J. M. (2017). Leg length versus torso length in pedophilia: Further evidence of atypical physical development early in life. *Sex Abuse, 29*(5), 500-514. doi: 10.1177/1079063215609936

Forrest, A. (2015). Why do we assume pedophiles look a certain way? *Vice Voices*. Retried from https://www.vice.com/en_us/article/nnqpg7/stereotypical-paedophile-look-189

Gassab, L., Aissi, M., Slama, H., Gaha, L., & Mechri, A. (2013). Prevalence and score of minor physical anomalies in patients with schizophrenia and their first degree relatives: A Tunisian study. *Comprehensive Psychiatry, 54*(5), 575-580. doi: 10.1016/j.comppsych.2012.11.007

Gooding, D. C., Tallent, K. A., & Matts, C. W. (2005). Clinical status of at-risk individuals 5 years later: Further validation of the psychometric high-risk strategy. *Journal of Abnormal Psychology*, 114(1), 170-175. doi: 10.1037/0021-843X.114.1.170

Gourion, D., Goldberger, C., Bourdel, M., Bayle, F. J., Lôo, H., & Krebs, M. O. (2004). Minor physical anomalies in patients with schizophrenia and their parents: Prevalence and pattern of craniofacial abnormalities. *Psychiatry Research, 125*(1), 21-28. doi: 10.1016/j.psychres.2003.06.001

Green, M. F., Satz, P., Gaier, D. J., Ganzell, S., & Kharabi, F. (1989). Minor physical anomalies in schizophrenia. *Schizophrenia Bulletin, 15*(1), 91-99.

Guy, J. D., Majorski, L. V., Wallace, C. J., Guy, M. P. (1983). The incidence of minor physical anomalies in adult male schizophrenia. *Schizophrenia Bulletin, 9*(4), 571-582. https://doi.org/10.1093/schbul/9.4.571

Happé, F., & Ronald, A. (2008). The 'fractionable autism triad': A review of evidence from behavioural, genetic, cognitive and neural research. *Neuropsychology Review, 18*(4), 287-304. doi: 10.1007/s11065-008-9076-8

Hata, K., Iida, J., Iwasaka, H., Negoro, H. I., Ueda, F., & Kishimoto, T. (2003). Minor physical anomalies in childhood and adolescent onset schizophrenia. *Psychiatry and Clinical Neuroscience, 57*(1), 17-21. doi: 10.1046/j.1440-1819.2003.01074.x

Ismail, B., Cantor-Graae, & McNeil, T. F. (1998). Minor physical anomalies in schizophrenic patients and their siblings. *American Journal of Psychiatry, 155*(12), 1695-1702. https://doi.org/10.1176/ajp.155.12.1695

Kato, T., Abe, Y., Sotoyama, H., Kakita, A., Kominami, R., Hirokawa, S.….Nawa, H. (2011). Transient exposure of neonatal mice to neuregulin-1 results in hyperdopaminergic states in adulthood: implication in neurodevelopmental hypothesis for schizophrenia. *Molecular Psychiatry, 16*(3), 307-320. doi: 10.1038/mp.2010.10

Lane, A. et al. (1997). The anthropometric assessment of dysmorphic features in schizophrenia as an index of its developmental origins. *Psychological Medicine, 27*(5), 1155-1164.

Lange, K. W., Reichl, S., Lange, K., Tucha, L., & Tucha, O. (2010). The history of attention deficit hyperactivity disorder. *Attention Deficit and Hyperactivity Disorders, 2*(4), 241-255. doi: 10.1007/s12402-010-0045-8

Levenson, J. S., & Ackerman, A. R. (2017). The relationship between sex offender height and pedophilic interest. *Deviant Behavior, 38*(12), 1383-1392. https://doi.org/10.1080/01639625.2016.1254986

Manouilenko, I., Eriksson, J. M., Humble, M. B., & Bejerot, S. (2014). Minor physical anomalies in adults with autism spectrum disorder and healthy controls. *Autism Research and Treatment*, Article ID 743482, 1-9. http://dx.doi.org/10.1155/2014/743482

McGrath, J., El-Saadi, O., & Grim, V. (2002). Minor physical abnormalities and quantitative measures of the head and face in patients with psychosis. *JAMA Psychiatry, 59*(5), 458-464. doi:10.1001/archpsyc.59.5.458

McGrath, J., Saha, S., Chant, D., & Welham, J. (2008). Schizophrenia: A concise overview of incidence, prevalence, and mortality. *Epidemiologic Reviews, 30*(1), 67-76. https://doi.org/10.1093/epirev/mxn001

McGrath, J. J., van Os, J., Hoyos, C., Jones, P. B., Harvey, I., & Murray, R. M. (1995). Minor physical anomalies in psychoses: Associations with clinical and putative aetiological variables. *Schizophrenia Research, 18*(1), 9-20. https://doi.org/10.1016/0920-9964(95)00016-X

Meehl, P. E. (1990). Toward an integrated theory of schizotaxia, schizotypy, and schizophrenia. *Journal of Personality Disorders, 4*(1), 1-99. https://doi.org/10.1521/pedi.1990.4.1.1

Miles, J. H., & Hillman, R. E. (2000). Value of a clinical morphology examination in autism. *American Journal of Medical Genetics, 91*(4), 245-253.

Miles, J. H., Takahashi, T. N., Bagby, S., Sahota, P. K., Vaslow, D. F., Wang, C. H., Hillman, R. E., & Farmer, J. E. (2005). American Journal of Medical Genetics. Part A. 135(2), 171-180. doi: 10.1002/ajmg.a.30590

Minahim, D., & Rohde, L. A. (2015). Attention deficit hyperactivity disorder and intellectual giftedness: A study of symptom frequency and minor physical anomalies. *Revista Brasileira de Psiquiatria, 37*(4), 289-295. doi:10.1590/1516-4446-2014-1489

Myers, L., Anderlid, B., Nordgen, A., Willfors, C., Kuja-Halkola, R., Tammimies, K., & Bölte, S. (2017). Minor physical anomalies in neurodevelopmental disorders: A twin study. *Child & Adolescent Psychiatry & Mental Health, 11*(57), 1-11. doi: 10.1186/s13034-017-0195-y

National Institute of Mental Health (NIMH). (2016). *Schizophrenia.* Retrieved from https://www.nimh.nih.gov/health/topics/schizophrenia/index.shtml

O'Callaghan, E., Larkin, C., Kinsella, A., & Waddington, J. L. (1991). Familial, obstetric, and other clinical correlates of minor physical anomalies in schizophrenia. *The American Journal of Psychiatry, 148*(4), 479-483. doi:10.1176/ajp.148.4.479

Ozgen, H. M., Hop, J. W., Hox, J. J., Beemer, F. A., & van Engeland, H. (2010). Minor physical anomalies in autism: A meta-analysis. *Molecular Psychiatry, 15*(3), 300-307. doi:10.1038/mp.2008.75

Schiffman, J., Ekstrom, M., LaBrie, J., Schulsinger, F., Sorensen, H., & Mednick, S. (2002). Minor physical anomalies and schizophrenia spectrum disorders: A prospective investigation. *The American Journal of Psychiatry, 159*(2), 238-243. https://doi.org/10.1176/appi.ajp.159.2.238

Sivkov, S. T., & Akabaliev, V. H. (2003). Minor physical anomalies in mentally healthy subjects: Internal consistency of the Waldrop Physical Anomaly Scale. *American Journal of Human Biology, 15*(1), 61-67. https://doi.org/10.1002/ajhb.10124

Steg, J. P., & Rapoport, J. L. (1975). Minor physical anomalies in normal, neurotic, learning disabled, and severely disturbed children. *Journal of Autism and Childhood Schizophrenia, 5*(4), 299-307. https://doi.org/10.1007/BF01540677

Thoma, R. J., Gangestad, S. W., Euller, M. J., Lynse, P. A., Monnig, M., & Yeo, R. A. (2008). Developmental instability and markers of schizotypy in university students. *Evolutionary Psychology, 6*(4), 586-594. https://doi.org/10.1177/147470490800600405

Turetsky, B., Cowell, P. E., Gur, R. C., Grossman, R. I., Shtasel, D. L., & Gur, R. E. (1995). Frontal and temporal lobe brain volumes in schizophrenia. Relationship to symptoms and clinical subtype. *Archives of General Psychiatry, 52*(12), 1061-1070. doi:10.1001/archpsyc.1995.03950240079013

Trixler, M., Tényi, T., Csábi, G., &, Szabó, R. (2001). Minor physical anomalies in schizophrenia and bipolar affective disorder. *Schizophrenia Research, 52*(3), 195-201. https://doi.org/10.1016/S0920-9964(00)00182-1

Waddington, J. L., et al. (2008). Congenital anomalies and early functional impairments in a prospective birth cohort: Risk of schizophrenia-spectrum disorder in adulthood. *British Journal of Psychiatry, 192*(4), 264-267. doi: 10.1192/bjp.bp.107.035535

Waldrop, M. F., Bell, R. Q., McLaughlin, B., & Halverson, C. F., Jr. (1978). Newborn minor physical anomalies predict short attention span, peer aggression, and impulsivity at age 3. *Science, 199*(4328), 563-565. doi: 10.1126/science.622559

Waldrop, M F., & Halverson, C. F. (1971). Minor physical anomalies and hyperactive behavior in young children. In J. Hellmuth (Ed.), *Exceptional infant: Studies in abnormalities, Volume 2* (pp. 343-380). New York, NY: Brunner/Mazel.

Waldrop, M F., Halverson, C. F., & Shetterly, K. (1989). Manual for assessing minor physical anomalies (1989 revision). Unpublished manuscript, University of Georgia.

Waldrop, M. F., Pedersen, F. A., & Bell, R. Q. (1968). Minor physical anomalies and behavior in preschool children. *Child Development, 39*(2), 391-400. doi: 10.2307/1126953

Weinberg, S. M., Jenkins, E. A., Marazita, M. L., & Maher, B. S. (2007). *Schizophrenia Research, 89*(1-3), 1-23. doi:10.1016/j.schres.2006.09.002

Weinstein, D. D., Diforio, D., Schiffman, J., Walker, E., & Bonsall, R. (1999). Minor physical abnormalities, dermatoglyphic asymmetries, and cortisol levels in adolescents with schizotypal personality disorder. *The American Journal of Psychiatry, 156*(4), 617-623. doi: 10.1176/ajp.156.4.617

Werling, D. M., & Geschwind, D. H. (2013). Sex differences in autism spectrum disorders. *Current Opinions in Neurology, 26*(2), 146-153. doi:10.1097/WCO.0b013e32835ee548

Xu, T., Chan, R. C. K., & Compton, M. T. (2011). Minor physical anomalies in patients with schizophrenia, unaffected first-degree relatives, and health controls: A meta-analysis. *PLOS One, 6*(9), e24129. doi:10.1371/journal.pone.0024129

Zhang, L., et al. (2016). Gray matter volume of the lingual gyrus mediates the relationship between inhibition functioning and divergent thinking. *Frontiers in Psychology, 7*, 1532. doi: 10.3389/fpsyg.2016.01532

Chapter 10

CONCLUSION

I am the beautiful reflection of my love's affection.

-Barbra Streisand in Funny Girl (1964)

Although our parents warned us, "Don't judge a book by its cover," the research we have reviewed in this book tells us that, after all, maybe there is a benefit to doing so on a scientific level. Research from evolutionary psychology, developmental neurobiology, behavioral neuroendocrinology, social psychology, anthropology, and other fields has evidenced compelling connections between morphology and psychology.

We agree with Pratt and colleagues (2016) that biological explanations—particularly, biological mechanisms predicting behavior and mental processes—can be very scary. Although the multitude of evidence we highlighted in this book points to connections between physical traits like face, symmetry, fingers, toes, body ratios, scents, and voice cueing us as to a target person's mate value, attitudes, actions, and even mental health, we urge caution in using physical markers alone to make critical judgments about others. It is not guaranteed that your best friend with a longer second toe is going to try to beat you up and steal your Pinot Grigio, or that your very masculine boyfriend will cheat on you, or that your friend with an iris coloboma has psychosis. Research on morphology and psychology presents statistical frequencies and probabilities that should be interpreted with extreme caution, and we urge you to consider this scientific evidence for what it is worth and proceed with the positive outlook that everyone has beauty and inspires wonder. Being inclusive and respecting pluralism makes the world a better place.

Image courtesy of Fly Me Home Handmade and Upcycle Décor
© flymehomedecor.com

Much of the research herein, some of it we ourselves conducted, speaks to prenatal influences mediating physical development and also mediating behavior and mental processes. We therefore must caution about the correlational nature of the data linking physical traits to behavior. As in the case of finger ratios, an androgenic milieu in utero likely contributes to both brain differentiation and to finger, toe, and genital development. It's not that a longer ring finger makes you have major depressive disorder or congenital adrenal hyperplasia. *Remember: correlation does not imply causation.* A significant correlation simply means that two numerical indexes vary with one another. Consider the reported correlation between ice cream sales and murder per capita, or the reported correlation between ice cream sales and drowning deaths. Ice cream does not, to our knowledge, kill. There is likely a third variable (the heat) causing an increase in both ice cream sales and swimming, and ice cream and aggression.

There are also correlations that occur spuriously. For example, TylerVigen.com (2019) reported there is a strong ($r = 0.67$) correlation between the number of movies per year in which Nicholas Cage appeared and the number of people who drowned by falling into a swimming pool (tylervigen.com, 2019). We are sure that Cage doesn't commit chlorine-fueled murders as a post-film celebration ritual.

As with all scientific information, there are important concepts to consider when interpreting these data. Remember that there is wide variation in individual preferences. All men do not prefer women with feminine faces. All women do not prefer men with a ripped, muscular physique. Remember, too, that there is wide phenotypic expression in the traits we described herein. Certainly, everyone with short legs is not a pedophile, not everyone with a nonrasied birthmark has schizophrenia, and not every man with a low voice has cheated on his partner.

Science continues to grow. Ancient Greeks knew that the brain was the center of reasoning, and we humans have continued to explore the biology of behavior for centuries. However, even though we are leaps and bounds ahead from just a decade or two ago in terms of the sophistication of research methodology, we still have a long way to go. There are a multitude of connections and concepts we discussed in this book that are far from conclusive. As an example, the connection between finger ratios and behavior is unclear given the number of conflicting findings. It appears something is there, but that something needs further exploration with refined techniques...even techniques that are on the edge of being developed.

For more reading about evolutionary psychology, or about any of the approaches to studying behavior and mental processes we discussed herein, we challenge you to visit the references section of our chapters and read the evidence-based articles from which this information was derived. Interpret the information for yourselves and be inspired by the scientific sophistication and theoretical acumen of our colleagues and students who created this knowledge. We appreciate their dedication and efforts in building upon the scientific body of evidence, and we appreciate the time you have invested reading this work.

With gratitude,
Marissa and Susan

ABOUT THE AUTHORS

Marissa A. Harrison and Susan M. Hughes each earned their Ph.D. in Biopsychology from the University at Albany, State University of New York with a specialization in evolutionary psychology under the advisement of renown evolutionary and experimental psychologist Dr. Gordon G. Gallup, Jr. Marissa and Susan each have over 20 years of experience in research and teaching psychology on topics ranging from the human voice to serial murder. They have published dozens of scientific papers and presented over 100 papers and posters, and they have spoken at national conferences, regional conferences, and colleges on evolutionary psychology and general psychology. They have collaborated for over 20 years on various research endeavors. This book is infused with examples of their own research findings.

Marissa A. Harrison, Ph.D. is senior faculty at Penn State Harrisburg in Pennsylvania, U.S.A. She teaches seminar, writing, and honors courses, and she mentors graduate and undergraduate student research in general and applied clinical psychology. She has published research on various aspects of the evolution of human sexuality, ranging from dating, to the locution "I love you," to serial murder. Her work has been covered by popular written and televised national and international media (e.g., *The Washington Post*, *The New Yorker*, *HuffPost*, *CBS.com*, *London Daily Mail*, and *Time Magazine*). She's been featured on programming by *Investigation Discovery (ID)*, *BBC Radio*, the *Jill Bennet Show*, *Room 104 Dublin*, and *CBS All Access*. Dr. Harrison earned her B.A. in Psychology and Ph.D. in Biopsychology from the University at Albany, SUNY. She is a proud native of Scranton, PA, *The Electric City*, and a proud graduate of Riverside High School. She sends a special "thank you" to her high school English teachers E.M. and P.J. She loves her family, friends, other animals, music, and inclusivity. *Stay Golden.*

Susan M. Hughes, Ph.D. is a Professor of Psychology at Albright College in Reading, PA, and is the Director of the Evolutionary Studies program at the college. She earned her B.S. in Psychobiology at Binghamton University, received her Ph.D. in Biopsychology at the University at Albany, and taught at Vassar College (NY) for 2 years prior to joining Albright College. Most of her research is in the field of evolutionary psychology, with an emphasis on the study of the human voice. Her research explores the idea that voice has evolved to be more than a natural mechanism for communicating semantic information through speech and the sound of an individual's voice, irrespective of content, can convey a host of social, behavioral, and biological information about a speaker. In addition to her work on voice, she has published several studies related to mate assessment, attraction, attitudes, and behaviors from an evolutionary perspective. Her work in the field has also received a considerable amount of both national and international media attention and has been featured in many popular media sources over the years (e.g., *New York Times, Washington Post, Reuters Health, BBC News, Dr. Drew Show, NPR, Time Magazine, Good Morning America*). Dr. Hughes is a proud native of New York City, from the borough of Queens, NY.